Fields of Sun and Grass

Fields of Sun and Grass

An Artist's Journal of the
New Jersey Meadowlands

John R. Quinn

R

RUTGERS UNIVERSITY PRESS
New Brunswick, New Jersey, and London

NJ
508
Q44

Library of Congress Cataloging-in-Publication Data

Quinn, John R.
    Fields of sun and grass : an artist's journal of the New Jersey
Meadowlands / John R. Quinn.
        p.   cm.
    Includes bibliographical references and index.
    ISBN 0-8135-2443-1 (cloth : alk. paper). – ISBN 0-8135-2444-X
(pbk. : alk. paper)
    1. Natural history–New Jersey–Hackensack Meadowlands.
2. Hackensack Meadowlands (N.J.)   I. Title.
QH105.N5Q55   1997
508.749'21–dc21   96-37700
                                                                              CIP

British Cataloging-in-Publication information available

Manufactured in the United States of America

Design by John Romer

To my grandfather, John D. Dempsey,
who opened the door to nature for a curious
eight-year-old, and to my father,
Raymond M. Quinn,
who encouraged his child to follow the path chosen
and never, ever look back in regret

Contents

Acknowledgments

*M*any people have contributed generously to this work—some through personal reminiscences of life in a bygone Meadowlands era, others through the contribution of facts, figures, and statistics that define the Meadowlands as they exist today. Without their interest and support, this book surely would not have seen completion.

Foremost my editors, Dr. Karen Reeds and Will Hively, deserve my undying gratitude for patiently and with good humor helping me whittle the original manuscript from a volume the size of the Special Area Management Plan down to a more manageable and readable text.

Special thanks must go to Anne Galli, Don Smith, Robert Sikora, Ken Scarlatelli, John Trontis, and Bob Grant of the Hackensack Meadowlands Development Commission for their assistance in many crucial areas. In addition, the HMDC's executive director, Anthony Scardino, Jr., was highly supportive of the project from the start and placed his agency's resources and historical materials at my disposal.

The following people also contributed personal input and historical materials: Dr. David Fairbrothers; Marj Reenstra of the Meadowlands Museum, Rutherford; Richard Fritzky of the Meadowlands Regional Chamber of Commerce; and Commissioner John H. Anlian and Mayor George D. Fosdick of the Village of Ridgefield Park.

To Bill Sheehan of the Hackensack Estuary and River Tenders, Brendan Riordan of the New Jersey Native Plant Society, and Andrew Willner and Steve Barnes of the New York–New Jersey Baykeeper, my thanks for the lively environmental input and for the good times on the river. William Greene, Richard Kane, Steve Royka, John Schulz, Carl Vercelli, Peter Poirier, and my brother, Steve Quinn, deserve more than a handshake for contributing materials and for their willingness to share their own memories of the Meadowlands past.

A sincere thank-you to staff writer Tom Topousis, formerly of *The Record* of Hackensack, for his invaluable input on public discussions of development and preservation in the Meadowlands, and to the *North Jersey Herald & News* of Passaic for kind permission to reprint Meadowlands articles written while I was in the paper's employ in the early 1980s.

And finally, my enduring gratitude to the countless human beings over the centuries who, regardless of their intentions and actions in the Hackensack Meadowlands, have contributed to making this still beautiful estuary the "New Jersey state of mind" that it surely is.

Fields of Sun and Grass

Introduction

> I believe a leaf of grass is no less than the journey-work of
> the stars.
>
> WALT WHITMAN, *Leaves of Grass*

Six miles—and ten thousand years—to the west of Manhattan's
Times Square lies one of the grandest environmental paradoxes
on Earth. Here, beneath a sun often obscured by smoky industrial ex-
halations, a river of many bends makes its way to the sea. And a sea of
grass flanks the river, moving and pulsing in long, leisurely wind-waves,
green in summer, rich sienna in winter, when the tidal creeks lie locked
beneath brine-ice.

This river has a timeless, enduring aspect; it has none of the exuberant action of a high-mountain freshet. When it was created by glacial ice thousands of years ago, the river and its valley was a place
of great sky-spaces, and wonderful silences. Mastodons, caribou, musk
oxen, and the formidable dire wolf lived here. They have long since
vanished, but the valley is far from empty of life. Birds in their multitudes still course above the river; more than 250 species either live in
or migrate through this valley. Many kinds of fishes still inhabit the waters, and other creatures too varied to name, from the smallest crus-
tacean to the web-footed muskrat, shuttle back and forth among the
arcing reeds of its banks. People live along the river as well—many,
many of them. And they are the source of the current paradox.

Geologist Kemble Widmer, in his *Geology and Geography of New Jersey*, posed the essential question about this unique habitat: "Where else
but in New Jersey, the state of contrasts, can one find a swamp where
muskrats are trapped only five miles from the world's most intensely developed square mile?" Indeed, nearly within earshot of Times Square,

*The Hackensack Meadowlands, looking northwest from Snake Hill and the
New Jersey Turnpike.*

amid the tangled traffic arteries of the great industrial-commercial
complex on the western edge of New York City, the original—and the
real—Meadowlands persist. Reviled more often than not as a toxic
wasteland, the geopolitical entity known as the Hackensack Meadowlands District nonetheless supports a vital, if not thriving, ecosystem.
While some of its once fabulously abundant wildlife has certainly disappeared, much remains; estuarine vegetation has even grown lush,
and increasingly varied.

And so it is here, in these urban fields of sun and grass, that the
probable environmental future of humankind—in all its overwhelming
ugliness, yet stark and haunting beauty—may be glimpsed from the air-
conditioned interior of an automobile.

In their fascinating book *Looking for America on the New Jersey Turnpike*,
Angus Gillespie and Michael Rockland note that the state of New
Jersey, exemplified in the public consciousness by its heavily industrialized northeastern corridor, has become the very image of environmental impasse, "the ultimate suburban state—the place where the
struggle between the machine and the garden has been joined and

where a compromise of sorts has been struck between competing visions of America." The machine's impact seems especially powerful at night, when the blazing lights of the oil refineries, the Newark International Airport, the Pulaski Skyway, and the Turnpike testify to the fearsome amount of energy that is both generated and consumed near the Meadowlands.

But the timeless heartbeat of nature pulses here as well; indeed, the modern meadows are a veritable urban wilderness. The federal Wilderness Act of 1964 defined the term *wilderness* as "an area where man himself is a visitor," and this great tidal marsh surely qualifies: even though throngs of people cross the meadows daily by rail and in motor vehicles, any adventurer who attempted a safari on foot would soon feel very much alone there. Among the impenetrable thickets of twelve-foot-high reeds a horizon cannot be seen, and many a would-be bushwhacker has become marooned in the dense, reedy fastness of the northern Meadowlands, assaulted by mosquitoes and greenhead flies and mired in the low-tide mud.

And yet, to the average traveler bearing down on Manhattan via the organized chaos of the Turnpike, the parts of the Meadowlands that can be seen from the roadway resemble nothing less than an industrial moonscape. It is a forbidding yet terribly beautiful panorama, seemingly in ceaseless motion, presenting the viewer with the absolute apogee in humankind's vaunted subjugation of the natural world. Nature here survives obscured amid a concrete and steel chessboard of oil refineries, warehouses, railroad marshaling yards, and factories of every description.

What can we make of this stark juxtaposition? The eminent British scientist James Lovelock, coauthor of the controversial Gaia hypothesis—which holds that planet Earth is a single living organism which, although not sentient, does regulate itself—insists that in spite of the profound and mostly detrimental effect humankind has had on its planetary home, "our species with its technology is an inevitable part of the natural scene." In the northern New Jersey meadows, this simple truth has been taken to (and perhaps beyond) its inevitable and logical conclusion.

In his milestone book *The End of Nature*, Bill McKibben points out that, natural origins or not, many of us today no longer perceive our vital oneness with planet Earth. He argues that, as the world around us has been transformed into urban landscapes, the ancient ties that bound our species to its natal environment have frayed. He writes that "an idea, a relationship, can go extinct, just like an animal or a plant." The idea in this case, McKibben says, is "nature, the separate and wild province, the world apart from man to which he has adapted, under whose rules he was born and died."

Surely the notion that the Hackensack River marshes are a part of nature, and we, thus, an inextricable part of them, escapes the average New Jersey Turnpike motorist idling, say, among the fumes of his fellows at the Exit 18W toll plaza, gazing absently at the roadside litter and the wind-rippled reeds beyond. How can such a place be construed as "nature"? And as the nation continues to build and grow, these sorts of isolated "Turnpike moments" have become more and more common. We have, in McKibben's words, "become in rapid order a people whose conscious need for nature is superficial."

The environmentally dysfunctional appearance presented by the meadows today is of relatively recent origin. In 1628 Isaac DeRaiser, a Dutch colonist, described the Hackensack valley as a potential, if not actual, paradise: "At the side of the . . . little river, which we call the Achter Col, there is a great deal of reedy land; the rest is full of trees, and in some places there is good soil, where the savages plant their maize, upon which they live, as well as by hunting." Although serious large-scale attempts to dike and drain the marshes began in the early nineteenth century, for the most part these early reclamation campaigns ended in failure. The meadows stubbornly refused to surrender their ecological integrity.

Rough-legged hawk hovering above reeds in search of prey. The coal-fired Public Service Electric & Gas power plant at Ridgefield is in the distance.

Something of the benign and bucolic nature of this ancient ecosystem existed even as late as the 1920s. It inspired the nearly forgotten work of a contemporary poet named Owen Terry, who in 1922 penned a paean to the meadows as they met the eye in that year. In *Windjammers of the Hackensack*, Terry celebrates the Meadowlands as only one who knew them with an intimacy born of exploration could:

> Oh, the marshlands of New Jersey
> Oh, the broad moors near the sea
> Where the salt winds off the ocean
> Wander far and fast and free!
>
> Oh, the tides in winding channels
> Hidden in the meadow grass
> Where the hulls unseen, ghost vessels,
> Gliding schooners seaward pass.
>
> And the nodding and the lisping
> Of the zephyr-haunted sedge,
> And the mallow's flaming petals
> On the sluggish ditch's edge.
>
> And the meadowlark, sky-scaler,
> Mounting up on tiny wings,
> Flooding upper space with music
> Largesse, free, but fit for kings.
>
> And the fleecy clouds of cloudland,
> Browsing o'er their sunny leas,
> And the flitting of their shadows,
> Playing with the vagron breeze.
>
> Oh, the brave life of the marshes,
> Jersey's moorland green and wide,
> And the brotherhood that crowns it,
> Blowing wind and flowing tide!

Terry's benign vision of the meadows—doubtless he sensed he was toasting a vanishing natural entity—reflects that of the late Bergen County historian Frances Westervelt, who wrote of the river in the same year: "From here [the city of Hackensack] to Newark Bay the Hackensack forms one of the finest features of this section of country. While the river varies considerably in width, the current is so gentle and still, except in the time of an early spring freshet, that the waters seem to be slumbering in quiet repose."

Although much of the Hackensack's main stem no longer affords passage to either windjammers or modern commercial shipping (the river is non-navigable beyond the Court Street Bridge in Hackensack), it very early on was the scene of heavy commercial traffic. By 1748 the river was considered navigable for vessels up to fifty tons "as far inland as New Bridge" in Hackensack. By 1834 sloops plied the river between Hackensack and New York "carrying . . . wood, lumber and agricultural products." In 1876 it was reported that "vessels and steam tugs run up to Hackensack with coal and lumber and other freight. Berrys Creek is navigable for vessels and steam tugs up to Carlstadt." By the 1890s commercial traffic on the Hackensack, including schooners loaded with bricks cast in Little Ferry, amounted to some 150,000 tons valued at one million dollars annually.

All this river traffic, combined with the industrialization of the sur-

Two cormorants fishing Overpeck Creek. This view is to the east, from Bergen Turnpike in Ridgefield.

rounding shoreline, began to take its toll. As though in rueful summation of the deterioration evident by the 1920s, Westervelt later noted that the Hackensack River "was a paradise for anglers a quarter of a century ago, but fishing is now a lost art owing to the pollution of the stream by sewage and contaminating matter from manufacturing plants."

Such visions and voices out of a gentler past are a far cry from the sights and sounds that assail the senses from the New Jersey Turnpike today. The pristine, prehistoric Meadowlands are lost to us forever. But if one views humanity as an integral part of nature and accepts the inevitability of change, then perhaps that fate is not altogether lamentable. In spite of the abuses heaped on them over the past two centuries, the meadows *have* survived, surprisingly intact. Today, the Hackensack meadows and estuary epitomize the travails and the tarnished glories of urban ecosystems everywhere; like Lake Erie, the modern Meadowlands have risen, Lazarus-like, from the tomb of their own destruction and can now be said to be in a state of healing, of regeneration. Though assuredly yet very much a degraded riverine complex, this estuary does appear to have a future, albeit an uncertain one.

HOME GROUND

Whether or not the meadows fill any sort of primal need for nature in the eyes of travelers who view them from the Turnpike, wilderness these broad, grassy plains surely are. For though defiled nearly to the utmost, they are yet filled with life—a complex, living biomass that has simply made the best of the industrial juggernaut that has all but overwhelmed it. The meadows have adapted, and endured. And in their own unique way they possess a living beauty that has not been obliterated. You simply have to know where to look for it.

Although sizable enclaves of intact tidal marshes persist in many sections of this drainage, perhaps the broadest stretches of undeveloped meadows, nearly all of them invaded by the ubiquitous, exotic reed called phragmites, will be seen from the stretch of the New Jersey Turnpike that runs north from Route 3 to the Turnpike's terminus in Ridgefield Park. It is here that at least some image of the ancient glacial estuary may be called to mind, the western vista bounded by the low, rolling Watchung Mountains a few miles distant. And it is on this part of the Meadowlands that many of the narratives, ecological perspectives, and artistic efforts of this book will focus. For it was to these places—some of their locations lost and fragmented amid the confusion of a modern road map—that I returned, to seek something of the meadows experience I had enjoyed so many years before.

All too often, we tend to regard the province of the amateur field naturalist, in the words of nature artist Cathy Johnson, as being "exotic, removed, remote, unique." But she counters that common misconception with her conviction that "the world is a wondrous place—*all* of it, not just the Galapagos or the Amazon rain forests, but the ditch by the railroad tracks . . . and my own backyard. It is the wonder of discovering the unexpected so close to home that makes the world so interesting."

I hope with this book to craft a portrait of my own backyard, albeit a rather spacious one—a profile in words and drawings of the Hackensack Meadowlands, their human and natural history as well as their projected future. It has been a personal odyssey for me, but one that also involves the thoughts and perceptions of others who have cast their die with this marsh complex.

Although at times I dispassionately describe the impact of the natural and sociopolitical forces that have sculpted this landscape over millennia, I have found that I, too, am inextricably a part of it, and on an intensely personal level. Born here, almost literally within sight and scent of the (then) largely untrammeled meadows, my life-experience is firmly rooted in the color, panorama, and history of this "good ground" of the Lenape people.

Scott Russell Sanders wrote in his wonderful book *Townships* that one's "home ground is the place where, since before you had words for such knowledge, you have known the smells, the seasons, the birds and beasts, the human voices, the houses, the ways of working, the lay of the land and the quality of the light. It is the landscape you learn before you retreat inside the illusion of your skin. You may love the place if you flourished there, or hate the place if you suffered there. But love it or hate it, you cannot shake free. Even if you move to the antipodes, even if you become intimate with new landscapes, you still bear the impression of that first ground."

When I eventually returned I found, of course, that the home-ground impressions one carries through life are not the same as the actual place. The meadows had changed—in places dramatically—over the intervening years. What had been an impenetrable and vaguely threatening natural landscape was now "tamed"; little of the mystique I remembered from my youth survived among the towering reeds. But this is the nature of life. A closer look, made over the course of a year, revealed that the old intrigue of the meadows I had known and felt as a child had simply aged right along with me.

From my new perspective I saw, not only an enduring river, but

Low-tide mud and ice, Ridgefield meadows. Although blighted by pollution and poorly planned industrial activity, this area is nonetheless attractive to waterfowl, who winter here in considerable numbers.

the longer flow of human occupancy of this planet. Our burgeoning numbers, coupled with our ability to manipulate an already overburdened biosphere, have made it abundantly clear that diverging paths lie before us. The choices we make now, today, in this very generation, will surely have great import for those who will follow us. The steps we take to forestall or alleviate the environmental calamities looming on our horizon will determine the kind of future our descendants will have—if they are to have one at all.

A glimpse of that future may be had here, in these fields of sun and grass that lie at the heart of the Great Eastern Megalopolis. In the

Kingsland Creek mudflats at low tide. This drawing was made on a brutally hot August day, but the exposed banquet table of the tidal flats was nonetheless well populated by gulls seeking edibles.

Hackensack Meadowlands, a truce of sorts has been declared and a compromise reached between nature and a technology that has long been estranged from it. The view from the Turnpike at once represents the very worst and the very best aspects of our species in its million-year relationship with this Earth. In the Meadowlands, something of a reconciliation and healing is under way. Its fruition will not be apparent the day after tomorrow, nor even in the next century; it will take time, perhaps hundreds of years, before this estuary once again fully assumes its role as inspiration and provider for, rather than adversary of, humankind.

But it must be accomplished, and it will be worth the effort. In the current attempts to phase out the haphazard destruction of these marshes and effect a more orderly development, as well as to preserve the viable habitat that survives, lie solutions to virtually all the serious problems of economic growth "versus" the environment that confront us today. Material prosperity in the now will not sustain our descendants in a toxic, biologically impoverished future. If the environmental maturity and wisdom acquired here, in the management of this threatened ecosystem, are applied wherever and whenever they are desperately needed, we will, just perhaps, bequeath a livable planet to those whose lives are yet to be lived.

Starting Point

What did you go out into the wasteland to see? A reed
swayed by the wind? What did you go out to see?

MATTHEW 11:7

The "meadows," as defined by nature and so called by local residents for more than three centuries, extend from the middle
Hackensack River and Overpeck Creek drainage (in the towns of Little
Ferry, Ridgefield Park, Teaneck, and Leonia) south to the river's outlet
in Newark Bay, a distance of roughly thirty-five miles as the crow flies.
They comprised, until quite recently, about 21,000 acres of natural salt
marsh and coastal white cedar forest habitats. The cedars have vanished, done in by both human and tidal encroachment, and the runways of Newark International Airport lie upon the reclaimed Newark
Meadows just to the south.

The boundaries of the modern Hackensack Meadowlands District,
on the other hand, were determined by the state-appointed Hackensack
Meadowlands Development Commission (HMDC) at its formation in
1968. The district is of slightly lesser area than the natural estuarine
marsh complex: it encompasses some 19,730 acres, stretching from the
lilliputian "airport borough" of Teterboro and Ridgefield, in the north,
to the industrial townships of Kearny and Secaucus, and Jersey City, in
the south. As defined by the HMDC, the district includes territory in
ten Bergen County and four Hudson County municipalities and is six
square miles larger than Manhattan Island, twenty times larger than
Central Park. Not all that long ago written off as noxious wasteland that
might be had for a mere dollar an acre, the Meadowlands today have
an aggregate value of $5.8 billion.

But neither of those geographic entities defines the world in which

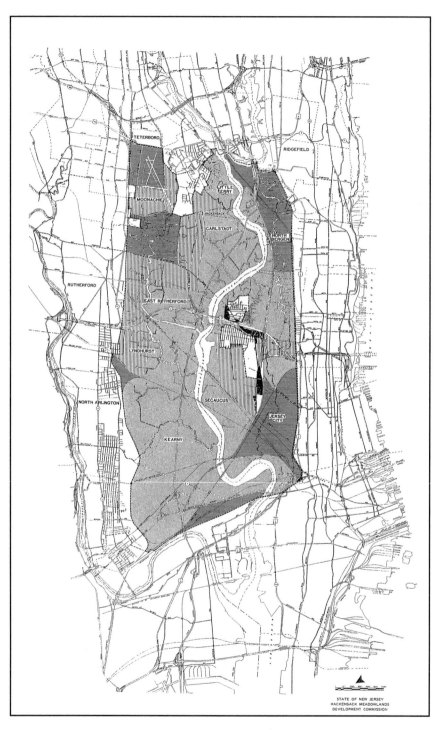

Map of the Hackensack Meadowlands District, showing the 14 Bergen County and Hudson County municipalities that lie within its jurisdiction. Courtesy of the Hackensack Meadowlands Development Commission.

Gulls moving toward the safety of higher ground—and their evening roost—on a nearby landfill. This Hackensack River tributary presents a scene of surprising natural beauty even though its banks and the surrounding lands are comprised primarily of fallow landfill.

I grew up—my own home ground. That was a smaller place: a broad shallow tidal basin, roughly three miles long and a half-mile wide, that forms the Hackensack Meadowlands' northernmost boundary. This is the place in which I first came to know the meadows, many years ago, as I ventured out from the security of my boyhood home. . . .

HOME GROUND REVISITED

The Village of Ridgefield Park is not large, as New Jersey municipalities go. It is less than two square miles in extent, occupying what was once a densely wooded ridge between two rivers. To the north, the village is separated from its neighbors—the borough of Bogota and the township of Teaneck—by another "river," this one made of concrete: Interstate 80 originates a continent away in San Francisco and terminates at the maze of access ramps and approaches to the George Washington Bridge. In effect the town is located on a peninsula, and through this fortuitous semi-isolation it has managed to avoid the featureless merging with neighboring towns that characterizes so much of the urban Northeast. It has an "identity," rather like that of a smallish medieval city casting a wary but not unfriendly eye over its potentially threatening surroundings.

Today, the "village" is such in the political sense only. It is one of only three incorporated villages in the state, the other two being Ridgewood and South Orange. Few villages, however—in the traditional sense of the word—would be home to slightly more than twelve thousand residents. Ridgefield Park is no longer pastoral; this small

Bucolic summer scene on Overpeck Creek, looking south from DeGraw Avenue Bridge, Leonia. A small colony of rough-winged swallows nests beneath the bridge.

Overpeck Creek in winter, looking south from DeGraw Avenue Bridge, Leonia. The Hartz Mountain Corporation's sprawling Overpeck Corporate Centre is just visible in the hazy distance.

town, like those of the rest of Bergen County, has become a bedroom suburb of New York.

But at one time, the local historical record assures us, "a time long gone in Ridgefield Park," there were "woods, sand banks on the Hackensack River, and clear streams for boating, swimming and fishing. Some folks say it was a time that was a paradise just made for boys and young men who had visions and dreams." This is an image of Ridgefield Park that few, if any, living residents can recall with eyewitness clarity. Some older residents—my mother is one—can recall swimming in the Overpeck Creek, where, she says, "you could see the sandy river bottom in the clear water." And few can revisit fading memories of the surrounding unbroken grasslands, where the only interruption of the seemingly limitless greenery, except the horizon itself, was "the tiny line of a toy-like train crossing the meadows from Ridgefield Park to Hoboken."

East Grand Avenue, Ridgefield Park. All roads lead down to the meadows—
or former meadows—in this village; the high-rise apartment houses of Fort Lee
loom in the background, to the east across the Overpeck valley.

My own experience with the meadows began here, in the Overpeck valley, in the late 1940s. At that time the town's population was somewhere in the area of ten thousand souls. This was a time, following the building of the George Washington Bridge in the 1930s and the end of World War II, in which Bergen County was poised at the brink of enormous change. But in a sense, my little part of it was always ripe for change—always a crossroads, always a choice piece of real estate. In centuries past, for instance, the site of my hometown was a favored encampment for the Lenape (or Delaware) Indians. The Achkinsac band of that great confederation once lived here:

> On the west bank of the Tantaqua creek, later known as English or Overpeck, on a high, widespreading knoll, with acres of land over hill and dale, extending to the Hacken-

sack River on the west, and north and south on a lower
plane touching the edge of the marshes, washed by tidal
waters, was located the Indian village of Achkinheshacky,
the home of Oratam, the sachem of the tribe that inhabited
this territory. In documentary records he is . . . listed as a
landowner. . . . The site is well chosen above the high water
mark on a stream that was one of the waterways to the Kill
von Kull on the south and the Tappans on the north, only
a few miles to the Hudson river via the Palisades trails,
thence to "Manhattan."

(*Westervelt,* History of Bergen County, *1923*)

The written history of the town offers this wistful description: "If
you close your eyes and imagine a virgin forest surrounded on three
sides by crystal clear waters, you will have an idea of of the land which
the Indians called 'Hacki Sak,' or 'good ground.' It is said that this name
arose from the fact that Indians traveling up the Hackensack River saw
nothing but swamps and unusable marshland until they reached Ridgefield Park. Here was the first 'good ground' north of the Meadowlands."
It looked inviting to the European settlers as well. "This area," the
town history continues, "provided the first suitable land for farming as
one sailed north from Newark Bay."

Historical Note. 1669, June 24. Patent, Gov. Carteret to Mrs
Sarah Kiersted, widow of Hans Kiersteden, late of New
York, Girugion [Doctor], for a neck of land given to her
by Oratan, the Sachem of the Hackingsacks, and lying between the Hackingsack River and Overpacks Creek, 2120
acres.

(*Westervelt,* History of Bergen County, *1923*)

Before Mrs. Kiersted got her patent, Overpeck Creek and its valley
formed the western boundary of a Dutch settlement called Vriessen-
dael, the first organized Bergen County hamlet. Founded as a plantation
in 1640 by Captain David DeVries, it extended from the Hudson River
at present-day Edgewater over the cliff of the Palisades to Overpeck
Creek; the settlement was destroyed by a war party of Lenape five years
later. Today, the aggregate value of the land and buildings that occupy
this former Lenape village site, the modern-day Village of Ridgefield
Park, is reported as $720.5 million.

As settlers continued to arrive, and as properties continued to
change hands, the surrounding meadows themselves remained much
the same. Although these extensive marshes dominated the view from

Mergansers and crows briskly trading back and forth above a frozen Overpeck Creek. The merganser is a common wintering waterfowl on the creek.

HOODED MERGANSER

COMMON MERGANSER

RED-BREASTED MERGANSER

Fish ducks

*The hooded merganser (*Lophodytes cuculla-tus*) breeds from Alaska, Manitoba, and Nova Scotia south to Oregon and Tennessee. In the Meadowlands it is a regular fall and winter resident, most often observed on the Hackensack River, the Kingsland Impoundment, and in the Saw Mill Creek area. The common merganser*

*(*Mergus merganser*) is a familiar winter visitor, usually in freshwater habitats. It may be seen in good numbers on the impounded Overpeck Creek, remaining there throughout the season as long as there is open, unfrozen water. The red-breasted merganser (*M. serrator*) makes occasional appearances in the estuary in winter, mostly on the Hackensack River, in the Saw Mill Creek area, and at Newark Bay.*

ANYBODY HERE NAMED OVERPECK?

Overpeck Creek is a six-mile-long waterway that drains the northern-most arm of the Meadowlands. Rising in wooded wetlands in north-ern Bergen County, the creek today is a suburban stream for its first two or three miles. Then, nourished by small, mostly human-engineered tributaries, it broadens just before joining the parent Hackensack River into a quarter-mile-wide watercourse landfilled and bermed right up to its banks.

Local opinion on the origin of the Overpeck's name has long been divided. Some old-timers in the village insist that its genesis lay in the word *Awapough*, "the stream behind a rock" (probably refer-ring to the nearby Palisades), in the vernacular of the Lenape peoples who inhabited the western ridge of the valley before any Europeans arrived. The other theory is that the creek is named for an early landowner, one Jeremiah Peck, who had an extensive holding on the west bank in the 1700s, in the present-day village. In a 1948 response to a query by a former resident bearing Overpeck as a surname, the late commissioner Herbert I. Lowe wrote that he had "heard the story that a man named Peck lived somewhere in the neighborhood and that this stream was known as Peck's Creek and that persons on one side of the creek in referring to a place on the other side would simply note that it was 'over Peck's creek.'" A faded survey map of the creek, drawn up by Peck himself and dated August 1712, shows such a holding, called "Peck's Meadow," on the west side of what we now call the Overpeck.

In some accounts, this name has been corrupted to "Overpack" or "Overprook," as in this 1830 description of early southeastern Bergen County: "Near the mouth of the bay, upon the side of Over-prook creek, adjacent to the Hackensack River, several of the rich valleys were then [1680] settled by the Dutch; and near Snake Hill was a fine plantation, owned by Pinhorne and Eickbe, for half of which Pinhorne is said to have paid 500 pounds."

most of the higher prospects, they received relatively scant mention in historical accounts. The "swamps" were considered as much an obsti-nate barrier to the march of civilization as a prominent natural feature. A few local entrepreneurs speculated in meadow acreage, buying up the Overpeck's swampland for between one and fifty dollars an acre. But up to the days of my youth, in the 1940s, most of my village's resi-dents chose to ignore the brooding wetlands just beyond their doorstep;

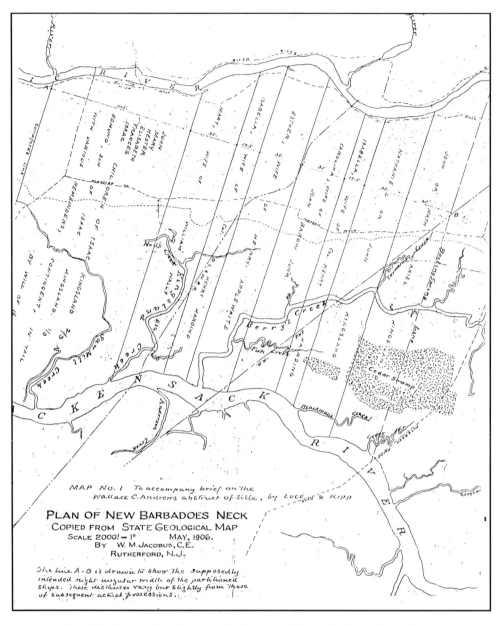

Map of the former New Barbadoes Neck section of Rutherford and Carlstadt, circa 1906. This map shows major landholders of the period as well as the remnant cedar forest that persisted in the area occupied by the present-day Meadowlands Sports Complex.

"the meadows" lay beneath the summer sun and winter ice, just as they always had.

In spite of this local ambivalence, the Village of Ridgefield Park would be the starting point of my journey of rediscovery. At its very outset, I left the thunder of the Turnpike. The village was still an orderly gridwork of relatively quiet streets flanked by the leafy descendants of the original forest, a place filled, for me, with the wind-echoes of memories: summer-night streets splashed with streetlight and inky shadows, lightning bugs, and the smoky aroma of burning cattail "punks" collected in the nearby swamps. Today, in broad daylight, the dignified old houses, though many are re-sided in vinyl and sport thermal windows, still evoke those summer evenings.

George D. Fosdick, Jr., is Ridgefield Park's current mayor. He is a lifelong resident whose tenure—at age fifty-six—extends back about as far as mine does; his was a childhood similarly influenced by the meadows, though he is one of those townsfolk who did not know them by that name. He recalls the twin rivers and their marshlands as places of both peril and promise.

Voices ∽

MAYOR GEORGE FOSDICK
"In the late 1940s, when I was about seven or eight years old, we didn't call them the meadows. It was 'the swamps.' And there was a great deal of fear about going into the swamps, because we all believed they were full of quicksand. That was the common belief among the kids—we were about eight, nine years old. Ten years old maybe.

"There were all sorts of trails through there. Trails were simply where the swamp grass had been beaten down by those who went before us—or, we made our own trails. That was the exciting part of it, making your own trail and finding your way [to the creek]. Of course, there was always a certain amount of hesitancy, about making your own trail, 'cause you were afraid you'd step into quicksand, that you were gonna get trapped. Now, I don't even know if there ever was quicksand out there, but I do know that Mickey Duncan's brother, back in the thirties, went out in the swamps at the end of Brinkerhoff Street and never came back.

"Up here in the north end of town, I can remember coming up with Charlie Seivers—who has since passed away—up in the area of what we now call 'the woods.' Of seeing deer, very definitely seeing deer, of taking pictures of the deer and other wildlife for completion of a second-class merit badge requirement or something. I specifically remember the deer, fox, down there; I never paid too much attention to birds, but there were box turtles, all over, snapping turtles too.

"In the late forties, before the building of the New Jersey Turnpike, I recall that the old Route 6 was just a two-lane cement road, going through the swamps, with a drawbridge across the Overpeck Creek. That's where Werner had his dump, and you'd go out Route 6—we used to go out there on our bicycles—and before the creek you would make a right into what was Werner's dump. Which of course was a fascinating experience, you know. Dumps had everything in them. 'Course there were muskrats—I never did any trapping, any hunting at all, but you saw these things.

"There weren't back then any concerns like 'environment.' The dumps were out there; nobody thought about these things. You didn't see the dumps as anything necessarily negative: 'That's the dumps.' I mean, the town had dumped there forever; Werner had the dump there forever. . . . The meadows were a resource to be used; it was exciting to be out there. The dumps were out there. Nobody thought about it then, about environment. But it was a very positive perception; it was a place of great adventure.

"I don't know of any young people today, with what little resource is left out there, who avail themselves of it. Today's young people . . . have missed an awful lot because so much is done for them. Everything

Overpeck valley as recalled from the early 1950s. This view looks down from the eastern slope of Veteran's Park, in the Village of Ridgefield Park.

Overpeck valley in the mid-1990s. This view also looks down from Veteran's Park, in the Village of Ridgefield Park. The scene now includes eight-lane Interstate 95 and, beyond, high-rise apartment houses on the Palisades bluff in Fort Lee.

is prepared, manufactured, or organized. . . . Television—we're waiting for things to happen. We sit in front of the television and we'll have the entire Second World War pass before us in an hour, maybe a half-hour. The computer—you miss the experience of God's creation.

"The surroundings—part of the adventure of growing up in Ridgefield Park was that. That was there. There was still a wild, natural place right here. We didn't have to travel to far-off places to find it."

Like the other South Bergen municipalities that abut the Meadowlands, my town was somehow inextricably tied to this wetland complex, but mostly in an undefinable way. Few residents, save the minority subculture of muskrat trappers, extracted any meaningful livelihood from the marshes, and in fact most people generally avoided them. It had been

American bittern on nest, Saw Mill Creek Wildlife Management Area. This large bittern, often well camouflaged, calls out in a ghostly voice from the marsh.

nearly three centuries since the Lenape held sway in the forested glens and broad marshes, and many decades since the last farmer had harvested a crop of salt hay. As the years fell away, these early pastoralists were gradually replaced by human inhabitants of another stripe: city dwellers fleeing the crowded urban core–the commuters, the planners, the empire builders, and the operators of the heavy machinery that would ultimately subjugate the meadows and bring them into the twentieth century.

But even as civilization crowded in on them, the marshes played host to millions of birds in their seasonal gatherings. Redwings, waterfowl, shorebirds, and a host of other winged folk obscured the reeds in their astonishing numbers, flowing up and down the eastern flank of the continent and gathering in this mid-Atlantic haven as they had for countless millennia. A habitat-group guidebook from 1930 describes a fair sampling:

AUGUST BIRD-LIFE OF THE HACKENSACK MEADOWS

The thousands of acres of marshland bordering the Hackensack River and Newark Bay, so familiar to travelers over the railways which pass through them, abound in interest to the naturalist.

In their lower portions, colonies of Florida Gallinules and Pied-billed Grebes have been found nesting; but it is August that birds are most abundant in the marshes, and they then possess the strongest attraction for the ornithologist. At that season the wild rice begins to ripen, bringing to the marsh a large, though ever decreasing, number of Bobolinks and Sora Rails that delight to feed upon it.

The Bobolink is then in its streaked, sparrow-like plumage, and is known under the name "Reedbird."

The Sora, in spite of its small size and sluggish flight, is ranked as a game bird, but at the present rate of decrease it will pay the penalty of this distinction by practical extermination in this region. Red-winged Blackbirds also come to feed on the rice.

During the latter half of July, August and September, Swallows (by far the most abundant birds of the meadows) use the marshes as dormitories, coming to them in incalculable numbers in the evening to sleep, and leaving them early the following morning to radiate to every point of the compass. During the day, and as the birds gather for their evening flight, they may be seen perching in long lines on roadside telegraph lines.

In August the marshes are as remarkable for their flowers as for their birds. The great rose mallow is doubtless the most beautiful, as it is also one of the most abundant species, acres sometimes being pink with the bell-shaped flowers. There are also brilliant cardinal flowers, pickerel weed, jewel flowers. . . .

Least bittern stalking killifish in the waters of Saw Mill Creek.

With the so-called "march of civilization," all this wealth of bird and plant life is bound to disappear, to be replaced by railways, factories and docks.

(Guidebook to the Habitat Groups of North American Birds, *American Museum of Natural History, 1930*)

Swamp sparrows and tidal ice, Overpeck marshes, Leonia.

The wonderful profusion of birdlife has perhaps been the Meadowlands' crowning natural attribute throughout their history. And even as the meadows contracted, the birds endured. Clouds of gulls swarmed above the expanding dumps, and bitterns nested among cattails at the very base of the advancing glaciers of municipal refuse. It was a place tailor-made for youthful adventure and discovery.

Journal ✒

WINTER 1949: THE VISION QUEST

I recall the day with clarity. It was on one of those opaque, silver-frost marsh dawns that occur only in the very first days of the young year that the bird and I crossed paths. A silent, bitterly cold realm of weathered, eroding snow, wind-dried shocks of brown reeds, sagging tidal ice yellowed and discolored with brine, the world to the east beginning to pale with the new day.

It was a winter dawn many years ago; I was ten years old.

It was at that precise point in time, when the landscape begins to

Low tide on a meadows creek. The Meadowlands have traditionally attracted the youth of surrounding towns, as a place of mystery and adventure.

reveal itself to the eye in its gradual emergence from the limbo of night, that a thin, barely discernible sound, much like the far-distant tolling of bells, began to make itself known to my ear. A phantom, the impression made more upon the mind's eye than upon the ear.

How I had managed to escaped my parents' supervision and witness that frigid dawn symphony is lost in memory. Perhaps best so.

As I stood there in the growing light and tried to determine the source of the sound, the low, ragged outline of the marshes emerged and assumed its place on a horizon comprised of nothing but snow and frozen river. The air, seemingly touched by the eye of a cold January sun I could not yet see, began to move. A gaunt reed, locked in ice, dried and shredded by weeks of unrelenting wind, stood alone above its fellows; lightly stroked by the rising breeze, it began to buzz with a dry, almost insectlike sound. Joined, too, by the music of the river ice in its drippings and millionfold rearrangements–shift, slip, and fall of crystal, changing, second by second.

I stood there, chilled to the marrow in the silvery darkness, watching the meadows move, seemingly in a million different directions at once. Try to isolate one! There! A distant swarm of gulls far away and high above the frozen creek. The birds rise in complete silence; they lift easily in slow, wide concentrics, hang against the cluttered tapestry of the vast, awakening urbs that surround this place on every side, a dark stirring flank of constructions and amber lights, wavering, thinning, extinguished one by one by the approaching light of day. The birds are familiar with this mad assemblage of roadway and concrete, wood and steel, for what it is—though not of their making it is as much a part of their world as it is of ours. They pass above it daily, exploit its variegated landfills; but they find home and sustenance in the remnants of the marshes, where they subsist on the debris of civilization. Higher and higher they soar into the evanescent heavens, mere flecks of life, avian scavengers, borne aloft in timeless grace and beauty by the warm thermals of the stirring landscape below.

"It's coming," I heard myself whisper, so as not to shatter the spell of that moment. "They can see it now—sure, they're high enough!" Indeed, as I spoke, gazing heavenward, the ascending birds moved into the fire of the new sun, one after another, bursting into cold flame, flaring into tiny sparks, white wings and bodies ablaze against the high, bright sky. Now their thin, joyful cries dropped down out of the sky and reached my ears; a dog, chained somewhere among the houses of the town, at once mourned and celebrated yet another sunrise.

Across the wind-motions and acoustical confusion of the broad valley, morning sounds came to me: the dry whisper of reeds, plumed heads leaning away from the freshening breeze; the drip and run of gray, tainted waters below the cover of snow and black ice; the rush of many, many wings, some hidden, most now on the move. Voices drifted across the meadow, inquiring, fresh, hopeful. An auto horn, hard, jarring, intrusive. An engine cranked into life; another. The urban world, the machine of the city, was shrugging, coughing, and groaning itself awake.

From the sediments below my feet, beneath the ice, I could sense the eyes of lesser beings fixed on their own heaven. How many glass shrimp and killifish would struggle to shake free of the torpor of winter and move toward the light? On this new day, what changes were now flowing and fleeing in the billions of cells, nameless tunnels and borings, through which circulated the very lifeblood of this, our water planet? How did those minute armies of living things, spinning out their lives in the darkness below, view that fragile light that so tenuously penetrated the boundary of a frozen world?

Then it appeared at the eastern edge of the world: a tiny point of brilliance so intense as to momentarily supersede all but the dense and massive flank of the valley rim with its multitude of night lights and buildings. Arcing to the north and south along the ridge, the light picked out the towers of the distant city in sharp relief, flooded like water, and moved down into the broad marsh. Its faint warmth touched my face. A clot of snow dropped soundlessly from a reed head; a raucous party of starlings fled by overhead; the roar of traffic grew.

I turned to the east and watched the sun rise, and fill the sunken hollows of yellowed tidal snow; sharply define the frozen leads under which coursed the tides; and pluck the meandering track of a bird from the anonymity of the snowfall's blank page.

Much like the tread of a barnyard hen, the spidery prints wandered with an oddly purposeful aimlessness, one track placed neatly before its predecessor, the whole strung across the dry snow from wind-dried reed shock to tangled briar. Long-toed, light, furtive, the trail moved off and away over this inert, frozen landscape, inviting pursuit.

In the now bright day, I followed the tracks, dogging their every convolution and doubling back, noting their freshness and their passage through latticed reed spaces of the narrowest dimensions. Such a trail, I reasoned, could have been laid down only by one kind of physically compressed marsh denizen—a rail.

But the meadows here, at their place of convergence with the artificial dunescape of an abandoned landfill and the town beyond, seemed of much less survival value to a water-loving rail than a desert to a duck. Overpeck Creek lay nearly a quarter-mile to the east, its flow locked in midwinter ice.

How would a bird so dependent on water finds its way through the maze of winter-dried plants and ice to the foods so desperately required to stoke its tiny fire at this forbidding end of the year? This particular rail, I decided, must surely be on the threshold of starvation and death among the frozen ruins of summer!

As the sun climbed in the eastern sky, I dogged that mysterious track, marveled at its author's inquisitive and exploratory nature. No aimless wanderer here; the invisible bird, somewhere ahead of me in the wilderness of reeds and cattails, was clearly scrutinizing every feature of its uncompromising habitat with the intensity of a medieval field gleaner. No tangled, reedy floral arrangement was scorned as a source of provender, no ice crevice or frozen cavelet passed by in the grim and relentless quest for access to the moving waters and unfrozen mud below the reach of the cold. There lay the rail's living prey, and its life.

I approached a bracken of matted and wind-flattened reeds and noted how the trail lost itself in the lattice of blue-gray shadows. Circling the thicket, I saw that there was no sign of exit: the small creature was hidden there, deep among the dry brown grasses. I knew at once that a wildling, a being of another sphere of existence, crouched there in silence and immobility, brought to bay but not yet violated, awaiting the next move of its pursuer.

Virginia rail prowling bleak winter reed beds near Overpeck Creek.

I can recall taking a shuddering, fearful breath (one would have thought a lion crouched there!) before pushing into the reeds to flush the bird. The grasses protested with dry, impossibly loud pops and clashings that shattered the stillness. I pushed ahead, amid the crackling and clinging reeds. Cattail fluff and nameless seeds flew into the air, and then, almost at arm's length, my quarry appeared before me: a small brownish form sprang aloft and for a second or two hung in startling contrast against the brilliant snow. Long-billed, rounded wings, leggy, a splash of dark, frantic motion in the cold blue air. It wobbled uncertainly; then, legs dangling, it fluttered weakly away over the reed tops and almost immediately dropped back into their protection.

SORA RAIL

VIRGINIA RAIL

CLAPPER RAIL

RAILS

Three species of rails may be regularly expected in the Meadowlands.

The clapper rail (Rallus longirostris) is a true saltmarsh wader, found on both coasts from California and Massachusetts to South America. Formerly breeding in considerable numbers throughout the Hackensack estuary, the clapper for centuries formed the basis of an active hunting enterprise. It is today restricted to the Saw Mill Creek area, Kingsland Creek, and, in smaller numbers, Kearny Marsh.

The smaller, rust-colored Virginia rail (R. virginianus) is found from southern Canada to southern South America in fresh and brackish marshes. Formerly much more abundant in the Meadowlands, this rail prefers freshwater sedge and cattail habitats, though it may breed in brackish phragmites marshes. It is most common in Kearny Marsh West, occasional in the Saw Mill Creek area. It still breeds in scattered surviving wetland habitats in the Overpeck Creek drainage.

The sora rail (Porzanza carolina) breeds from Canada to the west-central and northeastern United States, and winters south to Peru. It is the most common breeding rail in the Meadowlands, frequently observed and heard in the Kingsland Impoundment, and may be encountered almost anywhere along the Hackensack River shoreline or its tributaries.

The bird's heart-stopping explosion into flight became at once a revelation and a crossroads for me. I had read of the "vision quest" of the Lenape. In this rite of passage, preteen boys were required to enter the surrounding wilderness and seek a guiding spirit that would accompany them through life, rendering advice and counsel. This ethereal persona might be found in any natural aspect of the environment: in a rock or tree, or perhaps in an animal. The Lenape referred to such a spiritual escort as a *manitto*. As I recall tracking the railbird with startling clarity, even after so many years, I realize now that perhaps that bird had been mine.

Back then, on that winter day in 1949, I embarked on a quest that was to dominate my life for the ensuing three weeks. The adventure would end with my capture of that bird in a crude, homemade trap, its confinement in an outdoor cage, and its eventual release—following inner conflict—to its rightful freedom. My experience with the rail irrevocably influenced my view of the natural world and perception of the Meadowlands forever.

Ultimately, my life's journey would lead me far from this place. But by coming face to face with my own manitto, in a frozen waste of reeds in the winter of 1949, I acquired something that never left me: the first tentative soundings of an environmental conscience. I have never forgotten that event, or that rail. They have proved to be more than imaginary companions, who would accompany me back over the years to these once-beautiful meadows and allow me to discern them with the eye of an artist and the heart of a naturalist.

Today, unfortunately, I have the ear of a Turnpike traveler. Right now, my perspective on this part of the world is perhaps best expressed in a notice that appeared in the October 1994 *Village Newsletter*. It encouraged the Ridgefield Park citizenry to attend an upcoming New Jersey Department of Transportation "Information meeting" that was held in town to discuss the construction of sound barriers that would spare the village at least some of the din of Interstate 95, the six-lane superhighway that now floods the valley of Overpeck Creek. The road cannot be seen from the east-west streets near the center of the village, but it can be heard. At times, when the wind is out of the east, the roar of traffic is so overpowering that outdoor conversation is difficult.

Mayor Fosdick lives in a house of venerable lineage on the eastern ridge that overlooks the point of this highway's junction with Interstate 80. His opinions on the road are perhaps understandably negative:

Gulls on ice, Overpeck Creek, looking toward the Ridgefield side of the river.

Big red-tailed hawk cruising above the juncture of Interstates 80 and 95 in the bright mists of a winter dawn.

Voices ❧

MAYOR FOSDICK

"The building of Route 95, of what they call 'the missing mile,' has destroyed the area, and people tend to forget what we really had here. Down off the side of the hill, all along Ridgefield Park, from Route 46 all the way up to Fort Lee Road, off the side of the hill, you were in a true wilderness: the meadows, the streams and channels—peaceful, quiet. But you could walk all the way out to the creek. . . .

"That's all changed today, of course. Where 80 and 95 come together may qualify in terms of traffic as the busiest intersection in the

Original Fort Lee Road between Teaneck and Leonia. A casualty of Interstate 80, built in the early 1960s, this road now lies abandoned. Cobbles used in its early 19th-century construction are once again visible through the eroding asphalt.

United States. That has forever altered, negatively, the entire area. No more deer—it had a very negative impact.

"It's such a constant din, you don't even think about it. It's a problem when you think about it, though. Time to time, something will happen on the road; trucks, you know, have what they call Jakes Brakes. You'll hear a trucker put on his Jakes Brakes; then you'll become aware of it."

⤜ ⤛

The two great highways, Interstates 95 and 80, converge at Ridgefield Park, funneling a great volume of traffic over the ridge and across the Overpeck meadows toward the city and New England. The notion of their joining here, and the relentless movement of plastic, rubber, steel, and people across the meadows, would have been considered pure fantasy less than a generation ago. Now, their massive overpasses loom above, invading the spaces of distant, yet still vibrant, memories.

Journal ⤜

SUMMER 1946: GRANDPA AND THE RED HERRING
My maternal grandfather's death in 1954 at the age of eighty left a wide, seemingly unfillable void in my young life. Grandpa Dempsey was a pensive, gentle man of rather portly proportions; he was a veteran of the Spanish-American War and chronicled his service to his country in marvelously descriptive letters penned in handwriting so ornate and beautiful that it appeared to be the work of a skilled calligrapher. Surely it lived up to all the penmanship criteria demanded by the Palmer method.

Since I was the oldest of his three grandsons, he seemed to pay particular attention to my budding interest in nature, and he presented me with my earliest books on the subject.

My grandparents had lived for many years in a modest frame house halfway down Brinkerhoff Street. At its eastern end, the street descended the town's ridge and ended at the edge of the meadows. Brinkerhoff Street was named for one of the founding families of the town; its first patriarch, Hendrick, had purchased the land in 1685 from Epke Jacobsen Banta, who had in turn acquired it from Sarah Kiersted, a settler who had served as an interpreter for Oratam, the patient and resigned sachem of the resident Lenape.

The street has changed relatively little since the 1940s; the turn-of-the-century frame homes remain—some of them remodeled over the years—and so do most of the shade trees, or at least their descendants, planted by the village's current Shade Tree Commission.

The foot of the hill is different now, though. For one thing, the dead end is no longer such—it now continues into the wide parking area of an apartment complex, built upon the firm footing created by one of the earliest meadows dumping and filling grounds. I stood there at the bottom of the hill recently, trying to recall how this place looked in the forties, fifty years before, when, for people like my grandfather, civilization ended and "wilderness" began at this very spot. I gazed on an urban scene that included an exit ramp for I-95, a relatively new private thoroughfare called Challenger (after the ill-fated space shuttle) Road, and the modernistic Hartz Mountain corporate complex that the road services. Try as I might, I could not conjure up that forbidding wall of reeds which had marked the end of civilization here nearly five decades ago. And this troubled me, for that had been the portal through which I had entered the Meadowlands for the very first time.

My grandfather and I had an easy, front-porch relationship, uncomplicated by the need or desire to make superfluous conversation. We were both on the quiet side, me perhaps out of simple firstborn shyness, he because it suited him. This was in the days before television stole our social skills; he and I spent many a long summer afternoon on the porch, listening to each other's occasional ruminations on nothing in particular, I accepting as truths his little gospels on life in general.

Then, one hot July morning shortly after my eighth birthday, we were occupying our usual stations on the front porch when a large herring gull skimmed in out of nowhere and landed in the middle of the street. It snatched a scrap of bread from the pavement and flew off with it toward the meadows. I was stunned; I had never seen such a big, impressive bird that close. Grandpa explained that although the gulls were "sea birds," they lived in the meadows as well; he had seen clouds of them from the train as it chuffed across the wide, flat marshes toward the Hoboken ferry.

My grandfather was a city man—he worked for Stern's Department Store in midtown Manhattan as an accountant—but he knew what gulls were and that they lived in wet reedy places, often in the thousands. As he casually instructed me in these new facts, he had little notion that he was about to take a new step of his own. For in that moment, as I walked to the curb and gazed down the street at the impenetrable greenery at the bottom of the hill, I realized for the first time that another world lay outside the familiar one of my town.

Being an agreeable, accommodating soul, my grandfather offered no immediate resistance to my out-of-the-blue suggestion that we take an exploratory walk in "the swamps." I can recall him cocking his head

*Ring-billed gulls gathering for a midday siesta on the abandoned landfill in
Overpeck County Park, Ridgefield Park.*

and considering this odd request for a long minute, as though the idea
at once repelled and intrigued him. Finally he agreed to escort me on a
"short stroll" along one of the old drainage ditches that sliced arrow-
straight through the reeds, from the dead end out to the creek.

I can clearly recall the rush of fearful expectation that coursed
through me as we pushed through the curtain of reeds and entered the
swamp that day. I knew that I was crossing a threshold of some kind,
stepping through a doorway that offered egress into a plane of existence that until that minute had been totally unknown to me.

The scent of the marsh—one of rich and boggy antiquity—was
strangely intoxicating. Unlike most of my peers, I was not repelled by
the primal odor of the meadows but rather, oddly, attracted to it. The
towering grasses, shining green and moving regally in the light breeze,
were at once intimidating and wonderfully familiar. I felt as an ant
might, navigating the trackless rain forest of a suburban lawn. There
was only the sky above and the grass, and a silence into which none of
the noises of the town intruded.

Grandpa and I quickly connected with a trail through the reeds, a
vague, beaten-down track of dead phragmites that wound off and away
into the dense thicket. Soon we came to the drainage ditch, and here I
had my first look at the life of the meadows.

The ditch's water was brownish and murky and moved slowly in
the direction of the creek; it carried a small cargo of flotsam in the form

of reed stems, spindly tree branches, and a solitary pink rubber ball. A frog plopped from the bank and stroked away through the water; the head of a muskrat moved toward the opposite bank at the apex of its wake. From somewhere deep in the green reeds, a bird called with a lilting, creaky note.

Then, I looked down into the opaque water at my feet and saw a small fish. It hung there close to the surface, motionless, save its tiny pectoral fins, which waved back and forth in a wild rhythm. Fascinated, I slowly crouched down and examined the creature more closely. It seemed to be ignoring me, yet supremely aware of my presence; its tiny, jeweled eyes swiveled about as it took in its surroundings.

I had never seen anything quite so beautiful in a wild fish; its back was a rather plain brownish green, but its body—what I could see of it—was liberally speckled with bright blue, green, and gold spots. Most impressive, its lower fins and tail were a bright saffron yellow. The fish looked like an aquatic butterfly!

For a long minute I watched the fish, and then the instinctive urge common to all children crept into my mind: I pondered the possibility of catching it. Tensely, I stood and looked about for some kind of container with which to scoop the fish from the ditch. A rusted can lying about ten feet up the boggy bank caught my eye, but as I made a move toward it, my grandfather spoke. "I don't think that's such a good idea, John Raymond," he said, as though he had read my mind. I squinted up at him; the sun was behind him, and he appeared as a great, dark adult-silhouette, his fedora pushed back on his head, his face unreadable. Never before had he contested my childish desires, if he felt them to be reasonable, and I wondered why, at this exciting moment in my life, he felt it necessary to thwart my righteous desire to obtain a pet.

"How come?" I asked, mildly defiant.

The dark figure took a draw on its cigar. "Because you have no place to keep the fish besides the can, and it belongs here and not in a can," Grandpa said. "You shouldn't take on a responsibility until you're ready to," he added with gentle finality.

I stared at the ground and considered this; he was right, of course, but it was all nonetheless pretty unfair. But to whom? Me, I guessed, and undoubtedly not the fish. I glanced back at the water; the spot was empty: the fish was gone. I looked quickly at Grandpa and then back at the water, at the sadly vacant place in the muddy flow where only seconds before had been an incredible living jewel—in the dirty and forbidding swamps at the end of Brinkerhoff Street!

I wondered whether, in the end, I had actually seen the fish at all. "What kind of fish was it, Grandpa?" I asked. My grandfather was

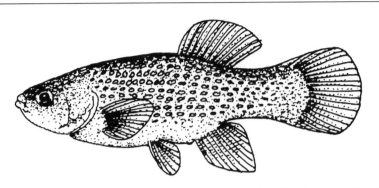

*The mummichog, or common killifish (*Fundulus heteroclitus*), is found in coastal brackish and marine habitats from Nova Scotia to Florida. It is also known as the zebra killy or chub. All Meadowlands waters affected by tidal influence, even those heavily polluted or near landfills, will harbor an abundant population of mummichogs. Studies have shown that this fish and the American eel can tolerate dissolved oxygen levels as low as 1.5 parts per million without apparent harm. In the 1960s surveys revealed that the mummichog was the only fish species able to maintain permanent breeding populations in the Meadowlands under the environmental conditions then extant.*

silent for a minute; he drew easily on his pungent White Owl and smiled. Then he chuckled: "Probably a red herring." I squinted at him. "A red herring? What kinda fish is that?" Grandpa laughed and tousled my hair. "Well," he said, "it's a pretty common fish; you'll come across a lot of them as you grow up, and they're not only found in swamps."

Later, as we shouldered our way out of the reeds and stepped once again upon the pavements of civilization, I persisted in my desire to identify that mystery fish with scientific certainty. "Grandpa," I probed, "that fish was brownish and yellow, with green spots, so why is it called a red herring?" My grandfather stamped the swamp mud from his shoes, then draped his arm over my shoulder. "Well, John Raymond," he answered, "maybe it's because a little mystery is as good a thing in a fish as it is in a person. And out there, in the meadows—and in the world—a lot of things are not really what they seem to be." He adjusted his fedora, tapped the ash off his cigar and grinned at me. "You'll see."

Within a couple of years of that adventure I finally captured a "red herring" in a different part of the Overpeck meadows. I placed the fish in a large glass fishbowl my mother had given me and then looked up its identity in a book on aquarium fishes. It turned out that my new pet was a common killifish, or mummichog. There was no mention of the species being called a red herring, but the book did note that the creature was hardy and adaptable and could be found in a wide variety of habitats.

Though I found myself irresistibly drawn to whatever wilderness remained tucked in among the seamless suburbs in the years following the Second World War, I knew that I was in fact very much a suburbanite and not the son of a wilderness guide. When the sixties blew in, my youngest brother, twelve years my junior, determined to walk that same philosophical "wilderness road," but he saw that the horizon toward which it led had edged a lot closer over the years.

My brother Steve has worked for New York's American Museum of Natural History for twenty-five years. He is an artist and designer of considerable skill and has brought his talent to bear on many of that institution's public exhibits. He is also something of an adventurer. He has served as ornithological leader for many of the museum's popular Discovery Tours, shepherding globe-trotting birders through places as varied as the Antarctic, Egypt, the Serengeti, and Manhattan's Central Park.

Steve bears some resemblance to actor Harrison Ford, and when he was growing up at the edge of the meadows, at the time of their final demise beneath the landfills of the sixties, to hear him tell it he occasionally behaved like Ford's Indiana Jones as well.

Voices

STEPHEN C. QUINN

"My first recollections of the meadows were of walking through what we called Barnes's Woods, near the edge of the Overpeck meadows. This was about 1957; I was seven or eight years old. I remember the horse stable, the old well, and spring. We'd look for salamanders there. In those days the trails went all the way up the edge of town to the creek and into Teaneck; that was before Route 80 came through. The woods were loaded with box turtles and full of raspberries; it was a half-day's journey to get out to the creek through the marshes, and you had to get wet to get there.

"I remember when they started the diking and draining there, in the early sixties. They would isolate big sections and dig the ditches to drain them, and the character of the meadows there began to change. Where before it was a cattail swamp, it became much drier and the

Overpeck marshes just prior to destruction by landfilling, late 1963–early 1964. The view is to the south, with the Public Service plant at Ridgefield visible in the distance. From a photo by the author.

phragmites moved in. Ironically, that's when my interest in birds and the natural world began. We formed a birding club called The Hazelton Heights Ornithological Club, after the old name for our section of the town. We'd meet under our various back porches.

"As kids, we seemed to understand the value of wetlands; it was something that was so obvious to us, but not, apparently, to adults. I recall that they were filling right through the nesting season. We'd find bittern, gallinule, and mallard nests in the reeds at the edge of the landfill, and the next day they'd be gone—buried under mounds of garbage. It was a terrible thing to see, and it made a lasting impression on me.

"This was the period when my friend Peter and I would go to the landfill when there was no one there and pull the spark plug wires and remove distributor caps and such in order to stop the bulldozers during

the nesting season. One time we were prowling the edge of the landfill
when a truck appeared. The guy got out as we ran into the phrags, and
we saw that he had a gun, a shotgun. We knew this guy; he was out there
all the time, sort of a guard. We waded out into the water, among the
dense reeds, and crouched there, motionless, hardly breathing. Suddenly we heard a shot, and pellets tore through the reeds near us. He
was shooting at us! We didn't dare move, and he kept loading up and
firing into the marsh. He finally left, but we hid out there for a couple
of hours, just in case.

"I told Dad about being shot at and he immediately called the police; however, I never told him about pulling the wires on bulldozers.
After being shot at, we ceased our tampering with bulldozers!

"When we were kids we'd trek out to the creek from the old

Paving the "missing mile" of Interstate 95, spring 1964. This view, looking east, shows heavy machinery preparing the roadbed after most of the landfilling in the Over-

Dexheimer Park; it was often a real adventure. One day my friend Louie and I came across an isolated pool at the edge of the dumps out near the creek that was full of fish, all of them gasping for breath, dying. We began scooping them up–big goldfish, carp, catfish–and moving them to the creek. It was pretty much a hopeless cause, there were so many of them, but we wanted to do it. Suddenly I stepped into an area of 'quickmud' and sank up to my neck in the stuff; only my head and right arm were above the surface. To make things worse, I had my good

peck valley had been completed. The level area in the immediate foreground is now occupied by Ridgefield Park's junior-senior high school. From a photo by the author.

clothes on. After a lot of hard work, Louie finally managed to pull me out; I don't know what I would have done if I had been there alone. We kids often made solo trips out into the meadows in those days. You could really get lost out there among the dense reeds, even in the Overpeck meadows. You had to follow sound, like distant voices, a car horn, or get a sighting on the sun; you couldn't see a horizon out there among some of the bigger stands of phragmites, and you might wander around in circles for a long time. The reeds might be ten to twelve feet high.

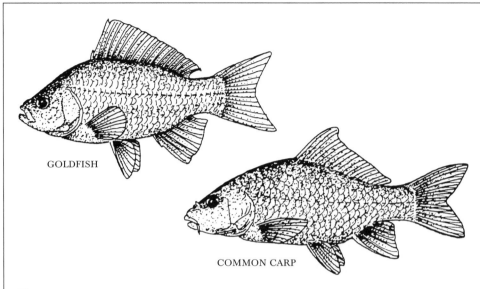

GOLDFISH

COMMON CARP

PISCINE INVADERS

The common goldfish (Carrasius auratus*) is native to temperate Eurasia and has been widely introduced worldwide, either accidentally or deliberately, as a bait fish and ornamental. In North America, feral goldfish are found from coast to coast in everything from farm ponds to large lakes. In the Meadowlands District the fish is common in mildly brackish and freshwater habitats such as Kearny Marsh, Overpeck Creek, and the Losen Slote area.*

The common carp (Cyprinus carpio*) is a native of temperate Eurasia but, like the goldfish, has been introduced all over the world, including Australia and Hawaii, as a food, game, and ornamental fish. In North America it is found throughout the temperate areas of the continent, often in waters so degraded as to be unable to support other fish. The carp is common throughout the district, both in freshwater impoundments and in the Hackensack River and most tributaries. It is highly regarded as a sport and food fish, and I have seen specimens caught in Overpeck Creek that measured 3 feet long and weighed 10 to 15 pounds.*

"Another time, a group of us were climbing on a huge earthmover on the dump when one of us must have hit the right button, because the thing started up! We all scattered and ran, leaving the big machine's engine running.

"In the mid-sixties Ridgefield Park was still a real meadows hunting and trapping town. I remember that the hardware store on Main Street had an entire wall of steel leghold traps for muskrat, fox, raccoon. Duck hunters built blinds throughout the area, and there was a lot of shooting in the fall. It would appear that they weren't only after waterfowl out there. Once we found a blind that had a dead barn owl stuck on a stick in front of it. There were dead crows all around the blind; they were obviously using the owl to lure in the birds, which they'd shoot at close range. We also found dead short-eared owls, bitterns, and teal in the area.

"We used to patrol the mosquito control ditches, looking for adventure. This was in the late sixties, when the mosquito control commission was still using petroleum distillates to spray the water in order to kill the larvae. I remember finding dead or dying black-crowned night herons, great blue herons, and egrets along the ditches, all because of the toxic oil spray they were using. Nobody knew, or cared, about the danger then.

"I recall all of my experiences in the meadows of the past as adventures that are unavailable to my own kids today. We had closer ties to the natural world then; it was much more a part of us and our life experience than it is for kids today. For example: hiding in the reeds near the creek and watching a flock of common mergansers come in and land no more than fifteen feet away; looking at those incredible, living jewels so close! Or a big male marsh hawk right overhead; you knew the nest was nearby, but you couldn't find it. Or a male sora rail, almost tame, stalking through the reeds a few feet away, like a little chicken.

"These were real life experiences, interaction with the other lifeforms that share this planet, and not any kind of 'virtual reality.' It was real. These things can't be duplicated today; they're gone . . . and that's very sad."

ᴥ ᴥ

Others, who predated my brother by generations, also recall experiences that cannot be supplanted by today's sophisticated entertainments. Rutherford's Charles Van Winkle, for instance, spoke of ordinary boyhood exploits at the turn of the twentieth century that rival those of the hardy subsistence hunters of centuries past. His adventures were the product of a land and fauna no longer accessible to youngsters, even if they were inclined to engage in them. Perhaps it is just as well.

Voices ᴥ

CHARLES A. VAN WINKLE
"On Saturdays a lot of the boys would go down to the meadows on shooting trips. At noontime we would shoot some railbirds and blackbirds, cut off the feet, wings, and head, and clean them. Then we would

pack the birds in meadow clay and put them in the fire to roast. Then we would take a stone, crack the clay, and the feathers would come right off with the skin.

"Some of the boys and myself went shooting every opportunity we had in the meadows. We noticed migrating birds that would fly about a mile in the air, so we figured that by making a nice bloody mess of skinned muskrats and putting a stake in the middle with a rattrap bound with cloth, and then making a hut of cattails, the migrating birds would come every spring and fall, come down on the stick, and the rattrap would catch them. I had traps on the ground also. I built a cage about eight feet by fifteen feet in the back of my father's barn to keep the birds in. I took two falcons, a chicken hawk, and a black Atlantic fish hawk [osprey]. They had six-foot wingspreads. With considerable difficulty I took them to the Central Park Zoo. I got a certificate from the zoo commissioners, and the birds were put in the eagle cage. I used to go over occasionally and look at them. I used to raise crows in the chicken yard. By clipping one wing on each bird, I could keep them from flying away. Crows were the easiest birds to raise, because they ate the same food as the chickens. I raised robins, thrushes, and blackbirds in cages on the second floor of the barn."

The marvelous profusion of birds was one of the more memorable physical features of the meadows; the "dry season" fires that swept the marshes in spring and fall were another. In recent years spectacular ignitions have occurred in the Hackensack marshes, most of the blazes blackening swaths of meadows turf where it still exists in sufficient acreage to allow a fire to work up a real head of steam. Although many of the blazes are doubtless triggered by what might be called "acts of God," such as the heat of the sun magnified through broken glass, others are likely the work or arsonists or of careless smokers flipping cigarette butts from cars on any of the busy roadways crossing the district.

Whatever the cause, a meadows blaze presents a rather odd analogy, not unlike that of a Great Plains wildfire transplanted to Central Park. Completely surrounded by city, a miniwilderness burns with all the ferocity and potential threat of a major forest fire in California. And no matter how many swamp fires one has seen, each leaves an indelible impression and irresistible urge to retell the tale. Mayor Fosdick recalls: "The thing that I was most impressed by as a kid was when the swamps burned. I mean that was—and I don't mean this to sound wrong—but it was spectacular. These big flames and that black smoke rolling up. And I specifically remember something that made quite an impression on me: when you thought that the fire was out, it turned out it wasn't. It was burning underneath the ground and the reeds, and all of a sudden it would erupt and this big explosion and a wall of flames flare up and the black smoke rolling."

Recent meadows blazes have arced over the Turnpike and brought traffic to a standstill, and they have at times threatened oil and chemical facilities. But in the past such grass fires were, for the most part, at best a diversion and at worst an inconvenience to residents of the surrounding suburbs. And aside from their dramatic effect on the landscape, they are not the environmental catastrophe they appear to be. Biologists recognize that in many habitats fire is crucial to the life cycle of some plants; the Long Island and New Jersey Pine Barrens would not be the unique ecosystems they are without the periodic fires that trigger germination in the pitch pine. These trees require the touch of fire in their eternal mission of procreation, and while the ubiquitous phragmites of the Meadowlands can survive well enough without a seasonal blistering by flames, there are indications that the heat and the elimination of detritus effected by a meadows fire invigorate subsequent growth in this hardy plant.

Renewal is as much a part of the meadows environment as it is anywhere else in the natural world. When the fires burn themselves into smoldering pockets and are then extinguished both above and below ground by spring rains, the land has been prepared for the promise of the new biological year. In abandoned dumps, where flames have swept away the dried tangles of last year's vegetation the aspect is one of a denuded, smoldering desert. By summer's end the amazingly resilient plants will have reclaimed in full their right to this place, covering it in lush profligacy—with bird-clouds now, instead of black smoke, darkening the skies above.

To my mild regret, most of my youthful investigative energies were expended in efforts to capture and confine the meadows' birdlife for my personal edification and amusement. In this I differed little from the great naturalists of yore; Audubon was as much the hunter as bird painter, shooting virtually every creature that flew, thereby gaining models for his art or new specimens for his personal "skin collection." In an age of seemingly limitless abundance, specimen collecting was not regarded as a wrong committed against nature but rather an act of violence in the interest of knowledge. The notion of animal rights was an alien concept destined for a peculiar future in which concern for the welfare of the "lesser creation" would supersede that rendered to others of our own kind.

But in spite of my often proprietary attitude toward the birds of the meadows, I saw them as fellow living creatures, fully deserving the

Killdeer calling from a pile of discarded tree stumps in the landfill near Overpeck County Park, Ridgefield Park.

very best intentions of my humanity when the need arose. Although the wild things more often bore the trials inflicted on them by an unforgiving environment with innocent brute patience, at times they required outside help to see them through an especially grim ordeal.

Journal ～

WINTER 1964: THE BIRDS

My youngest brother, Steve, and I went out into the meadows behind the park one bright and bitterly cold January day. I was a young, just-married guy then and had recently grown a beard. It was so cold—about ten below—that my breath quickly condensed and froze on the beard and created a solid chin-cap of ice. My brother was about thirteen.

We were looking for winter birds, and we ended up finding them, all right. In an open area of mixed cattails and phragmites near the edge of the landfill we saw what looked like hundreds of black pinecones on the snow and lodged up among the reeds. We never suspected they were anything alive, because they were absolutely motionless; they simply lay there, these black inanimate objects, stark against the white snow and dried brown reeds.

As we stood there, taking in this vaguely Siberian scene, we saw that a rather foul, grayish water was leaching from the landfill's flank. It gathered in steaming pools that sent clouds of faintly odorous vapor into the air among the reeds. It was bitter cold that morning, and the snow and reeds near the dump were coated with clear ice.

We crunched over to the strange objects, and as we got close, one of the pinecones feebly lifted a wing and made a thin, creaky noise. We realized with amazement that our "pinecones" were in fact birds—dozens, maybe hundreds of starlings. Most of them lay immobile on the hard-packed snow, but a number of them clung awkwardly to reed stems, stiff and seemingly very dead. Apparently, we speculated, the birds had been bathing in this unexpected supply of warm water and

Starlings roosting in reeds on a frozen winter dawn.

had been overcome by the severe cold as soon as they attempted to roost in this exposed, windswept place. And they had frozen to death.

But not all of them. As we hurriedly checked them over, we found that some were still alive, though just barely. The obvious course of action was one of immediate rescue. We ranged about a bit and found a large, battered, but serviceable cardboard box at the lip of the dump, and within a half-hour we had filled it with about sixty frozen, near-dead starlings.

Back home, as we lugged the boxful of birds down into the cellar that would serve as a sort of recovery room, my father observed the proceedings dubiously, but protested only halfheartedly. He had strong reservations about this campaign of mercy, but he was accustomed to the furred and feathered menagerie that had made its way in and out of the family home over the years, usually without misfortune, due to the outdoors avocations of his oldest and youngest sons.

He seemed to accept the essential rightness of rendering aid to these avian unfortunates, but we could tell that he found the notion of bringing sixty wild birds into his house a vaguely unsettling one, even if the creatures were in a cooperatively frozen state, like so many starling potpies. We were soon to experience for ourselves the folly of smugly brushing aside the gentle concerns of parents—even if they weren't naturalists.

My father was an easygoing and deferential man brought up in an era when respectable males did not cuss—preferably never, but especially in the presence of the opposite sex. My siblings and I, over all the years we loved him and lived under his roof, had never heard him utter anything more blistering or profane than a restrained "dammit," and then only under extreme duress, as when he would regularly bang his head on the low-slung hot water pipe while stoking the cellar's old coal furnace.

My brother and I left the starlings in the capable ministrations of the cast-iron furnace's heat, and vacated the cellar to pursue more immediate interests. In short, in the truncated attention span of youth, we had forgotten completely about the birds. But then, less than a hour later and from the depths of the cellar, we heard that fateful epithet. And we knew, this time, that it had nothing whatsoever to do with a recalcitrant water pipe.

We found the cellar a veritable blizzard of sable wings; our starlings had effected a marvelous recovery, but we saw to our dismay that the cure was surely worse than the disease. We found the recovery chamber empty—every single starling had flown the box and was either airborne or perched upon every available object in the cellar. Horrified, we surveyed a floor already liberally speckled with bird droppings and witnessed the painful spectacle of panic-stricken blackbirds battering themselves dizzy against the cellar's windows in their frantic efforts to escape.

For precious minutes we sprinted about ineffectually, trying to corner the now truly wild birds and rebox them while Dad sternly surveyed the bedlam from the head of the stairs. But it was hopeless, a classic can-of-worms exercise—a scene of mad and utter confusion. Starlings darted everywhere, disoriented, rasping and screeching in terror; they flew into packing boxes and shrouded family heirlooms, up the stairs, behind the washing machine, and, worst of all, up into spaces between the walls. A bird landed on my head, defecated there, and dashed away even as I moved to grab it.

Finally, my father had had enough of our obvious lack of bird-catching expertise and resorted to "that word" for the last time: "Dammit," he shouted, "open the cellar door!"

Epiphany! As the old wooden hatchways swung wide the starlings saw their opportunity and in a flood of flying bodies made haste toward the light of salvation. In a mad stream they poured forth, out into the backyard, over the garage, above the trees, and eastward, toward the meadows from whence they had all come.

Well, most of them, anyway. Back in the cellar, as Dad orchestrated the cleanup, we heard strange, furtive sounds, emanating, it seemed, from the very deepest recesses of the house. We looked at each other: "Good grief, they're up in the walls!" my brother breathed with dismay.

It took us the better part of two days to evict the last starling from its temporary refuge in the walls of the house. Using a long stick, a broom, and a flashlight, we discovered that starlings are not only superb fliers but accomplished climbers as well; some of them had retreated upward at least seven feet, above the level of the first floor, in the narrow spaces between studs and lathing. In the end, we were pretty sure we got them all.

As the birds took wing, my father returned to his usual self—a patient and kind man, tolerant of the many small crises that confronted him in life. He knew they came with the territory, with the assembly of a large family. Still, the incident has, over the ensuing years, become one of the more enduring items of family lore, and speculation remains that at least one desiccated holdout remains entombed, resolutely and eternally grasping the lathing, deep within the walls of the house.

✒ ✒

So much of the essence of a place is contained within the memories of those who called it home. The sum of our experience is ultimately expressed in the word *yesterday*. My own yesterdays span more than five decades. My father is gone nearly ten years now; his yesterdays would go back a few decades more. But the cumulative yesterdays of the Meadowlands themselves far exceed my own, or any conceivable human timeline.

Yesterday

The Hackensack meadows, in the form in which they meet the eye today, have been in the making for some 20,000 years. Although the modern perception of this estuary is one of rapid and continuous change–this no doubt enhanced by the industrial hubbub and ceaseless flow of traffic that dominates the scene today–there is an essence of timeless immunity to the meadows. They are, in fact, a product of patient forces working over a time span that ultimately reaches back 4.6 billion years, to our planet's very beginnings.

Geologist Don Eicher, in his book *Geologic Time*, compresses the history of the earth into a one imaginary "year" in order to offer us a humbling perspective on our biological tenure here. In Eicher's timetable, the earth's oldest known rocks date from about mid-March. Living things, mere single-cellular entities, first appear in the primordial seas in May. Terrestrial plants and animals emerge on a forbidding landscape in late November. The vast, steaming swamps that formed the coal deposits laid down in the Carboniferous period hold sway for a mere four days in mid-December; they vanish on the twenty-sixth of the month, at about the same time that the Rocky Mountains arise. Ancestral humans first appear late in the evening on New Year's Eve, and Columbus makes landfall in the New World about three seconds before midnight. Within the perspective of Eicher's timeline, the grand sweep of human events that have occurred since European "discovery" of the Western Hemisphere has thus flashed by in the space of time it takes to draw a breath.

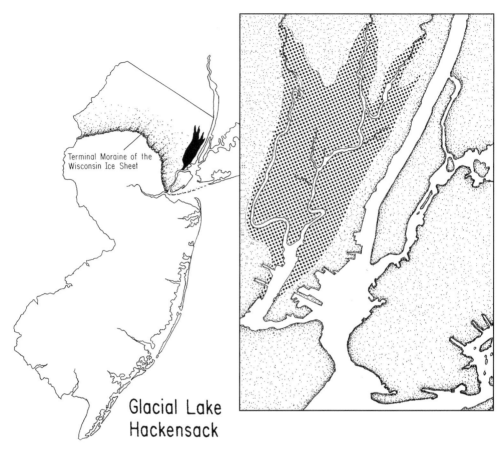

Glacial Lake
Hackensack

Map of Glacial Lake Hackensack. Adapted from Schuberth, 1968.

The Tertiary period of the earth's history began about 65 million years ago, with the geologically abrupt extinction of the dinosaurs,
and ended at the onset of the Quaternary, roughly 1.75 million years
ago. This span of time includes the Pleistocene period, in which the
greatest movements of glacial ice took place in North America and Europe. Four major ice advances occurred during this million-year time
span: the Nebraskan, Kansan, Illinoian, and Wisconsin. Three of these
glaciations–all but the Nebraskan–reached New Jersey, and the last,
the Wisconsin, was most instrumental in the formation of the Meadowlands region.

The immense weight and scouring capability of the Wisconsin glacier, estimated to have been between twenty-five hundred and thirty-
five hundred feet in depth, destroyed virtually all vegetation in its path
and carved great, bowl-like depressions in New Jersey's Pleistocene
landscape. These glacial bowls are known today as northern New

Jersey's largest water bodies, Lakes Hopatcong and Greenwood, and Budd Lake. At its greatest southerly extent in New Jersey, the ice sheet reached the area of present-day Staten Island and Perth Amboy.

As the ice melted and withdrew, rocks and debris it had carried down from the north, known as glacial "drift," were dropped in vast, rubbled windrows called terminal moraines, these deposits being the widest—up to one mile—and thickest at the far southern limit of the glacier. The terminal moraine as it exists today is a ridge of rocks and gravels—obscured by vegetation and houses, of course—that is up to three hundred feet deep in the area of Dover, New Jersey. By the beginning of the Holocene, or Recent period, dated at about 10,000 years ago, climatic warming was well under way, and the massive ice sheet had receded, at a rate of between sixty and one hundred feet per year, closer to its Greenland birthplace.

The northern New Jersey and southeastern New York landscape was left with several large but relatively shallow glacial lakes. Four of the largest were Glacial Lakes Passaic, Hackensack, Hudson, and Flushing. When these lakes eventually drained, much of the land around the Jersey side evolved into one of the world's largest coastal estuaries, melding with an ocean that had since risen three hundred feet.

Glacial Lake Passaic, at its greatest extent, reached a width of more than ten miles and stretched from present-day Far Hills to the city of Paterson, with a maximum depth of 240 feet. As the lake's ice plug at Little Falls in Paterson melted, the frigid waters plunged to the sea, leaving a series of extensive marshes. They are known today as the Troy and Great Piece Meadows and the three-thousand-acre Great Swamp in Chatham, the latter a national wildlife refuge surrounded by the suburbs of northern New Jersey.

Lake Hudson, the narrowest of the glacial lakes, occupied the present-day valley of the Hudson River. It apparently joined Lake Hackensack in the area of what is now Elizabeth, and it probably covered all but the highest elevations of Manhattan Island when at its greatest depth. Glacial Lake Flushing, considered an arm of Lake Hudson, extended northeastward through northern Queens County and well into Nassau County. It can be considered a prehistoric arm of what is today Long Island Sound.

Glacial Lake Hackensack, its eastern shoreline situated about two miles west of the Palisades, was the progenitor of the river and marshes that would one day occupy my home-ground landscape. This wide but relatively shallow lake filled the Hackensack valley from the earthen and rock-rubble dam of its terminal moraine at modern-day Perth Amboy north to slightly beyond the present New York–New Jersey border, a distance of about fifty miles. The lake was about fifteen miles wide at its greatest extent in the Upper Pleistocene, at the present-day

*Maximum extent of Wisconsin ice sheet (*left*) and of Glacial Lakes Passaic, Hackensack, Hudson, and Flushing (*right*). Adapted from Schuberth, 1968.*

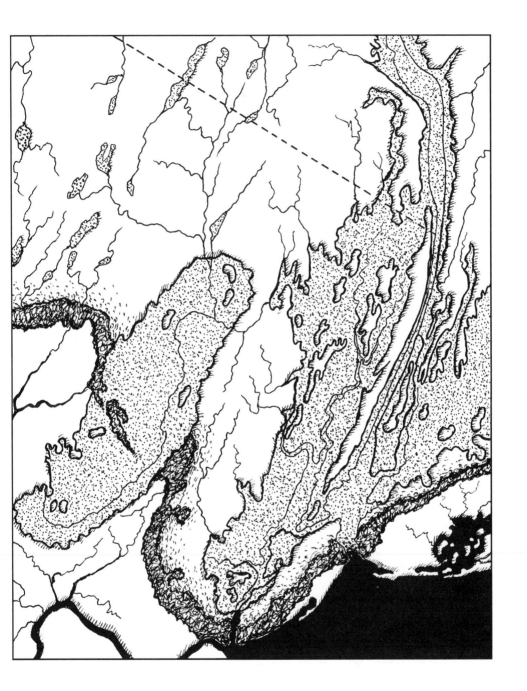

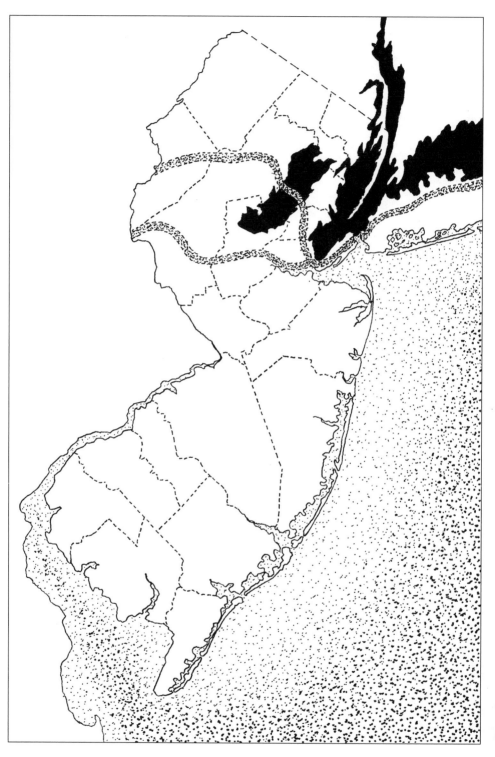

The four major glacial lakes in the present states of New Jersey and southeastern New York. This map also shows the terminal moraines of two successive ice advances.

city of Hackensack. Following a life span of 2,550 years, the lake's terminal moraine was breached between 8,000 and 10,000 years ago, and its waters drained seaward, leaving behind the rich estuarine clays and the complex ecosystem that would become known to the European arrivals on the continent as the Jersey meadows.

But near the end of the Pleistocene period, some 12,500 years ago, the Hackensack valley and much of the exposed Middle Atlantic continental shelf was a wide coastal plain of bogs, marshes, and taiga forest—a very different sort of place than it is now. Try to imagine the scene: mist-shrouded, parklike tundra clothed in the cold-resistant plants common to the steppe and arctic environments of today was the predominant topography of the coastal plain, which extended about fifty miles east of the present seashore. Swampy floodplains, marshes, and freshwater meadows graced the inner lowlands, while freshwater lakes and ponds dotted the ridges and valleys of the interior. Historian Kevin Wright notes that "alpine firs as succeed in cooler latitudes have been suggested as the original biotic community to colonize the drained lake

*Impression of the Passaic and Hackensack River valleys (*left and center*) at the time of glacial withdrawal, ca. 12,000–14,000 B.C.E. Drawing not to scale.*

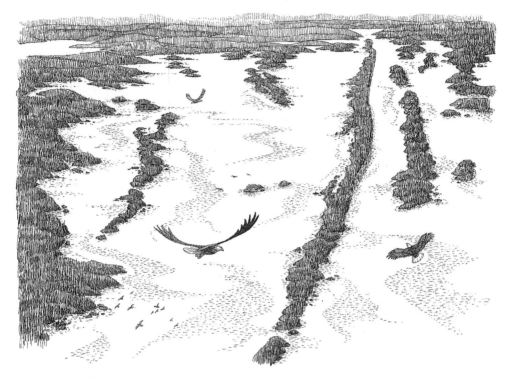

Impression of Hackensack valley at the greatest extent of Glacial Lake Hackensack,
ca. 10,000–11,000 B.C.E. Jutting from the far shore in the center distance is the
Teaneck–Ridgefield Park ridge; the long thin ridge to its right is the Palisades,
with Manhattan Island farther right. Drawing not to scale.

bed. Such forests could have provided mast for browsing herds of mastodon. The earliest record preserved in the peat deposits indicates that the clay bed of the lake was anciently transformed into a black ash swamp. There are indications that open grasslands composed of sedges, grasses, and alders also prevailed. The combination of lowland forest and grassy meadows would have supported grazing herds of caribou, elk and deer."

Temperatures in that distant epoch averaged eighteen degrees Fahrenheit cooler than those of today. This was the age of the storied beasts of the prehistoric past: the moose-elk, a giant beaver weighing four hundred pounds, a twelve-foot-high ground sloth, peccary, caribou, the dire wolf, saber-toothed cats, the huge short-faced bear, woolly mammoths—and mastodons.

The American mastodon (*Mammut americanus*), slightly smaller but stockier than the huge mammoth, was an abundant mammal in the ancient valley of the Hackensack, favoring the boggy shoreline of the gla-

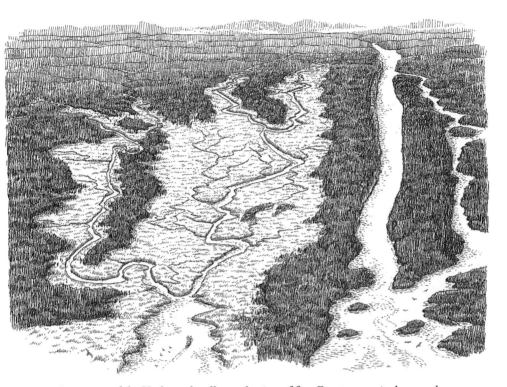

*Impression of the Hackensack valley at the time of first European arrival, ca. early
17th century. Drawing not to scale.*

cial lake. Although the remains of more than one hundred mastodons
have been found in the Middle Atlantic region, the notion of huge,
tusked creatures in the manner of elephants inhabiting the environs
of modern-day Manhattan—one was unearthed at Broadway and 141st
Street—is certainly an alien one. The discovery of ancient proboscidean
remains, nevertheless, is a fairly common occurrence, one of the better-
known finds being the so-called Hackensack mastodon. This animal,
discovered by two teenagers in the winter of 1962 near Polifly Road in
Hackensack, was recovered by scientists from the American Museum
of Natural History and the Bergen Museum of Art and Science. The
dig lay at the site of the former shoreline of Lake Hackensack, and excavators uncovered the remains of an Indian food midden on a slightly
higher and thus more recent level of the substrate. The bones of the
Hackensack mastodon, a young female, saw the light of day again after
some thirty centuries, during construction of Interstate 80.

The reality of the mastodons' recent tenancy in this land is perhaps brought into sharper focus by a firsthand description of its diet. A
researcher of the last century described the stomach contents of one

interred specimen, the Warren mastodon, thus: "In the midst of the ribs, embedded in the marl and unmixed with shells or carbonate of lime, was a mass of matter, composed principally of the twigs of trees broken into pieces of about two inches in length, and varying in size from very small twigs to half an inch in diameter. There was mixed in with these a large quantity of finer vegetable substance, like finely divided leaves; the whole amounting from four to six bushels. From the appearance of this, and its situation, it was supposed to be the contents of the stomach; and this opinion was confirmed on removing the pelvis, underneath which, in the direction of the last of the intestines, was a train of the same material, about three feet in length and four inches in diameter."

Geologically speaking, the mastodons did indeed fade from the North American faunal scene only yesterday. The lay of their Pleistocene landscape can still be glimpsed here today, in the shallow glacial valley flanked on the east by the ridge and ramparts of the Palisades and on the west by the Watchung Mountains. It requires only a small stretch of the imagination to picture the hulking forms of these powerful beasts as they moved with ponderous grace through the mists of boreal shorelines, around the icy-cold lake that lay where the urbanized Meadowlands now ripple in the sun.

The Paleo-Indians of New Jersey may well have hunted the mastodon here in the ancient past; in any event the Lenape, their distant descendants, explained the mastodons' disappearance in the Yah-qua-whee myth. The huge beasts, they said, were placed on Earth by the Great Spirit to benefit humanity. But the normally complacent creatures instead rebelled against such servitude, and in a subsequent battle between the mastodons and the humans (who had animal allies), the mastodons were defeated when they became mired in the blood-soaked mud of the battlefield.

New Jersey historian Earl Miers writes of the ultimate end of the great conflict in *Down in Jersey*: "The anger of the Great Spirit grew awesome. He stood upon the mountaintop, hurling bolts of lightning at the mastodons. One by one he killed all but an old bull, whose defiant tusks knocked aside the lightning bolts. In its rage, killing all who approached it, the old bull fought with a splendid, silent heroism. At last wounded, the bull dragged itself from the bloody mire. It bounded across the Ohio River, or so legend insists, and then across the Mississippi. It swam the Great Lakes and disappeared into the Far North where it lives to this day."

There are also, of course, current explanations of the mastodons' disappearance based on modern scientific research. The relatively sudden extinction, not only of the mastodons, but of many large Pleistocene mammals in North America, occurred within a narrow time frame about 11,000 years ago. In New Jersey, the demise of the American

Impression of mastodons at Glacial Lake Hackensack's eastern arm, near what is today the Teaneck–Ridgefield Park area, ca. 12,000–11,000 B.C.E.

mastodon seems to coincide with the disappearance of Glacial Lake Hackensack and the replacement of the animals' primarily coniferous food plants by less favorable deciduous species. It is thought that these animals depended on conifers and other nonflowering trees and shrubs; as the climate warmed, these plants were gradually replaced by angiosperms and grasses, and the mastodons–browsers in the manner of deer rather than grazers like bison–found themselves threatened by a steadily shrinking food supply.

One other hypothesis adds an all-too-modern, disturbing touch. Anthropologists and paleontologists have long debated the question of whether the arrival of Paleo-Indian big game hunters in eastern North America contributed to the sudden disappearance of mastodons. It is known that ancient peoples systematically hunted both mammoths and mastodons in western North America; indeed, a sudden influx of sophisticated, well-armed humans migrating across the Bering Strait from Asia (or perhaps just a rapid spread of new hunting tools and techniques) may well have exterminated all the big, slow-breeding, easily hunted mammals, according to a hypothesis known as "Pleistocene overkill." But the archaeological record in the East is inconclusive, being limited to artifacts uncovered in the higher, more recent strata of

Impression of Paleo-Indian hunters cautiously sizing up a passing herd of mastodons at the boggy shoreline of Glacial Lake Hackensack, ca. 11,000 B.C.E. Native Americans may have hunted the great beasts here; archaeological evidence is not conclusive.

digs. While it is probable that the earliest human inhabitants of the Hackensack valley knew the mastodon and may possibly even have hunted it, the sites containing mastodon remains found to date have not confirmed either of those speculations.

Although Lenape sachems of the seventeenth century insisted that their immediate forebears had known, and hunted, the mastodon—they regaled European newcomers with legends and purportedly eyewitness accounts to that effect—most paleontologists agree that these tales were likely cultural myths handed down from generation to generation. It is now believed that the huge beast was already a creature of the irretrievable past when the Meadowlands began to take their present form some 9,000 years ago, and that only the Paleo-Indians could have known them firsthand.

The current, meandering course of the lower Hackensack River established itself in the centuries after the glacial lake drained. No one knows by what name the earliest Paleo-Indian inhabitants may have known it, but the river's modern name, bequeathed on it by the Native Americans of the Late Woodland period, probably stems from one of two Lenape phrases: *Hackink Saquik*, meaning "a stream that unites with another on low ground," or *Hocquan Sakuwit*, meaning "hooked mouth of a river." Both names allude to the Hackensack River's curving juncture with the Passaic River at Newark Bay, near Bayonne. The Lenape root word, *Hackingh*, meaning "land of the pipe," refers to the clay found in the region suitable for the manufacture of pipes, and may also figure in the old name for the river.

In pre-Columbian times, the meadows consisted of extensive freshwater marshes and coastal white cedar forests, the remains of which lie beneath the dense mat of marsh detritus and embedded in the mud of some tidal creeks today. Historian Wright notes that at about 1400 C.E., more southerly, warmth-loving species of vegetation "migrated into the Hackensack Meadowlands. White cedar invaded the estuarine bog, transforming thousands of acres into a boreal swampland. The periphery of this cedar forest was invaded by marsh species such as rush, sedges, and cattails. Notably, the appearance of white cedar in this locale coincided with the advent of the Little Ice Age. Possibly, a lowering of sea level by the conversion of water to glacial ice occasioned the northerly spread of the cedar. By the historical period, approximately one-third of the meadowlands was cedar swamp."

But whatever spurred the cedars' advance, they seem to have pushed north a little too far. In *The Geology of New Jersey* (1868), George H. Cook, New Jersey's state geologist during the 1860s, commented on the evident decline of the coastal white cedar forest: "The marshes about the mouths of the Passaic and Hackensack Rivers are filled with the remains of cedar timber; and every traveller who crosses them by any of the railroads going to New York, can see the roots in the ditches; the stumps standing in the meadows and occasionally a log projecting from the mud. . . . Farther up the valley . . . there are cedar swamps in which the gradual dying out of the trees is seen now to be in progress."

A few decades later the construction of the Oradell Reservoir and the closure of its dam, in 1922, severely reduced the flow of fresh water reaching the estuary, and forever changed its ecology. Under the combined effects of diking, drainage, and the invasion of salt water from Newark Bay, the meadows' transformation from a freshwater marsh and coastal cedar forest into a brackish estuary dominated by the invasive reed called phragmites rapidly approached its conclusion.

LENAPEHOKING

The three major divisions of the native peoples who for more than 10,000 years occupied the piedmont and coastal plain of the Middle Atlantic region—the Munsees, the Unalachtigo, and the Unami—are known today as a loose confederacy under the name Delaware Indians. They are the only major American Indian tribe to be assigned a name based entirely on an English word: Lord De la Warre, the English title of Thomas West, a colonial governor of Virginia. The name these people themselves used, Lenape–traditionally thought to have meant "the original people"–is now variously determined by linguists to have been derived from two Native American words, *eren*, meaning "real" or "true," and *apeu* or *napeu*, meaning "a human being." Over time, the *r* in *eren* fell into disuse and was replaced by the letter *l*. Thus Lenape: "real people" or "true human beings."

The Hackensack Meadowlands lay at the heart of Lenapehoking– in the Munsee dialect, the Land of the Lenape. This land in toto encompassed present-day New Jersey, southeastern New York State, eastern Pennsylvania, and northern Delaware. The Munsee branch of the Lenape, known as the Hackingsauk, had their headquarters at Gamoenapa, located at that section of Jersey City known today as Communipaw. Native American life then was centered on the great estuary

Cormorants resting on a mud spit, summer evening, Overpeck Creek, Leonia.

of the Hudson River, known to the Lenape as Mahikanituk, the name stemming from *ma* ("great"), *hikan* ("ocean), and *ittuk* ("river"): Great Oceanlike River.

The historical Lenape appear to have evolved in situ from ancestral peoples, or Paleo-Indians, who had been living in Lenapehoking for many thousands of years. Scientists now believe that American Paleo-Indians derived from northern Asiatic peoples living in the basins of the Lena and Aldan Rivers in Siberia some 20,000 to 40,000 years ago, some of whom crossed the Siberian land bridge into North America between 13,000 and 15,000 years ago. These were of modern *Homo sapiens* stock and not of Old World Neandertal lineage; they, like their Cro-Magnon contemporaries, possessed a fairly sophisticated tool technology and fire-making skills.

These earliest Native Americans continued to live in a Stone Age tradition during what has become known as the Paleo-Indian period; this lasted from about 14,000 to about 10,000 years ago, during the retreat of the Wisconsin ice sheet and the ultimate drainage of Glacial Lake Hackensack. Archaeologist William Ritchie speculates that the first inhabitants of Lenapehoking, and the Northeastern Woodlands region in general, were likely "a wide scattering of tiny bands, in all likelihood limited to a few families, of great mobility and primarily dependent for sustenance on large game mammals." Ritchie traces the Paleo-Indian migration from the point of North American entry at the Siberian land bridge eastward to the Atlantic through the recovery and dating of flint spear points and other stone artifacts: "The thin scatter of fluted points in the Northeast follows the principal river systems, and it would appear that the primary movements had originated to the south and southwest of the area. Thus a trail of fluted point users seems to ascend along the Ohio and Allegheny rivers into southwestern New York; another to follow the Susquehanna and Delaware systems from Pennsylvania into central New York; while yet another to lead northward through the Hudson Valley."

Just when the ancestral Lenape arrived in the Middle Atlantic region in general and New Jersey and the Hackensack valley in particular is still a matter for some conjecture, but radiocarbon dating of archaeological sites in New York, Pennsylvania, and Connecticut places initial occupancy of those areas at between 12,580 and 10,190 years ago. They were certainly present—as true Lenape—in the Hackensack valley by 9,000 years ago.

Exclusive of the Paleo-Indian period, the history of the Lenape occupancy of this part of the North American continent extended through what are known to archaeologists as the Archaic and Woodland periods.

Red-tailed hawk, Overpeck County Park, Teaneck. This hawk was hunching possessively over a muskrat it had captured near a frozen tributary of Overpeck Creek.

The native peoples of the Archaic period were true hunter-gatherers. They relied entirely on the bounties of nature, practiced no agriculture, and kept no domestic animals except the dog, descended in North America probably from the wolf. Anthropologist John Witthoft described the Archaic-age Indian as "a small man, rarely more than five feet, five inches tall . . . of very slight build, and . . . probably no more than 130 pounds." Nonetheless, these people, according to Witthoft, were doubtless "wiry, strong and extremely tough." But despite this physical hardiness, the earliest Lenape were subject to all the diseases and physical wear and tear that plague modern humankind, and the average warrior "seldom lived to his fortieth birthday, usually dying before he was thirty-five." Witthoft further notes that the Archaic Indian's "diseased teeth and the infections they caused were probably a prelude to death. Hunger, exposure and hunting accidents were probably the other major causes of early death. Various arthritic and rheumatoid diseases were remarkably frequent and often severe, judging by evidence from the skeletons."

In sum, the ancestral Lenape of the Archaic period, who may have shared the sylvan pathways and broad meadows with the mastodon and dire wolf, faced not a benign and lushly abundant Eden but an unforgiving, though pristinely beautiful, natural world. As such, they did not necessarily fit the popular imagery of the "noble savage" but possessed instead, perhaps, the determined innocence and corporal vulnerability of the wild creatures who shared their world. Witthoft again: "The [Archaic period] Indian was . . . constantly exposed to the worst rigors of our climate. He slept curled into a ball, with his knees under his chin, a habit acquired during a lifelong struggle against a cold and brutal natural world. He was a man who lived very hard and died young. This is not the Indian of our romantic literature, but it is most certainly the Indian whose bones we study."

At the time of their contact with white Europeans, the Lenape peoples congregated for the most part in small, permanent communities situated in locations that offered both strategic protection from human enemies and ready access to reliable plant and animal food sources. "There is no historical or archaeological evidence that the Late Woodland Indians of Lenapehoking lived in large villages, as that term is generally understood; neither is there any evidence that their houses were protected by stockades," writes anthropologist Herbert Kraft in his scholarly work *The Lenape.*

European perceptions of the Lenape residents they encountered were apparently at strong variance from the image of disease-ridden and misfortune-prone Paleo-Indians conveyed by the archaeological record. Dutch colonist Nicholas van Wassenaer, writing in 1624, remarked: "It is somewhat strange that among these most barbarous people, there are few or none cross-eyed, blind, crippled, lame, hunchbacked or limping men; all are well fashioned people, strong and sound of body, well fed, without blemish." Another contemporary observer, Van der Donck, wrote in 1650: "The natives are generally well set in their limbs, slender round the waist, broad across the shoulders, and have black hair and dark eyes. . . . The men generally have no beard or very little, which some even pull out." Others found the New World style of personal adornment bizarre, in the manner of "savages" known to Europeans at the time: "Their pride is to paint their faces strangely with red or black lead, so that they look like fiends."

David De Vries, an early Dutch colonist and large landholder in the Overpeck Creek area, obviously was not an admirer of the Lenape he encountered; he wrote them off as "very foul and dirty." William Penn, on the other hand, observed in 1682 that the Lenape "are tall, straight, well-built and of singular proportion. They tread strong and clever, and walk with a lofty chin." Penn was also an unabashed admirer of their language, noting that the Lenape "do speak little, but fervently, and with elegance." He described the Munsee dialect as "lofty, yet narrow, like the Hebrew. In signification full, like short-hand in

writing: one word serveth in the place of three, and the rest are sup-
plied by the understanding of the hearer. I have made it my business to
understand it, that I might not want an interpreter on any occasion."

At the time of European arrival in New Netherland, it is estimated
that there were between 8,000 and 12,000 Unami living in what would
become the state of New Jersey—roughly one per square mile. Where
the Lenape settled down to plant crops in the Late Woodland period,
the population density must have been greater. It is now, statewide,
about a thousand persons per square mile, and no doubt higher in the
industrialized northeastern corridor. A modern footnote to these dry
statistics is the effort on the part of present-day persons of claimed
Lenape-Delaware ancestry to gain recognition as a tribe in New Jersey;
they number about 15,000 persons of mixed ancestry.

The first significant Lenape, or Unami, contact with modern Europeans probably occurred in 1524 with the arrival in Lower New York
Bay of Florentine navigator Giovanni da Verrazano and the crew of the
French caravel *Dauphine*. He named the bay The Sea of Verrazano, a
name that has not endured. Verrazano, however, was the first known
European to catch sight of the rocky, wooded shore of Manhattan Island, long known to the Lenape as Minna-atan, Island of Hills, or simply, Hill Island. He never returned.

The ensuing decades saw little or no further contact with Europeans; the Hackensack flowed on toward the sea as it had for countless millennia. One might well imagine that the wisest of the Lenape
sachems, perhaps plagued by troubling dreams and visions inspired by
that first encounter with the pale, oddly attired strangers, kept their
watch over the broad meadows and the waters of Newark Bay—
wondering if, or when, another sail would appear on the horizon.

In the year 1609, that sail did slip up over the curve of the world.
Henry Hudson, an English navigator in the employ of the Dutch East
India Company, entered Lower New York Bay and dropped anchor off
the Narrows. Over the following week, he and his crew explored the
"Shatemuc River" of the Lenape as far north as the site of present-day
Albany. John Colman explored coastal inland portions of the land of
the Lenape, coming upon Newark Bay and the confluence of the Passaic and Hackensack Rivers. Samuel Groome, an explorer-successor of
Hudson, wrote several years later of the Raritan River and Newark
meadows: "Well, here is a brave country, the ground very fruitful and
wonderfully inclinable to English grasses such as clover. Those swampy
lands bear great burdens of grasses and the land is four times better
than I had expected."

Among the distinct Munsee bands or subtribes that occupied lands
in the meadows region at the time of European arrival were the Ca-

narsees, Esopus, Hackensacks, Kitchtawanks, Navasinks, Raritans, Tappans, Warranawankongs, and Wiechquaeskecks. These peoples saw the Meadowlands not as a noxious "swamp" that might be improved but as the only homeland they knew, a life-sustaining landscape of spiritual significance. Writes Herbert Kraft: "The Indians adapted to the landscape; they lived in harmony with nature and shared in its bounty." He adds that "the Lenape built no mounds or monuments, established no governmental organization, and invented no written language or complex sciences. Their way of life required none of these, and they certainly were not concerned about the judgments future historians or archaeologists would make about them.

"As European trade grew in volume and importance," Kraft continues, "the Indians' attitudes towards the white man's peculiar notions of commerce changed, and many now had but one thought: beaver pelts could be used to buy exotic trade goods and liquor, and the more pelts, the more riches could be obtained in return." Such contamination of the Lenape by the "civilized" credo that every feature of their world, whether living thing or the land itself, ultimately had a price tag and was thus reduced to cash value was, Kraft says, one of the root causes for the deterioration of their culture and their eventual disintegration as a people.

Dr. Kraft's view of the ecological correctness of the aboriginal North Americans and of the reasons for their decline is no doubt the prevailing one today, but is it in fact based on truth? Was the Native Americans' so-called Earth Mother view of the natural world really at loggerheads with that of the European invaders of this continent? Historian Fergus Bordewich, in *Killing the White Man's Indian*, insists that "there is no certainty that native tribes even possessed the idea of nature as a whole." He notes that nearly all tribes living in pre-Columbian North America "used the means at their command to bend nature to their use" and that within the limits of their technology they "were no less inherently exploitative of it." There can be little doubt that the Lenape of the Hackensack valley, like their counterparts in other areas of the continent, often used effective food-gathering techniques—such as the wholesale burning of forests and marshes to flush game, and the overexploitation of game animals—that would certainly be regarded as ecologically unconscionable today.

Whatever the truth of the Native American land-ethic mystique, it is plain that the Lenape were ultimately unable to resist European influence and persevere in the face of Western concepts that were generally alien to them. A culture based on a ruling elite, ownership of land, and the erection of self-aggrandizing monuments—"the Lenape would have none of," writes Kraft, "for they were fiercely egalitarian. Every individual had dignity and worth, and every leader was regarded merely as 'first among equals.' It was a world of mutual support and community."

But the clash of cultures intensified, and the Lenape stewardship of the Meadowlands soon drew to a close. "Perhaps it was inevitable," Kraft writes, "that misunderstandings arising from differences in language and culture, as well as a natural distrust of unfamiliar people, should occasionally lead to quarrels and violence," hastening the suppression and eventual displacement of the native peoples.

The subsequent steady decline in the fortunes of the original inhabitants of New Jersey, launched by the brutal February 25, 1643, massacre of eighty Hackingsack Indian men, women, and children at Pavonia by Dutch under the command of Willem Kieft, culminated with the 1798 removal of the Lenape to Brotherton, the first American Indian reservation, located in southern New Jersey. By the close of the seventeenth century, most of Lenapehoking from Sandy Hook to Bear Mountain in New York had been appropriated by Europeans, and the majority of the Lenape had migrated west to Pennsylvania and Ohio. Others, through various agreements and treaties with their conquerors, were removed to alien lands in Canada, Wisconsin, Oklahoma, and Kansas Territory, where they gradually intermarried with whites or members of other tribes, ultimately relinquishing their identity as the Lenape, "the real people." Within little more than a century, the Lenape had met the Old World and had been vanquished by it.

THE GOLDEN DOOR

On the eve of Henry Hudson's arrival, the Passaic and Hackensack Rivers ran sweet and pure, the "silver river bottom" so admired by the earliest European settlers readily visible through the transparent flow. Wildfowl and game animals abounded in the meadows. Then, as to a diminished degree now, the marshes were a marvelously complex nursery for life, a bountiful table of riches for those attuned to its mysteries and secure in the skills of their harvest.

The new European inhabitants of the Hackensack valley looked on the "bright, unstained expanses" of a land yet unpopulated by throngs of humanity—a New World Eden of "island-dotted and stream-divided meadows of tall sea grass," as Bergen County historian Frances Westervelt describes the scene. The Dutch burghers and farmers of the 1600s, accustomed to an Old World in which all game and fowl belonged to the king and his minions, here encountered a land in which all wild creatures were free for the taking. The newcomers "walked forth in untroubled dignity with enormous guns to shoot the wild fowl whose wraithlike flights filled that sky," Westervelt writes.

For a while, the vast new land easily absorbed such assaults. John E. Pomfret, in *The Province of East New Jersey*, notes that, as of the late 1600s, the Hackensack valley was still very sparsely settled. Describing a landscape in which "there were both fresh and salt meadows, so useful in supporting livestock through the winter, and great resources of fish, both salt-water and fresh-water," he mentions "John Berry's and other plantations on the Hackensack," and little else north of those isolated agricultural outposts, save a few scattered Lenape villages. "The town of Bergen . . . contained 70 families with 350 inhabitants, while the out-plantations occupied 60,000 acres. Northward lay the tiny village of Hobuc [Hoboken]. Further north Edsall owned a plantation and one Beinfield another, both as yet without tenants. A few smaller farms were found further north, but on the whole this area was uninhabited as late as 1680."

Less than a century later the picture had changed considerably; the region was well on its way to becoming the New Jersey of today, the most densly populated state in the union. By the first decade of the 1700s, the fledgling Province of East Jersey—which the English had

*The red fox (*Vulpes fulva*) occurs over much of North America, from arctic and subarctic Canada south to the Carolinas, Texas, and the central Great Plains, and in the West from central California to Washington. It is a fairly common, though nocturnal and secretive, mammal in the Meadowlands. Look for it on closed landfills, highway verges, waste areas, and town edges. The slimmer, more strikingly marked gray fox (*Urocyon cinereoargenteus, not illustrated) has been reported in scattered locations in the district; it was observed in the Berrys Creek area and at the present site of the Sports Complex in surveys made in 1972.*

*The eastern cottontail (*Sylvilagus floridanus*) occurs from Minnesota, the Great Lakes region, and central New York south to Florida and Mexico. It is fairly common on the drier portions of the Meadowlands but avoids wetlands subject to tidal inundation. It may be especially abundant near buildings having extensive lawns, abandoned landfills, and roadway verges. This rabbit may be observed browsing at the edge of the meadows along the northern sections of the New Jersey Turnpike.*

wrested from Dutch control–boasted seven bona fide European-style towns, Pomfret writes, "inhabited by a sober and industrious people." Englishman Andrew Burnaby, traveling through New Jersey in 1760, commented on a landscape "exceedingly rich and beautiful" but noted that "the number of its inhabitants is supposed to be 70,000: of which, all males between the [ages of] sixteen and sixty . . . are obliged to serve in the militia."

By then, memories of any real or perceived Indian threat had faded. Already, the once-feared and disdained "savages" had become the stuff of twice-told tales and local legend. With the solid entrenchment of European civilization, a far more benign and idealized perception of the Lenape as displaced victims, and of the fast-vanishing wilderness as an irrevocably lost Eden, was subtly taking root. This yearning after the passage of the frontier, and its misunderstood and mistrusted "wilden," was a precursor of the collective guilty conscience over the fate of Native Americans in evidence today.

Some of the seventeenth-century colonists' land-use practices were not what one might consider environmentally friendly. In *As We Were*, a history of Elizabethtown, Theodore Thayer writes: "Like the Indians before them, the pioneers burned over the woods and fields in the spring or fall. All men and boys were required to turn out to help. While some saw to the burning, others were posted to shoot game as the frightened animals sped away." Thus, well before the dawning of the eighteenth century, a new people, industrious if not yet industrial, set in motion the inexorable process by which the Meadowlands would be transformed from a trackless wilderness to the cityscapes of the twentieth century. Less than a hundred years later the original forests were gone, stripped of their old-growth trees by the king's procurers of ships' masts and by the land-clearing and game-driving conflagrations of both the resident Lenape and the constantly arriving settlers.

PATRIOTS, LOYALISTS, AND NEUTRALS

During the Revolutionary War, the strategically important region of northeastern New Jersey witnessed numerous campaigns, engagements, and sorties. Where they involved passage through the meadows, the military must have found these extensive wetlands to be every bit the obstacle as would their dikers and drainers a century later. Historian Kevin Wright notes that "the spongy expanse of salt grasses and cedar thickets which composed the meadowlands was unlikely terrain for the maneuver of armies." However, he describes an extensive and well-developed system of cedar-plank causeways linked by ferries that "formed vital links in the primitive network of roads leading from the Hudson opposite Manhattan to Philadelphia." These eighteenth-century precursors of the immense transportation grid that transects the meadows of today doubtless made the business of conducting a war in such a marshland a possible, if rather arduous, enterprise:

> A detachment of 150 men from the 57th regiment under the command of Major Brownlow landed upon the New Ark Meadows, yesterday morning at two o'clock, in order to surprize a small body of Rebels quartered in the town; upon the march of the troops to that place, Major Brownlow fell in with a small patrole close to the town, one man of which running off, gave the alarm; by this means the greatest part of them made their escape, thirty-three excepted, four of whom were killed, the remainder taken prisoners, with the loss upon the part of the King's troops, four men wounded, three of them very slightly.
>
> (The Royal Gazette, *May 27, 1780*)

In the fall of 1776 the British, following a series of engagements that routed General Washington first from Manhattan and then west to Hackensack, took control of the important port of New York City. For the remainder of the war the invaders would occupy the city, appropriating food and supplies from the farms and towns that lay in the hinterland of the extensive meadows of the time. During the darkest days of the war, Wright says, the local population of Bergen and Hudson Counties, much of it still of old Dutch stock, "was divided in its sympathies."

Military and naval commanders utilized the Meadowlands' principal waterway throughout the war. A news item of May 1780, for instance, reported that "a fleet of twenty-six vessels sailed up the Hackensack River, their intentions unknown." These were perilous times for meadows residents trying to go about their ordinary business, such as the Loyalist Joshua Smith.

Voices ℞

JOSHUA HETT SMITH
"On the evening of the 4th of June, 1782, my two pilots crossed this [Passaic] river in a small cedar canoe, or boat, to the opposite shore, which was a salt meadow, sometimes overflowed by the tide, which leaves a muddy slime over which a light boat may be easily drawn. We passed a large tract of meadow, some miles in length, before we came to another river called the Hackinsack River, on the opposite shore of which, near the foot of Snake Hill, we discovered a party of men, who hailed us—not answering, they fired several shot, but they fell short of us. We now judged it prudent to hide the boat in the sedges and retire, as they could not pass to us; this being done, we hid ourselves—and, soon after, heard several vollies, appearing to us as if two parties had been attacking each other; this ceasing, we again ventured to the margin of the river and observing no person on or near the opposite shore, we boldly launched our bark, knowing that no parties but British would venture to stay there long in broad daylight; we crossed in safety and soon reached the town of Bergen, where halting for a few minutes for refreshments, we proceeded to Pryor's Mills, near Paulshook."

With the advent of peace in 1783, travel throughout the Hackensack valley became less of an adventure. No longer fearing the wartime perils of shot and shell, travelers rediscovered the joys of touring. They often commented on the progress-impeding bogginess everywhere, and on the fresh, eye-pleasing vistas of this yet bright land:

Voices ℞

ROBERT HUNTER, JR.: TRAVEL DIARY, 1785
"New York, Friday, October 28: . . . I called on Mrs. Lott this morning to settle about going to Paulus Hook with Mrs. Aursenclever, and on my way back met Charles McIvers and his father. . . . We took leave of the family of the Lotts, and walked to the ferry, where we met the servants with our baggage and sailed precisely at four with a fair wind.

"We were just a quarter of an hour crossing the North River to

Paulus Hook, in the state of New Jersey, where we found the coach ready to set off with us immediately. We sent the servants with our baggage in the stage wagon. About four miles on we ferried the Hackinsack River, which is half a mile across and empties itself into the sea near Newark. Half a mile farther on we crossed the Posaic River [in a scow], which is the third in the course of sixteen miles. It's astonishing what an immense quantity of water you meet with in this country."

OF MOSQUITOES AND MEN

> Didja hear the one about the ground crew at Newark Airport that pumped a thousand gallons of gas into a jet plane— until they realized it was a mosquito from the Jersey meadows?"
>
> *(Jersey joke, 1950s)*

Derogatory comments about Meadowlands mosquitoes are quite common in the historical literature. This excerpt from an eighteenth-century account of a sightseer's trek from New Jersey to Manhattan is typical:

> We were ready to proceed on our journey at sun-rising. Near the inn where we had passed the night, we were to cross a river, and we were brought over, together with our horses, in a wretched, half-rotten ferry. . . . The country was low on both sides of the river, and consisted of meadows. But there was no other hay to be got than such as commonly grows in swampy grounds; for as the tide comes up in this river, these low plains were sometimes overflowed when the water was high. The people hereabouts are said to be troubled in summer with immense swarms of gnats or musquitos, which sting them and their cattle. This was ascribed to the low, swampy meadows, on which these insects lay their eggs, which are afterwards hatched by the heat.
> *(Peter Kalm,* Travels in North America, *1751)*

Local residents and travelers alike have been cussing and swatting mosquitoes for centuries, and relief from the depredations of these bloodthirsty little insects was one of the principal rationalizations behind the first efforts to dike and drain the Meadowlands. Mosquitoes, in fact, are probably the single most important force in the historical coevolution of European humankind and the Meadowlands.

Worldwide there are some 2,700 recognized mosquito species, the great majority of them innocuous to humans. Many are highly specialized, extracting blood meals only from birds, caterpillars, turtles, or even ants. The island of Madagascar has 500 mosquito species; the citizens of Central America swat some 750 different kinds. About 130 species of mosquitoes are found in North America; perhaps 5 of these, including a recent Asian immigrant, the tiger mosquito, are of any real concern as disease vectors or nuisances.

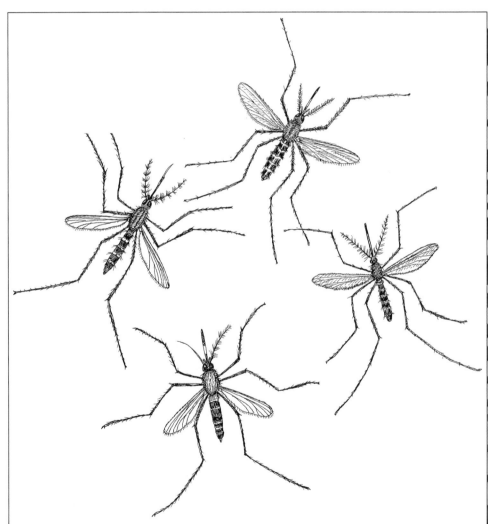

*New Jersey mosquitoes (clockwise from top): white-banded saltmarsh mosquito (*Aedes sollicitans*), house mosquito (*Culex pipiens*), small saltmarsh mosquito (*A. taeniorhychus*) and swamp mosquito (*A. vexans*).*

Canada geese greeting a winter dawn on the ice, Kingsland Impoundment, DeKorte Park, Lyndhurst.

About 25 species of mosquitoes occur in the state of New Jersey, but only 4 of these might be considered world-class pests or significant disease transmitters. Two of them, the house mosquito (*Culex pipiens*) and the swamp mosquito (*Aedes vexans*), occupy a variety of habitats, including cities and suburbs; both can be a significant backyard nuisance. The other two species, the so-called small saltmarsh mosquito (*A. taeniorhychus*) and the white-banded saltmarsh mosquito (*A. sollicitans*), are more specific in their habitat requirements. It was toward the control of these two abundant and eminently pestiferous saltmarsh species that most of the largest diking and draining operations carried out in the meadows were directed.

Further justifying these efforts was the long-standing conviction that the meadows might also be tamed and pressed into agricultural and industrial use. As George Cook, New Jersey's state geologist, wrote in 1868, "The tide marshes occupy a large surface in the vicinity of Newark, Elizabeth and Jersey City, and lying as they all do, within a few miles of the great centre of business in our country, the condition of them is of great public interest. They must soon be reclaimed, so as to be fit either for cultivation, or for occupation with buildings."

Doubtless with that encouraging vision in mind, test borings into the substrate had already been made in the Meadowlands. The results of one made by the Jersey City Water Works "on the bank of the Hackensack River at the aqueduct crossing" revealed "thirty-two feet of mud from the surface of the meadow; eight feet of blue clay; ten feet of blue and red clay; ten feet of red clay; four feet of red clay with some fine sand and four feet of hard, red clay, with small pebbles and stones." In the tidewater sections of the river, soundings revealed the alluvial deposits to be "twelve feet deep on the right side of the river" and "nine feet deep on the left bank."

None of these formidable geological statistics–the accumulation of centuries of varved clays from the bed of Glacial Lake Hackensack–were viewed as insurmountable obstacles to reclamation, even given the limited technology of the day. "The solution of the problem is to shut out the sea and remove such water as occurs behind the barrier either by gravity through sluices or with pumps," writes Thomas Headlee in *The Mosquitoes of New Jersey and Their Control.* That, in essence, is the simple formula for draining and drying out a living tidal marsh.

The earliest attempts at draining, or ditching, the meadows were carried out by crews using hand tools in what must have been an extremely arduous and difficult task. In the early years of this century, the "Manahan shovel," equipped with a ten- to twenty-inch-wide blade, was wielded by hand, but power machinery soon made the job far easier. The so-called Eaton plow had separate gas-powered winching and plow units; the ditching procedure involved moving the power plant from point to point on the marsh and then hauling the ditch-cutting plow up to it. The more sophisticated Reiley ditching plow consisted of a mobile power plant–a tractor–that simply hauled the ditch-cutting unit along behind it. In both of these techniques, sod removed from the ditch was simply deposited alongside the channel. In time it dried out and floated about in great unsightly windrows on high tides. The State of New Jersey's Agricultural Experiment Station later developed a combined "swamp tractor" and plowing unit that operated at a (1930s) cost of one cent per linear foot of ditch; this technology shredded the excavated sod and spread it on the marsh surface in a thin layer that did not inhibit the growth of grasses.

But draining was only half the battle; the other half was preventing water from creeping back onto the reclaimed land. According to Headlee, the construction of dikes was an arduous, time-consuming, and even rather complicated procedure:

> The early dikes as they were built stood three feet above the meadow surface, were two feet wide at the top and six feet wide at the bottom. When the construction of the dike began, a trench ten inches wide by twenty inches deep was cut along the line to be occupied by the structure, and the sods taken out were utilized as part of the dike. A row of sods composed of pieces approximately ten inches wide,

Ditch construction in the Meadowlands, 1930s. From a photo in Headlee, 1945, courtesy Rutgers University Press.

twelve inches thick, and twenty-six inches long was laid on each side of this trench with the grassy ends out, enclosing a space twenty inches wide. Mud was then tamped into the trench until its surface was flush with the upper surface of the sod layer. Then another layer of sod composed of pieces ten inches wide by twelve inches thick by twenty-four inches long was placed on top of each of the other two rows. Again the grassy ends were out but the ends of the upper layer were six inches nearer the dike center than were the ends of the lower layer. The central cavity thus formed was tamped full of mud. Then a third layer of sod was placed on the second in a similar fashion with a similar approach to the center. The space formed between the two parts of the layers was tamped full of mud. In some cases the dike thus constructed was covered by a layer of sod while in other cases the crest was simply rounded up with mud.

"During the summer the grass in the sods grew vigorously and transformed the dike into a wall of green," Headlee writes, adding that the sods used to cap the dike "dried out and separated until they looked like the battlements of a wall."

> *Bend your knees,*
> *Straighten out,*
> *Something's got to give.*
> *It's either the sod or back,*
> *See which one will give.*
> *(Meadows ditchers' chant, 1920s)*

In the northern sections of the meadows, Headlee says, the ubiquitous phragmites were frequently used in early diking projects, the plants being "cut and laid in the mud crosswise, forming a mat over the soft spot or stream to be crossed. The soil is then thrown upon these reeds and tamped down, giving a crosswall . . . fairly satisfactory in preserving the dike."

At points where streams or large ditches crossed dikes, they had to be given passage. Sluice boxes, tide gates, or corrugated iron pipe did the job. The largest of the modern tide gates may be seen at the point where the New Jersey Turnpike crosses Overpeck Creek at the Ridgefield–Ridgefield Park border.

Dutch settlers who lived in the area of what is today the borough of Ridgefield may in fact have been the first to attempt drainage and reclamation in the Meadowlands. (Headlee notes that Vernon Conant, a former superintendent of the Bergen County Mosquito Extermination Commission, wrote that he had long been puzzled by the long, regular canals his workers discovered when they began digging their own ditches in 1915.) Whatever the Dutch may have done, certainly among the earliest large-scale efforts to reclaim the Hackensack meadows for the purpose of agriculture were those of the Swartwout brothers–John, Robert, and Samuel. Prominent New Yorkers, the Swartwouts began acquiring meadows acreage shortly after the War of 1812 and by 1816 owned several thousand acres in the area between Newark and Hoboken. In 1816 they formed the Hackensack & Passaic Meadow Company and began diking and draining large tracts of the meadows. In 1819 they reported expenditures of $130,000 for purchasing land and "the erection of 7.5 miles of dikes, and the construction of 120 miles of ditches." The entrepreneurs reported that they had reclaimed thirteen hundred acres on which "grain, vegetables, hemp and flax were growing, together with a herd of 80 to 90 grazing cows to supply the New York market with milk."

A number of natural calamities eventually did in the Swartwouts' efforts and dreams. Abnormally high spring tides in 1820 severely damaged both crops and dikes, and the rooting shenanigans of the Meadowlands' ubiquitous muskrats, which persisted in riddling the dikes with their extensive tunnels and burrows, eventually convinced the would-be Meadowlands farmers that a salt marsh was not, in the end, an agricultural gold mine. Ironically, by 1918 muskrat pelts had become far more valuable than any food crops or salt hay obtainable from the marshes, and thus these animals were encouraged on the meadows.

Another famous reclamation endeavor, this one for the purpose of converting the Meadowlands into a vast cornfield, was undertaken shortly after the Civil War by the partnership between Spencer P.

Driggs and Samuel Pike, a Cincinnati millionaire and philanthropist. *The Record* of Hackensack in 1955 recounted how Driggs held a patent for an iron levee and canal system which he claimed could tame the meadows. He proposed to convert five thousand acres just south of the Bergen County border into productive farmland. "Driggs, an engaging fellow, got financial help from Samuel Pike, who had made a fortune in a Kentucky liquor business. All in all, Driggs and Pike spent $300,000 on their scheme. The result: a leaky levee system which failed completely when the meadowlands behind the metal wall began to shrink because they were deprived of their normal water supply. Driggs did get one section fairly drained and planted corn there one year. The stalks grew 10 feet high and looked just fine. But they didn't yield a single ear of corn."

The Driggs reclamation scheme, while it ultimately failed, in part due to the untimely death of Pike, its principal financial backer, was probably the largest agricultural project ever attempted in the Meadowlands. Its method was described in the June 12, 1868, issue of the *Bergen Democrat*: "A ditch four or five feet wide is excavated, the earth from which forms the embankment for the dyke, and an iron plate is placed in the centre, reaching down below the low water mark to prevent the burrowing of muscrats. The ditch serves to collect the drainage of the meadows, which can be discharged at low tide, or pumped out by engines, while the embankment prevents the flooding of the land. It is an immensely important work and promises to be completely successful in reclaiming these vast wastes and making them fit for profitable cultivation." Such optimism was, of course, very premature, for in the end the ambitious venture had become a classic case of throwing good money after bad; the only return on the partners' investment was realized through the eventual sale, at a loss, of large sections of the reclaimed tracts to real estate speculators.

Not all harvests, however, depended on reclamation. In their natural state the meadows were far from barren. For nearly three centuries they remained a steady source of another important item of commerce: salt hay. The harvest of saltmarsh cordgrass (*Spartina patens*) was an industry of such economic importance that it was regulated by a series of so-called Meadows Laws. Between 1697 and 1783, seventy-four statutes are recorded, most of them related to the protection of meadows and the maintenance of salt marshes for the purpose of harvesting the grass.

Toward the end of large-scale harvesting, in the late nineteenth century, the price of salt hay varied from two to ten dollars per ton; at the turn of the twentieth century the Hackensack and Newark marshes were producing an income of between ten and forty dollars per acre

Dragline excavating a mosquito control ditch in the Hackensack meadows, 1940s.
From a photo in Headlee, 1945, courtesy Rutgers University Press.

when drained and diked, which produced an increasingly lush growth of *Spartina*. Prior to 1900, most of the harvest was used for animal bedding, stock feed, manure mulching, and roof thatching; after the 1890s a number of banana import firms opened in Newark and used much of the Meadowlands salt hay crop to layer and protect the ripening fruit.

With the growth of the glass-making industry, salt hay was increasingly used in packing this breakable product. As markets for salt hay expanded, in the late nineteenth century, the grass was used as traction on winter roads, in the manufacture of paper, and in the building of new roads over the marshes themselves. Under normal conditions—a dry, firm footing that offered easy access to men, horses, and machines—one square mile of salt marsh yielded about a hundred tons of hay.

By the 1950s productive *Spartina* acreage in the Hackensack meadows had been all but destroyed through dumping and the invasion of phragmites, and commercial hay cutting had ceased there, although it continued elsewhere in the state. By the late 1960s the New Jersey salt hay harvest was of insignificant size, the bulk of it coming from the Salem and Cumberland County marshes bordering Delaware Bay. At that time retail prices ranged from forty to fifty-five dollars per ton, with most of the crop destined for mink ranch bedding, commercial mulching, and the prevention of land erosion in new suburban housing developments.

RAILROADS

The development of rail transportation, like ditching and diking, was among the earliest of the technological impacts on the natural Meadowlands. Shortly after the turn of the nineteenth century, people began contemplating the laying of track across the wide marshes to connect the various rural hamlets of Hudson and Bergen Counties with the growing metropolis of New York City. By 1830 their dreams had become reality, and even before conventional roads transected the swamps, a modest network of rail lines offered passage to picturesque "Currier & Ives" locomotives and the ornate, gas-lighted cars they hauled.

For the most part, travel by rail across the meadows has traditionally been a benign, if somewhat monotonous experience, fraught only with the usual delays and scheduling glitches inherent to a complex urban transportation system. But sometimes it can be deadly. In February of 1996 two New Jersey Transit commuter trains, one pushed, the other pulled by 180-ton locomotives, collided on a stretch of Meadowlands track; the two engineers and a passenger were killed and 235 other commuters injured. News accounts of the tragedy noted that rescue teams were hampered in reaching the accident site, located in "a baleful tract of flat Jersey City meadowlands."

Usually, though, the modern story of rail travel through the meadows is not one of terror and death but of uneventful reliability and, sometimes, romance. Especially in the days of steam.

The sight and sound of steam trains are among my earliest memories of the Meadowlands. In the pre-television age of the mid-1940s, one of my anticipated weekend entertainments as a small child was the blissful hour or so spent Saturdays "waiting for the morning train" in the company of my father and younger brother and sister. At the time, Dad was classified advertising manager for the now-defunct *New York Herald Tribune*. Although he endured a high-pressure environment filled with unforgiving deadlines that descended on him daily and was often forced to bring unfinished business home for the weekend, he nonetheless recognized the importance of meaningful weekend interaction with his kids. Prior to the construction of the Port Authority Bus Terminal in midtown Manhattan in 1950, my father rode the train twice a day, five days a week, to and from the Hoboken terminal and ferry slip, so one would assume that by Friday night he would have had more than enough of the thundering mechanical behemoths and the foul smoke, gritty cinders, and rattling, drafty cars that went with them. This may have indeed been the case, but in one of the many paternal sacrifices he accepted as part of the job, Dad once or twice a month would yield to our passionate entreaties and drive the three of us down to the West Shore station at the foot of Mount Vernon Street or the creek rail crossing at Bergen Turnpike, here to await the Saturday freight locomotives that would haul their seemingly endless caravans of boxcars and tank cars out of the emptiness of the meadows and through the town.

In those days the West Shore Railroad, operated as part of the New York Central system, ran regular passenger and freight service from Haverstraw, New York, and the Pascack Valley in northern Bergen County all the way to Weehawken; in its heyday during the 1940s and 1950s the line carried some 12,500 commuters daily. And most of the southern portion of that route crossed the Meadowlands east of the Hackensack River.

In the 1940s train locomotives were still objects of awe-inspiring, baroque wonder; they were all "bells and whistles" and huge, malevolent headlights and thrusting, steaming pistons and drive wheels as high as a Mack truck. The engineer always seemed to be a middle-aged guy in a pinstriped engineer's cap, bandanna around his neck, leaning out of the cab, at the reins. He dressed for the job and seemed to appreciate his crossing audience of little kids and their patient parents and never went through a town without wearing out his arm waving to them.

Although my siblings and I welcomed many a train across the rusty old Overpeck Creek bridge in the five or six years my father indulged us in this pastime, one arrival in particular remains bright in my memory.

Rock doves taking their ease near the Conrail lift-bridge, Overpeck Creek, Ridgefield Park.

Journal ❦

FALL 1948: THE SHOWSTOPPERS

Dad had parked the faithful 1937 Ford Tudor in the Saturday-empty commuter lot by the tracks, and we all sat in the car and eagerly scanned the flat meadows to the south for signs of an approaching train. Unless the wind was out of the south, trains were heralded by the sight of the engine's distant smoke plume rather than by the heavy chuffing sound of its vast cylinders. Except for its rhythmic pulsing, the smoke looked more like that of a meadows fire. It was at the first glimpse of the locomotive's black smoke on the horizon that my father would sometimes break into a heartfelt rendition of "She'll be comin' 'round the mountain when she comes. . . . She'll be drivin' six white horses when she comes. . . ." and stay with it until the roar of the approaching engine drowned him out.

Of that particular morning, I remember the faraway smoke plume and the tune and the little knot of expectant kids and their parents. And the birds. As I stood beside the tracks and watched the advancing train, I noticed what seemed like millions of blackbirds among the reeds just across the rail bridge over the creek. It was fall, and the flocks were massing as they always had, but for some reason this was the first time I can recall noticing them. They seemed to be everywhere, feeding and screeching in the reeds and scattered all over the track bed.

As the train drew nearer, its steaming thunder and my father's accompanying serenade growing ever louder, I found myself watching the birds. The locomotive was still hidden behind the last curve in the tracks before the bridge, but it was getting close, and I wondered if it would suddenly appear around the bend and like a monstrous vacuum cleaner swallow up these fragile creatures in a great inhalation of smoke and steam. The noise rapidly grew in volume and the smoke rose higher and higher into the sky, but still the birds squabbled and chattered with complete unconcern.

At last the track under my foot began to vibrate, and I stepped back as the huge engine, leaning slightly to starboard as it banked into the curve, swept into view and neared the bridge. I watched in amazement as the blackbirds held their ground; under the very nose of the monster their daily affairs clearly took precedence. The reeds and the tracks were stubbornly black with birds.

But then, just as the birds seemed fated to be sucked beneath the engine's cowcatcher and spewed out into the air with the smoke via its roaring stack, they grudgingly gave ground. Those on the tracks, mere feet from the looming monster, swept from the ground and swirled aloft. They were followed by hundreds more, and as the train, whistle shrieking, rumbled over the bridge there were two clouds in attendance—one of smoke, the other of flying birds. The surrounding reeds emptied of birds until the sky seemed black with them. I had not realized that so many were hidden there in the grass; it seemed as though all the birds in the universe had collected here, waiting for the train, just as we were.

Until that day I had never seen such an impressive display of the poetry of living things; at that time in my young life I maintained, like many youngsters, an abiding interest in dinosaurs and other prehistoric animals, and although these had surely been more spectacular in life

Steam train emerging from the Meadowlands and crossing Overpeck Creek, 1940s.
Adapted from a photo, courtesy Ridgefield Park Historical Society.

than mere blackbirds, I would never see them in the flesh. Here for the first time I experienced, firsthand, the power and vitality of creation, as well as its innocent defiance of the technological authority of my own species.

As the train passed by, the huffing roar of the engine faded and a

long line of boxcars, tankers, and gondolas swayed and rumbled by. Each the size of a bus, they were strung together by life-size editions of the "knuckle" couplers we saw reproduced in miniature in our Lionel trains at home and bore strange faraway names like "Erie & Susquehanna," "Norfolk & Southern," "Rock Island," "Baltimore & Ohio," and

"Lehigh Valley." After what seemed like hours of breezy and clanking passage the freight cars came to an end and the soot-grimed red caboose trailed by, its wheels whisking and squealing against the shining rails; a man in coveralls stood on the rear platform and saluted us solemnly as the long freight labored on toward Hackensack and points north.

Through all this the swarm of blackbirds remained in the smoky sky overhead. After the first five or so boxcars had passed, I lost interest in the train and found myself seeking their whereabouts. The flock had quartered back and forth, out over the meadows, "like as the starlings wheel in the wintry season in wide and clustering flock, wing-borne and wind-borne"; shifting, unfolding and folding gracefully upon itself like a dusky silk scarf cast into the wind. Then, as though on universal command, a tail of the scarf abruptly dipped toward the ground and, much as one would imagine a mythical genie retreating back into his bottle, the birds peeled en masse out of the sky in absolute silence, settled down over the marsh, and vanished again among the reeds, as though swallowed up by the earth itself. Where, moments before, the technology of man and the energy of nature had met and mingled in a profusion of noise and action, now there was only silence and a recalled sense of inquiry that suddenly revealed to me the world that lay beyond the West Shore tracks.

My encounter with the blackbirds was a small natural happening that made the ordinary experience of watching a train go by a unique and lasting one. But from that day on my interest in railroading flagged, and I began to wonder about the pulse I felt, coming from the creek that ran under the bridge, from the larger river it joined, and from the strange, wild marshes that spread far and away from them on all sides.

The West Shore Railroad of my childhood memory, which opened to service in 1879 and folded its tracks for good eighty years later (to be replaced by today's Conrail), was one of the early meadows lines, but it was far from the first. The Paterson & Hudson Rail Road, begun in 1829 and completed in 1832 at a total cost of $300,000, can be considered the genesis of railroading in the Meadowlands. The cost of track bed grading diagonally across the meadows alone, a five-and-one-quarter-mile stretch, was $45,578. The fare from Paterson to New York, about fifteen miles, was fifty cents one-way, a hefty sum in those days.

An excerpt from the original survey for the line betrays the prevailing nineteenth-century bias against the meadows as a natural obstacle to progress, along with a utilitarian view of nature: the ancient cedar forests of the region might supply timber to support the tracks.

*Ring-necked pheasants near the Conrail right-of-way, northern boundary of
DeKorte Park, Lyndhurst.*

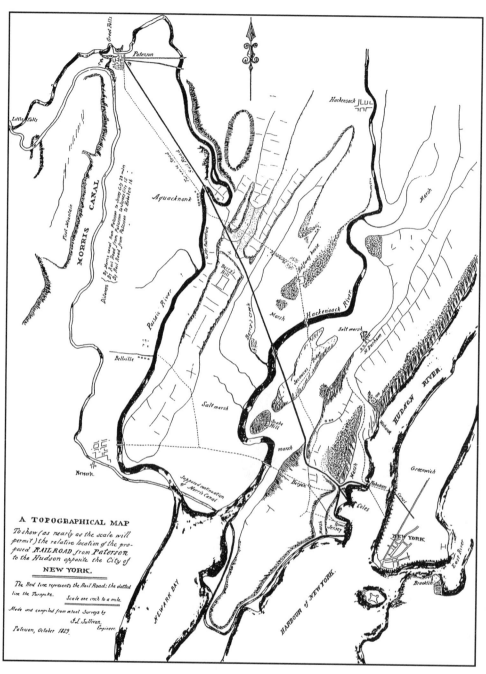

Map showing the proposed route of the Paterson & Hudson Rail Road, 1829.

SURVEY FOR A RAIL-ROAD FROM PATERSON TO NEW YORK, 1829

. . . a course from Berry's Hill to the centre of New-York takes the line through a depression in Secaucus Ridge, to a point at the foot of Bergen Ridge, three-fourths of a mile south of the [New Barbadoes] turnpike, whence the ascent may be very gradual. . . .

The extensive marsh to be traversed may to some, at first, appear to be an obstacle or occasion of heavy expense. But it will be perhaps the least costly part of the way, because the foundation will be on piles. The native growth of cedar on some parts of the marsh will furnish at once a cheap and durable timber, and the substratum of clay the best ground into which to drive them.

By 1832, with the railroad fully operational, a modest but unique adventure–a day trip across the meadows by rail!–was marketed to the city dwellers of that less pressured age:

The passenger is scarcely aware of the movement except by the rapidity with which he passes objects. He feels in perfect safety, although at times his elevation above the surrounding meadows may be fifteen or 20 feet there is not the least danger to be apprehended from a deviation from the rails. . . .

[The Railroad] will . . . enable thousands of our citizens–who have not weeks of leisure upon their hands, to spend in the country–to pass a leisure day occasionally at a very small expense in the enjoyment of as pure air and as enchanting scenery as can be found either at Saratoga Springs, at Trenton, or at Niagara Falls.

The roadbed of the original Paterson & Hudson line has long since become obscured or obliterated entirely by subsequent rail and industrial development; sections of the old right-of-way survive just north of Snake Hill, within the current confusion of tracks, switches, and sidings that are being expanded and improved to accommodate the Secaucus Transfer Station proposed by New Jersey Transit as part of the original Master Plan for the Meadowlands.

And yet despite the apparently slender scars they left behind, barely noticeable today, these early railroads had a subtle but devastating effect on the ecology of the Meadowlands. The filling and grading of railroad rights-of-way across the marshes upset the natural hydrologic

*Flock of starlings, Linden railyard and refinery complex. The birds seek
nourishment around this unpromising site, built on reclaimed marshland
in the former Newark meadows.*

cycle of the tidal estuary and contributed to the disruption of the ecosystem in ways not yet fully understood. By the turn of the century, railroad track beds, constructed without a thought being given to natural
drainage patterns, had increasingly fragmented and isolated sections of
the natural salt marsh. The result was that the invasive cattail and
phragmites, plants of much less commercial value than the native salt
hay, took over, and by 1932 the meadow grass harvests of the past had
gradually slipped into history.

The reduction of the "mosquito nuisance" to tolerable levels, in
turn, helped usher in the twentieth-century era of reclamation–this
time with an eye toward comprehensive industrial and residential development, now that railroad tracks crisscrossed the Meadowlands.
Property values soared, and speculators grew restive. A new, and to
some a more ominous, chapter in the Meadowlands story was about to
begin. This time, garbage paved the way.

A "MONSTROUS VISUAL SYMBOL"

The environmental deterioration of the meadows between Hackensack and Secaucus accelerated during the first quarter of the twentieth century. As Beryl Robichaud and Murray F. Buell reported in *Vegetation of New Jersey*, manufacturing plants "maltreated the waters by emptying oil and dye stuffs into it," so that by 1926 the Hackensack River was "so polluted that the boards of health have prohibited persons from bathing in it."

Indeed, it was the time-honored practice of disposing all kinds of refuse in wetlands that eventually came close to destroying the meadows completely and permanently. The most destructive practice of all was called, with no intended irony, "reclamation."

> A scheme to canalize the northern valley of the Hackensack River between New Milford and Piermont, New York, and open navigation from there to the Hudson River was submitted to the Legislature in February of 1926. An even grander plan for canalizing the main stem of the river between Hackensack and Newark Bay was also projected. Accordingly, a Meadowlands Reclamation Commission was appointed by the New Jersey Legislature in 1928 at the instigation of the Bergen County Chamber of Commerce. Reclamation of the Hackensack Meadowlands had been the third major objective of the Chamber since its organization in 1927.
>
> The Chamber of Commerce concluded that 30,360 acres of meadowland were "the logical location for the region's industrial development." Raising the level of the marsh with 172 million cubic yards of fill was estimated to cost $125,000.
>
> *(Hackensack Meadowlands District Commission,*
> The Hackensack Meadowlands, *1970)*

By the early 1970s the Hackensack meadows were being filled with waste "at the rate of 30,000 tons a week," according to Robichaud and Buell. This massive, deliberate infusion of municipal and industrial garbage, along with "drainage, fill-in, and development of the land for industry, housing, or highways," plus the "pollution from industries, oil spills or urban sewage," they concluded, had left the species diversity of the meadows "severely depleted of their biological integrity." The deadly invasion by refuse was nevertheless, in some peculiar sense, awe-inspiring.

Trash-littered shoreline of Overpeck Creek, Overpeck County Park, Leonia.
Although dumping has long since ceased here, refuse continues to tumble and
float from the former dumps and drift to the creek's banks. Pencil drawing.

"Garbage has an undeniably large symbolic presence. It lacks the
tidiness of merely being itself, representing as it does the back end of
our lifestyles." So write the self-described "garbalogists" William Rathje
and Cullen Murphy in *Rubbish!*, their fascinating analysis of the nature
of the twentieth-century garbage beast. Although the sheer volume of

the national solid waste problem is an abstract concept to the average homeowner setting the week's trash by the curbside ("garbage passes under our eyes virtually unnoticed, the continual turnover inhibiting perception"), there exists a place where the physical dimensions of the so-called garbage crisis can be readily perceived.

Not far from the Meadowlands lies the largest landfill on Earth. Sprawling over more than three thousand acres–or about two thousand football fields–of once-sylvan Staten Island, the sardonically misnamed Fresh Kills landfill is an artificial mountain, rising more than 150 feet above the surrounding landscape. The City of New York delivers more than 14,000 tons of municipal refuse daily to the huge landfill.

Fresh Kills was once a thriving tidal marsh, rich in life and aquatic diversity; it is now a toxic biological desert inhabited by swarms of scavenging gulls, rats, feral cats and dogs, numberless multitudes of bacteria, and garbage truck and bulldozer drivers. Its mass has been calculated at 100 million tons, its overall volume at 2.9 billion cubic feet, and growing. By the time this monster dump is closed early in the next century it may well more than triple in altitude, reaching 500 feet at its apex. The vast dung heap will then be the highest physical prominence on the eastern seaboard south of Maine's Mount Desert Island. Indeed, it is often wearily referred to as "the Mount Everest of garbage dumps" by the unfortunate Staten Islanders who must live in its odorous shadow–though they, of course, contribute to it daily as well.

The Fresh Kills landfill had its origins in what was once a living wetland. The plan for the marsh–in 1948–was simply to fill it with municipal garbage, cover the mess with topsoil, and then develop it into residential and commercial properties, a process that Robert Moses, then the city's master planner, thought would see completion in about twenty years. But the accelerating volume of garbage generated by New York residents and businesses forced the city to keep the landfill in operation through the ensuing decades–though officials have set an optimistic "last load" date of December 31, 2001.

But for the intervention of the state of New Jersey in the form of the Hackensack Meadowlands District Commision (HMDC), such a dismal and malevolent landscape would also likely have been the ultimate fate of the entire Hackensack meadows. Although the technology for coping with the disposal and recycling of garbage has undergone great improvement in recent years, the rising tide of refuse generated by our consumer society has not abated. Conversely it has, in spite of a "greener" conscience on the part of the populace, continued to flow undiminished. In 1960 Americans generated 88 million tons of garbage yearly; by 1990 that figure had ballooned to 195.7 million tons. Americans today produce about 4.3 pounds of garbage daily per capita, for a nationwide solid waste volume in excess of 410,000 tons *daily*, and 221 million tons yearly. Much of the recent increase in the trash flow consists of "nonendurables" such as paper and clothing, "durable" items such as major appliances and automobile tires (242 million per year), and a virtual avalanche of paper and plastic containers and other packaging materials. The packaging category has seen the most spectacular increase in volume, rising from some 25 million tons annually in 1960 to 65 million tons in 1990; it is expected to reach 75 million tons annually by the year 2000.

The Australian archaeologist Rowland Fletcher some years ago coined the term "Monstrous Visual Symbols," or MVSes, for those oversize monuments that any society constructs in the course of its development. He noted that as people's motivations and ideals change, so does the nature of their MVSes. Where once the pharaohs built temples and pyramids, we build huge dams, skyscrapers like the World Trade Center, and gargantuan dumps. According to Rathje and Murphy, modern landfills are among the most massive and space-consuming artifacts on the planet. They note that landfills in the Hackensack Meadowlands, for example, far exceed the volume of the biggest monuments of antiquity—such as Mexico's 75-million-cubic-foot Pyramid of the Sun at Teotihuacan—"a potent reminder that the largest MVSes in American society today are in fact its garbage repositories."

Initially, the logic of marsh landfilling, wherever it took place in the United States, was as direct, to the point, and environmentally unfriendly as it could be. The process, as it was carried out in the lower Hackensack valley until the 1950s, is succinctly described by the HMDC: "Landfills in the Meadowlands were originally created by landfill operators to fill unproductive swampland with the intention of eventually producing tracts of developable land, while simultaneously disposing of garbage." Period. And it was a new "technology" at its basest: "The land was usually leased from the towns for a small yearly price. The landfills were 'dug out,' and garbage was then dumped into the water. The garbage was usually burned at the end of each day. At the time . . . no environmental controls existed, and no one regulated garbage disposal. After years of haphazard dumping, the Meadowlands became an extremely undesirable area."

Such short-sighted environmental degradation has not, of course, been unique to the Meadowlands. As late as 1990, 67 percent of the nation's solid waste, including superfluous packaging materials, was still being disposed of in its six thousand active landfills.

The dictionary defines a landfill as "a place, usually of a marshy or swampy nature, where garbage is disposed of, compacted and covered with soil." A clear enough explanation of the theory of refuse dumping, but what about its practice? How is a landfill operated? Rathje and

Murphy describe the odious but exacting process in terms understandable to the layman:

> The daily tipping of garbage into a landfill is an orchestrated mechanical pavane that may begin as early as midnight, but more usually starts at around 5:30 in the morning, when big mother-hen trucks or rigs pulling rectangular packer rolloffs from transfer stations file in noisily and deposit their cargoes across that day's "open face," in rows of piles, each tens of feet long and ten to twenty feet high. The piles are laid either on the top rim of the existing garbage glacier or in the front of the bottom of the garbage pack—that is, either on top of or directly in front of the previous day's garbage. Next, bulldozers and machines called compactors that have five-foot-wide studded rollers push or squash the fresh, supple garbage into tight communion with the dirt-covered and somewhat more wilted deposits of the day before. By early afternoon all the garbage from a single day—a "cell" in the jargon of many landfill operators, although the terminology is not universal—has been pressed into place. From the side, the row upon row of cells looks like an arrangement of dominoes on their sides, leaning one against the other as if frozen at the moment of mid-collapse. As the garbage trucks become less frequent, special double-jointed vehicles with bays for bellies crawl up the dirt mounds near the garbage pit, fill up, rumble over to the latest cell, drop their loads, and return for another bellyful. Bulldozers coax the dirt so that it neatly covers the garbage.

Thus was the filling of the Meadowlands accomplished, day after day, year after year, until most of the dumps were barricaded for good in 1979.

But dump closure today does not mean out-of-sight-out-of-mind abandonment. As Rathje and Murphy explain: "Even after the final cap is bulldozed into place and the landfill is officially closed, the site will continue to produce methane gas for another fifteen to twenty years, and methane wells therefore must continue to operate. Nevertheless, soon after closure most contemporary landfills are landscaped and developed, and embark on second careers as golf courses, parks, or industrial estates, with only the methane wellheads, poking up like periscopes, to hint at the location's previous identity." Just such a closed and sealed landfill forms the base for the manufactured Richard W. DeKorte Park in Lyndhurst.

The "reclamation" of much of the 20,000-acre marsh known as the

Garbage disposal in the Newark meadows, 1930s. The then-recently constructed Pulaski Skyway is in the background. From a photo courtesy Rutgers University Press.

Hackensack Meadowlands was accomplished almost entirely through the agency of refuse disposal. The eventual destruction of this extensive littoral habitat converted much of it from a wetland to an upland "habitat" such as DeKorte Park and, conversely, into an environment much better suited to other, uniquely human activities. Among the first and the largest construction projects undertaken using reclaimed marshland were those involving the Newark and Teterboro airports.

Newark International Airport was established in October 1928 on a mere 68 acres of reclaimed Newark meadows. Of its construction New Jersey aviation historian Pat Reilly writes: "Preparing the swamp land for an airport was a tremendous undertaking. The level of the land had to be raised six feet to avoid flooding. Sand from Newark Bay was hydraulically pumped into the area. Within nine months the swamp was transformed to what the pilots called the 'Newark Cinder Patch,' because of the hard packed cinder runway."

The original airport cost $1,750,000 and soon featured a sixteen-hundred-foot-long asphalt runway, the first hard-surface strip on any commercial airport in the country. By the fall of 1930 Newark Airport was the busiest air facility in the world; it was the first to offer passenger service to the West Coast: total travel time, thirty-six hours. Today, the international air terminal covers some 2,500 acres of reclaimed marshland and is the ninth busiest airport in the world, processing 28 million passengers annually. The development of the airport was greatly facilitated by the construction of the Pulaski Skyway in 1932, which opened easy access to the facility—and destroyed, of course, even more of the natural meadows.

Another Meadowlands airfield, the much smaller Teterboro Airport in the lilliputian borough of the same name, was completed at a cost of $500,000 in 1941. It was built on 550 acres of a formerly extensive marsh and riverine lowland forest. The combined airport and borough, slightly over one square mile in extent, was originally an undisturbed brackish and freshwater wetland drained by Losen Slote Creek. Department store mogul Walter Cooper purchased the land in 1905, his intention being to drain and develop it as a summer resort for company employees. In the end, Cooper balked at the economics of such corporate largess and in 1914 sold the property to investment broker Walter Teter; the plan then was to build the first "meadowlands racetrack," but the cost of draining the marshes gave Teter second thoughts as well, and the land was again sold, in 1917, to Wittman-Lewis Aircraft Corporation, which began the construction of a small airfield for trial-running its product. The Bendix Aircraft Corporation bought the airport in 1937, built a $3 million plant there, and enlarged the airport runways.

Song sparrow and jet aircraft, Newark International Airport. Birds of many species frequent the reedy verges of this major airport's runways, unconcernedly feeding and nesting as the giant planes noisily arrive and depart.

Today, the 1.1-acre borough of Teterboro has twenty-two permanent residents in nine households, a very large industrial base, a low tax rate, and an increasingly important little airport that serves a growing flock of conventional private aircraft and corporate jets.

The recent history of the Meadowlands is, of course, dominated by many instances of marsh reclamation; airports were only a small part of the picture. By 1968 the itch to launch big projects had inspired real estate people to join forces and persuade the New Jersey legislature to help them cut through what they considered a thicket of red tape placed in their path by apprehensive local governments preoccupied by the notion of home rule. In that year the legislature cooperated by creating a new state agency—the Hackensack Meadowlands Development Commission—with a mandate to formulate a master plan for the area and with the power to override the towns' zoning.

Thus were set in motion the plans to determine, once and for all, the future of the meadows. In 1970 *Forbes Magazine* voiced the prevailing optimism of the business community when it noted in an editorial that "even on a not-so-clear day you can see Manhattan, and that was the reality that eventually would override the obstacles. The developers went to work buying land and making plans. . . . When all the hearings and protests are over, the developers almost certainly will be out looking for more Meadowland-like situations where they can turn know-how and patience into big projects and big profits."

By the mid-1970s, at the end of the most intense dumping and filling period in the Meadowlands, much of the acreage was, indeed, in the hands of large developers and speculators, most planning major commercial or light-industrial complexes for their holdings. Among the primary landowners in the meadows were the S. J. Sisselman Berrys Creek tract (Bergen County Associates), Hartz Mountain Industries (Mori tract), the Empire Ltd. tract, and the Bellemead Development Corporation tract. For many years, however, about all that the major developers managed to build in the Meadowlands were a few small industrial parks consisting mostly of warehouses and distribution facilities that mainly served Manhattan garment makers.

Meanwhile the garbage flow continued. During the 1960s, when refuse disposal was at its height, the Meadowlands District received about 40 percent of the state's solid waste stream; another 70,000 tons per week were trucked across the Hudson from New York City. The state's tourism promoters and publicists were hard-pressed to counter the popular image of New Jersey conjured up by this growing waste disposal bad dream; the view of the state most visitors got from the Turnpike was anything but inviting.

But if the state's public image suffered, so, too, did the senses of the residents whose tree-lined streets overlooked what had become an environmental Armageddon. They soon found themselves literally under physical assault by a rising tide of garbage—the odious underside of the American dream.

MARCH 1981: GARBAGE JOE AND
THE LOOSE-LOADERS

All day long, five days a week and half a day on Saturdays, the big 10-wheelers roll down Schuyler Avenue and the Belleville Pike, heading for the vast landfills in North Arlington and Kearny.

Packed full of the variegated refuse of the surrounding megalopolis, the huge rigs fill the air with diesel fumes and thunder and set the roadway to trembling with their passage, on their way to building mountains in the meadowlands....

Most of these guys [who drive the trucks] are the hard-living and hardworking employees of the many public and private trash hauling firms servicing cities as far away as Newark, Hackensack, and, illegally, New York City. Their temperament and machismo reflect the nature of the work they do: it's a job that close to nobody else would want to do, but it pays well and the need is always there. . . .

"We may run outta clean air and water and space, but we'll sure as hell never run outta garbage—and that's good news for guys like me," says one driver for a North Jersey trash hauling company.

The majority of the haulers are pretty careful about the manner in which their loads are packed and secured for the trip to their final destination in the meadowlands. But sometimes human error and the sheer volume of the stuff overwhelms even the most conscientious of operators. The loads are lightened through accidental spillage en route, littering the landfill approach roads with everything from beer cans, cardboard boxes and plastics to discarded lumber and scrap metal. This major league littering combines to create a dangerous hazard to passing motorists and an eyesore for local residents.

Most of the meadows towns in southern Bergen County regard the problem of roadside litter as something of a minor annoyance, but the borough of North Arlington, seemingly the ultimate destination for every garbage truck ever built, does not. Truckers using Schuyler Avenue there had better be sure that load is secure and legal or they'll find themselves on the receiving end of a "loading to spill" citation written by Joe Sheedy, a single-minded and dedicated patrol officer. Last year Sheedy, known with some notoriety across the CB airwaves as "Garbage Joe," wrote more than 1,000 "loading to spill" citations. He averages 20 tickets a week, six on a particularly busy day.

At 41, Sheedy is a hometown boy and an 11-year member of the North Arlington Police Department. He has made the cleanup of his town's approach roads to the big meadows landfills his own personal crusade. Sheedy, like the majority of residents of South Bergen, is unschooled in the ecological intricacies of the meadows but he nonetheless harbors an intense dislike for the often careless—and illegal—behavior of those who are gradually filling in the swamps with trash as part of a day's work. The sheer volume of the odorous mess, both inside the landfill and all-too-often outside its fences, fills him with a quiet anger.

"You know, I lived on Schuyler Avenue for a long time, when I was a good bit younger, and I've seen what's happened to the place," he says. We're sitting in his cruiser by the side of the road, at one of his three ambuscades along Schuyler avenue and the Pike. The bright, hazy March sun heats up the interior of the patrol car; the place is dusty and litter seems to be everywhere along the road. "Look at it–have you ever seen such a mess?" he asks. The question is rhetorical. It is indeed that–a multicolored confetti of road-side refuse, seemingly in restless motion as the draft of pass-ing vehicles whisks the trash along the pavement, in the general direction of the dump.

Outside the car, the roadway is glaringly bright, gritty, and noisy with the passage of heavy vehicles, most of them garbage trucks. Sheedy watches them thunder by, takes in the gaping rear bays, looking them over, checking them out. He points out the paper and plastics festooning the nearby chain-link fence surrounding North Arlington's Holy Cross Cemetery. "Dammit, it burns me up–this is my town, too!" He speaks with a passion inspired by one's natal place, yanking his cap visor low over his eyes. "That, really, is why I'm such a buster about this litter thing; if these guys violate the law I'll get 'em and they know it."

As though on cue, the roadway jumps and vibrates and a huge rusty green collection of wheels, levers and hydrau-lic pistons rumbles by, bearing the words "DPW Town of Irvington" on its side. The big truck trails an aromatic wake of ammonia and grayish water rains from its gaping bay. A beverage can bounces off the tailboard and skitters across the pavement, glittering in the sunlight.

As the can is crushed flat by a passing car, Sheedy flicks on the light bar and siren whooping, takes off in pursuit of what looks from behind like a moving, swaying manmade mountain of trash. Bringing the monster to bay at the very gate of the landfill, Sheedy walks toward the truck like some kind of avenging angel; he slaps his ticket book lightly against his palm, humming softly, carefully looking the ve-hicle over, speculatively. The driver, a middle-aged black man, watches Sheedy approach in his rear-view mirror. Now he climbs out of his cab and stands there, an expres-sion of bemused unease on his face. They walk to the back of the truck. Sheedy squints at the load, then, abruptly, points at the truck's rear tandem tires. "Those tires, they're bad–illegal." "Uh-huh," the driver says. "Where's your left wheel flap?" "Don't know," the driver says. "I just drive it, I don't repair it." "Uh-huh; well, that load is where you're goin' to be cited," Sheedy says. He brusquely instructs the driver in the legal shortcomings of his sodden cargo, but does not touch any part of the truck or its load. "Uh-huh," the driver says.

The ticket book flips into action. "You're going to get one [a loading to spill citation] and the town of Irvington's going to get one," Sheedy says, peering closely at the vehicle's faded registration papers. The driver nods, smiling a little.

As the overloaded truck climbs wearily out of the pullover and onto the roadway Sheedy calls after it, "And clean off that license plate—you'll get stopped again for that!" The driver waves: "Okay!" and then he's gone, a rumbling, heaving hunk of flotsam in an endlessly flowing river of refuse. . . .

Sheedy, with some pride, notes that trash haulers "are under orders to avoid this area if they can, to come in from the east, from Tonnelle Avenue in North Bergen or Jersey City, to avoid me. But, hey, if they're loaded properly and legally they have nothing to worry about, you know?"

Sheedy's dedication has rubbed off on other towns. Kearny police have stepped up patrols on their side of the landfills, and the city's sanitation-enforcement officer Joseph Camino said he has been busy issuing summonses as well.

"The problem has improved by 50 percent over the past year," he said, adding that Kearny has had to cope with the problem of New York drivers who use trucks registered in New Jersey to haul trash across the state line.

"When they're straight they know it, and when they're not, I'll get 'em, and they know that too, it's as simple as that."

At the dump, the dialogue goes on. "Still bustin' tail, Joe?" the drivers of the rigs call out as they lumber and sway into the landfill. A bearded hauler high in the cab of a red Autocar garbage truck leans out of his window, crumples a wad of plastic wrap and lets it fall, blown away on the hot wind. "I'm legal today, Joe!" he hollers. Joe Sheedy smiles thinly, nodding. His eyes shaded beneath the bill of his cap, he surveys his domain: the dusty, rutted Baja of the landfill, the mountains of trash, the swirling birds, the men and the machines of modern garbage disposal, the meadows beyond. And in the distance, the city.

(John R. Quinn, The Record*)*

*Abandoned motorcycle, Lyndhurst meadows near DeKorte Park. Off-road vehicle
use has increased dramatically in the Meadowlands over the past 20 years;
although most dirt bikers stick to the unpaved service roads that grid the
district, some cut their own raceways, greatly impacting habitats
and wildlife.*

Though there are more than 2,500 acres of landfilled marsh in the
Meadowlands today, dumping has all but ceased in the district. The
scarcity of available land and the changing economics of trash disposal
have combined to bring the days of unregulated dumps and fill to a
close. "In the past 20 years, the business of picking up trash from New
Jersey's curbsides and garbage bins has evolved from a fairly simple
formula—pick it up and dump it at the nearest landfill—into a complex,
corrupt and costly burden on New Jersey's government, residents, and
businesses," writes Neal Thompson in a May 1996 *NJ Reporter* story on
the garbage crisis. Twenty years ago, Thomspon says, "it cost a few
bucks to get rid of a family's weekly garbage; today, the average is about
$100 per ton, more than double what it costs to get rid of trash in most
other states."

And what happened in the Jersey meadows was only one part of what happened all over the country. In the past hundred years, more than half of America's wetlands–some 100 million acres–have been destroyed by agricultural drainage, dredging and filling, stream channelization, pollutant discharges, and mining. Today, despite legislation designed to prevent it, about 60 acres of wetlands are still lost *every hour* in the United States. The HMDC has slowed the rate of destruction in northeastern New Jersey, at least for the time being. But from the very beginning of this century, the wetlands of the Hackensack and Passaic estuaries became casualties of the rapid expansion of the human population, and the transportation and industrial infrastructure required to service it.

> *O Lord and Master, not ours the guilt,*
> *We build as but as our fathers built;*
> *Behold thine images, how they stand,*
> *Sovereign and sole, through all our land.*
> (JAMES RUSSELL LOWELL)

As one approaches the Meadowlands from the south on the New Jersey Turnpike, the soaring arc of the Pulaski Skyway rises before the windshield as an unofficial gateway to the region. From the road here, the distant, angular mass of Snake Hill first becomes visible through the Erector Set superstructure of the span. As one tops the crest of the Turnpike bridge, a strange cloud comes into view and then takes on a more distinct form, off to the right. The air at its base shimmers and ripples with heat.

The landscape behind this cloud appears almost gauzy; buildings and roadways dance and vibrate, distorted by the glassy-hot vapors. The sight is particularly impressive at night, when the stark white and amber lights of the surrounding industrial complex give the scene the look of an alien starship viewed through a waterfall. The cloudlike emission flows from a series of huge vents; it is the superheated exhaust of a power plant, one of several situated in the southern sections of the Meadowlands District.

To me, the sight of such relative intangibles as smoke, transparent fumes, and the omnipresent haze that hangs over the Meadowlands on all but the clearest of days best exemplifies the predicament in which we have placed this ecosystem. The far more obvious factories, highways, motor vehicles, power plants, and other artifacts of civilization in and of themselves are not the root cause of the deterioration of the meadows. The primeval river and marshes could well survive the mere presence of such a blighted, monotonously utilitarian, yet chemically

Black skimmer cutting the calm waters of Kingsland Creek for edibles. The looming artificial mountain of an abandoned landfill rises in the background, one of the "monstrous visual symbols" of the modern Meadowlands.

benign urban surrounding. Rather, it is the cycling of resources through our machines–their respiration of clean air, water, and carboniferous fuels–as they are used in the service of our society, that places a huge burden on a vulnerable wetland environment.

Fossil fuels provide the energy that flexes the industrial muscles of the Meadowlands District, and it is likely that they will do so for the foreseeable future. The consequences of their combustion, whether in power generating plants or in the engines of countless motor vehicles, are ubiquitous in the environment here; acid rain, oil spills, refinery emissions, and the global warming and rising sea levels likely to follow the gradual buildup of carbon dioxide in our atmosphere all contribute directly to the debasement of the natural meadows. In combination with the decades-long contamination of the river and its estuarine sediments by countless tons of heavy metals and other toxic industrial compounds, the incidental chemical campaign conducted against the meadows as a result of our technological society has grown in recent decades into an assault of appalling proportions. The healing capabilities of the river are being sorely tested today; its waters are perpetually murky with suspended sediments whose content and origin one can only speculate on with apprehension.

Biologist Peter Lord wrote of England's once-beautiful River Trent in the early 1970s: "It seems almost to be in hiding, ashamed of what it has become, a receptacle for the sewage effluent . . . and the waste from dozens of gruesome outfalls. It is as though only darkness could blot out the memory of an upstream landscape so grotesque it could not be imagined. . . . The flora does not extend beyond the indescribable rush, nor the fauna beyond the brown rat."

Lord could as well have been describing the Hackensack River and its Meadowlands of the recent past. The HMDC has effected the termination of the worst of the dumping and has even worked resurrectional wonders with the retired landfills. But less than two decades ago–as I reported in 1982, in the following article–they were a grim habitat indeed.

HOME, HOME ON THE LANDFILL

Last Monday, a bird succeeded in doing what legions of environmental activists and recycling advocates have been trying to do for years. It closed a garbage dump.

Seagulls have fared so well by the dumps that they have multiplied and subdued the trash and now fill the air above the bulldozers and garbage trucks in vast numbers.

A judge ordered the 21-acre Kearny dump to close for

Feral cat in winter, Overpeck County Park, Ridgefield Park.

the day Monday to head off the influx of hungry gulls from the nearby Bergen County Landfill, which was closed for the Presidents' Day holiday. It seems the smaller birds were straying into the flight paths of those bigger birds landing at Newark International Airport and their sheer numbers made the prospect of dangerous mid-air collisions very real.

Most people think of gulls and rats as the only living things besides bulldozer operators and garbage truck drivers likely to be found in dumps. But they're wrong. A virtual Ark of other birds and beasts call the landfills home, some of them natives attempting to hang on in a hostile environment, others interloping opportunists like the rats, but unlike these rodents, not nearly as dangerous.

The dumps, euphemistically renamed "sanitary landfills" when city planners were trying to come up with a better image for garbage in general, today occupy more than half of the 20,000 acres of marshes, tidal creeks and

Haphazard dumping in the Meadowlands, ca. 1960s. The birds are killdeer, a ground-nesting species that has adapted well to the creation of open treeless upland habitats where once there was uninterrupted marshland. From a photo courtesy the Hackensack Meadowlands Development Commission.

river course designated in 1968 as the Hackensack Meadowlands District.

The District's two remaining active landfills, or dumps, receive upwards of 60,000 tons of garbage a week from more than 140 northern New Jersey municipalities. Hundreds of ten-wheeled garbage trucks deliver their 10- to 20-ton loads to the dumping grounds daily, where the trash is spread and compacted by huge 'dozers and then covered with a layer of fill dirt.

So the question is: what happens to all those frogs and turtles and herons and muskrats once their marshy homes vanish beneath tons of variegated refuse?

And what kinds of creatures, if any, replace them?

Chester Mattson, chief environmentalist for the Hackensack Meadowlands Development Commission and thus a dump-watcher by profession, points to the Meadowlands and its landfills as a classic example of industrialization usurping natural land and altering it completely and for good.

"Using the land in this country's brief history has come to mean using *up* the land," Mattson says, adding that "when the natural flora and fauna are displaced, nature will fill the vacuum with another set of plants and animals able to exploit the new environment." Most of the more environmentally sensitive animals and vegetation are forced out of an altered habitat, never to return, Mattson says. "There is little fare for ducks in the tread tracks of bulldozers."

But many other species—including the gulls that forced Monday's dump closing—have remained to take advantage of the scavenging bonanza of the dumps and the gulls have actually become something of a symbol of the sprawling landfills in the eyes of the general public.

"If anything, there seems to be a lot more of them now than there was even a couple of years ago; they're all over the place," a veteran garbage truck driver observed recently. He stands on the running board of his big rig, gazing at the swirling, screeching horde overhead while ducking a soft, pattering rain of gull droppings.

"I'd guess they do some good, cleaning up some of the scraps that attract the rats, but hell, there's almost too many now," he says, recalling that several years ago many drivers, himself included he admits, routinely carried .22 caliber rifles in the cabs of their trucks to shoot the birds for sport.

Most people lump all gulls together generically as "seagulls," but there are actually three distinct gull species that frequent the South Bergen landfills. Two are true "survivor-type" organisms; the other, the largest species, is something of an adaptable wannabe.

The aggressive herring gull is the most numerous of the "dump gulls" and often nests in isolated sections of the landfills. It is without a doubt the most visible example of a wild animal moving in to fill a suddenly created scavenging niche.

The two other gull species—the graceful ring-billed gull and the nearly eagle-sized black-backed gull—are less common on the dumps but they maintain an ever-stronger wing-hold on the chow line in spite of their more boisterous brethren.

Gulls aside, when people think of dumps, they think of rats. And there are rats aplenty in residence in every dump in the world except those in the frozen Antarctic.

GREAT BLACK-BACKED GULL

HERRING GULL

LAUGHING GULL

RING-BILLED GULL

GULLS

*Gulls are as much a part of the Meadowlands' popular image as are muskrats and egrets. The big, sassy herring gull (*Larus argentatus*) is circumpolar in the northern parts of the Northern Hemisphere and has been expanding its breeding range southward on the Atlantic Coast in recent years. Abundant and highly visible in the Meadowlands, it is found throughout the district, especially near active landfills.*

*The great black-backed gull (*L. marinus*) breeds on the US coast south to the Carolinas, occasionally to Florida. Although frequently seen throughout the Meadowlands, it is the least abundant of the three common gull species of the region.*

*The ring-billed gull (*L. delawarensis*) is found throughout much of Canada and the northern United States; it winters south to Mexico and Cuba, though many remain as far north as open water can be found. The ring-bill, abundant year-round throughout the district, is exceeded in numbers only by the larger, more aggressive herring gull. It is usually the gull found hanging around fast-food outlets and shopping mall parking lots.*

*The attractive laughing gull (*L. atricilla*) occurs on the Atlantic coast from Nova Scotia to Venezuela. This bird is common along the Hackensack River in summer; it is the typical "summer gull" of the mid-Atlantic states.*

The brown, or Norway rat abounds in the landfilled areas of the Meadowlands. Nobody has ever tried to count them, but there surely must be many thousands, perhaps millions. The rat, despite the popular image of sneaking cowardice, is in fact an aggressive, adaptable creature that will not hesitate to defend itself if cornered. They have been known to leap from bags of trash in garbage trucks and into the faces of startled operators.

Rats are primarily nocturnal scavengers but they have no aversion to prowling about the trash heaps during the day and can be serious predators on the young of birds and mammals. They refuse nothing, alive or dead, as potential food. They are also disease carriers of the first magnitude who have successfully resisted centuries of intensive campaigns to eradicate them.

For some hawks and owls, the dumps are made to order, duplicating to some degree their native hunting grounds: marshes and open fields. Short-eared and barn owls patrol the landfills, the former while the sun shines, the latter under cover of darkness. Both species make at least some inroads on the rat and mouse hordes.

About a half-dozen species of hawks have been reported among the surprising total of some 250 bird species

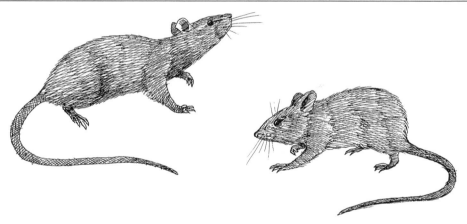

MAMMALIAN INVADERS

The brown rat (Rattus norvegicus*) was introduced from the Old World in the 18th century; it now occurs throughout North and Central America as far north as coastal Alaska, the central prairie provinces, and southern Quebec and the Maritimes. Common on the drier portions of the Meadowlands, it may forage in areas under tidal influence at night. Where abundant, it may be an important predator on nesting birds. Formerly much more common near active sanitary landfills, the rat has declined somewhat due to the closure of dumps and more effective control measures.*

The much smaller house mouse (Mus musculus*) is also an immigrant—via humankind—from the Old World in the late 18th century. It occurs with the brown rat throughout North America as far north as it can avoid extreme low winter temperatures and find shelter and a reliable food source; its populations are highly variable from year to year. It inhabits the drier portions of the district and is especially common near buildings, refuse piles, and landfills.*

PEREGRINE FALCON

KESTREL

ROUGH-LEGGED HAWK

RAPTORS

Birds of prey, both resident and visiting, have long been observed in the Meadowlands. Yet spotting one is always exciting.

The magnificent peregrine falcon (Falco peregrinus) is cosmopolitan in distribution, occuring in several races throughout temperate and arctic North America, Greenland, and Eurasia. This beautiful falcon was once abundant in North American but, due to shooting and contamination by the pesticide DDT, it underwent a spectacular decline in the 1940s and 1950s. By the early 1970s there were only an estimated 40 breeding pairs remaining in the contiguous 48 states. Although the peregrine falcon is not currently known to breed within the Meadowlands District, in 1994 there were 12 pairs known to live within a 15-mile radius of the region. A pair currently nests on the PSE&G plant in Kearny.

The much smaller kestrel, or sparrow hawk (F. sparverius), has also declined throughout much of its range, including the Meadowlands, over the past 20 years; individuals may occasionally been seen watching for prey along roads, including the northern section of the New Jersey Turnpike.

The rough-legged hawk (Buteo lagopus) of the Arctic winters anywhere from New

RED-TAILED HAWK

NORTHERN HARRIER

Jersey south, where it is almost always observed in open treeless areas, just the type habitat found in the Meadowlands. The big, rangy rough-leg is a fairly common winter raptor in the meadows, frequently observed coursing over, or hovering above, an expanse of reeds in search of rodents.

The red-tailed hawk (B. jamaicensis) is found from Alaska and central Canada south to Central America. It is probably the most abundant and conspicuous raptor in eastern North America as well as in the Meadowlands. This large soaring hawk may be observed at all times of year in DeKorte Park, as well as along most of the traffic arteries through the district. It is the large, stocky hawk most often seen perched in trees and scanning the surroundings for prey. Several individuals inhabit the area surrounding Snake Hill. Stephen Sautner, manager of conservation communications for the Wildlife Conservation Society, says he considers the New Jersey Turnpike "between exits 14 and 18W" to be among "the best red-tail spots I know of" in the New York metropolitan area.

The marsh hawk, or northern harrier (Circus cyaneus), is another circumpolar raptor characteristic of the Meadowlands. In North America it breeds from the Aleutian Islands, Hudson Bay, and Newfoundland south to Virginia and northern Mexico, wintering as far north as Washington State, Nebraska, and New Brunswick. This hawk was formerly much more abundant in the meadows: I can recall two breeding pairs in the Overpeck meadows in the 1950s. Though a fair number of migrants and transients are observed in fall and winter, there are at this time (1995) but two known breeding pairs in the entire district, both in the Berrys Creek area. The nesting sites are carefully monitored by HMDC naturalists and the New Jersey Audubon Society to prevent undue disturbance of the birds.

Sparrow hawk, or kestrel, at the base of the now-closed Bergen County landfill, DeKorte Park, Lyndhurst. The open, weed-grown expanses of abandoned landfills offer prime hunting habitat to birds of prey such as hawks and owls.

recorded in the meadowlands by birders. Some of the birds of prey are just passing through but others, such as the near eagle-sized rough-legged hawk and the diminutive kestrel, or sparrow hawk, spend a great deal of time and energy searching for the house and white-footed mice that skitter through the reeds and rubble.

The list of dump-oriented birds goes on and on—from the drab, tuneless house, or English sparrows and virtual blizzards of starlings to such gentle, elegant feathered residents as the killdeer, a strikingly attractive shorebird that thinks a dump is a fine place to raise a family. Killdeer nest

on the bare, open ground—just the kind of terrain found on landfills—so the threat of rat attack is a real one for these birds.

Four-footed predators and scavengers, besides rats, abound in and around landfills. Raccoons and opossums occupy virtually all sections of the meadowlands except those affected by the tides. Many a motorist doing 60 on the Turnpike has swerved to avoid a 'coon or red fox braving its life in the fast lane to get to greener pastures in Secaucus or East Rutherford.

Both the mink and the muskrat of fashion furs infamy

*The killdeer (*Charadrius vociferus*) is a widely distributed and abundant species, breeding from Canada to central Mexico, the West Indies, and Peru. It is probably the most common—and noisy—breeding shorebird in the Meadowlands, possibly exceeded in abundance only by the spotted sandpiper. It is found primarily on abandoned landfills and other open, treeless areas, including lawns, parks, and dredge spoil banks; several pairs nest on the open shrubby area at the base of Snake Hill in Secaucus.*

*The raccoon (*Procyon lotor*) is found from Alberta and northern New England south to Florida and Mexico, and throughout the West except for the higher elevations of the Rocky Mountains. It is found virtually throughout the Meadowlands except in the most heavily industrialized areas and is a common mammal in the surrounding suburbs. The coon's presence is usually unsuspected by humans because of its nocturnal habits. Within the meadows, raccoons may be serious predators on such ground nesting birds as waterfowl, and they often tear open the grass lodges of muskrats, devouring the young they find inside.*

tenant the dumps, the latter far more common and restricted to the surviving marshy ditches and creeks at the perimeters. The engaging otter, in centuries past a common resident of northern New Jersey, was thought to be extinct in these parts but one was reported rummaging along the margins of an abandoned landfill on the Overpeck Creek in Leonia several years ago. Wildlife experts speculated that it was an escapee from an area zoological collection.

The muskrat, a modest rodent that to its misfortune happens to possess a gorgeous pelt, was, and to some extent, still is, the true natural resource of the meadowlands. According to Chet Mattson, some 12,000 are trapped each year in the meadows, contributing to an underground economy of no small proportions. Muskrat trappers, diminished in number today, are "the true meadowsmen," far more than any developer, urban planner, or land speculator could ever hope to be, Mattson says.

Talk to any "'rat trapper" and you'll get a unique view of the life of the meadows, and the encroaching landfills, that you'll never hear in corporate boardrooms, Mattson says. "They (the trappers) are one of the best reasons we have found for working to save this marsh."

Dogs and cats, of the homegrown variety, regrettably call the dumps home as well. Hundreds of thousands of unwanted pets are abandoned by their owners each year in the United States and many simply adopt a feral, or semiwild

*The opossum (*Didelphis virginiana*) occurs from Florida and Arizona north to central Minnesota and central New England. It may be encountered throughout the Meadowlands but generally avoids dense phragmites stands and extensive muddy areas below low-tide levels. Common in residential areas, it is often overlooked due to its strongly nocturnal habits.*

*The muskrat (*Ondatra zibethica*), a Meadowlands keystone species, occurs over most of the North American continent, from Alaska and the Northwest Territories to northern Labrador and Newfoundland, and south to the Carolinas, Texas, Arizona, and Washington State. An abundant aquatic rodent throughout the natural and mitigated marshes of the district, the 'rat is, historically, the single most economically important mammal of the Meadowlands. Trappers took them by the thousands annually, well into the 1960s, for their fur. Muskrats tend to wander in the spring and fall and may then be seen grazing, along with woodchucks and cottontails, on the shoulders of the New Jersey Turnpike.*

*Feral dogs and cats (*Canis familiaris *and* Felis domesticus*) may be found living in a semi-wild though not necessarily self-sustaining state throughout most of temperate North America. Feral populations are much more common near larger urban areas, where food and shelter are more readily available, natural predators are absent, and hunting is generally prohibited. In the Meadowlands, both dogs and cats may be encountered anywhere throughout the district, though they are always more common near landfills, industrial parks, and town edges. They generally avoid moist areas under tidal* influence and dense stands of phragmites. The incidence of feral dog packs in the Meadowlands has declined considerably in recent years due to more effective control measures as well as continued construction of busy highways, which fragment formerly extensive open habitats. Few feral cats survive for more than a year or two in the harsh Meadowlands environment; those that persist are usually seen along roadways and near dumps and abandoned buildings, where food and shelter are more readily available to them.*

lifestyle. In the meadowlands, this often means the hostile environment of the landfills. Police reports of a decade or two ago averaged about 10 incidents of dog attacks on people a year, most of them carried out by free-ranging packs of domestic dogs roaming the dumps and other isolated areas of the meadowlands. Today the problem seems to have abated due to more efficient control methods and because so many busy highways transect the meadowlands that fewer dogs are able to reach the relative sanctuary of the dumps in the first place.

Feral cats adapt quite well to the dump environment. Secretive and wary, they avoid people while preying on birds, small mammals and any insects they can catch. Semi-wild house cats, unlike their truly wild relatives, may breed at any time of year and are extremely prolific. Where the food supply is adequate and populations are large, stray cats are a significant factor in the destruction of songbirds and other desirable wildlife.

In a 1978 report outlining the effectiveness of steps taken to clean up the Hackensack and Passaic River basins the HMDC spoke of the meadowlands and its sprawling, pungent garbage dumps as "a swampy, mosquito-infested jungle . . . where rusting auto bodies, demolition rubble, industrial oil slicks and cattails merged in unholy, stinking union." Anyone driving through the reedy plains and viewing the still-active dumps today would be inclined to suspect that the picture here hasn't changed all that much. The landfills, though carefully regulated and fast reaching the limit of their capacity in Bergen County, seem to be bigger and smellier than ever, topped by clouds of flying dumppickers that get in the way of airplanes.

But if the meadowlands planners realize their dream and the dumps are replaced by the green expanses of the 2,500-acre DeKorte Park and stately condominium complexes and glossy shopping malls rise where once rats prowled at will, one has the feeling that the gulls, the raccoons, the mink and the muskrats will still be around. Perching on the balconies of luxury, riverside townhouses and patrolling the midnight lawns of multinational corporate headquarters.

There just may be fewer of them.

(*John R. Quinn,* The Passaic Herald-News, *Feb. 18, 1982*)

A GATHERING OF GRACKLES

The great influx of seagulls around the dumps was only one–very recent–manifestation of habitat change. As the marshes began to undergo intensifying environmental degradation in the early twentieth century, the character of the resident and migratory birdlife was already changing, with large, noisy roosts of urbanized, so-called pest species, such as starlings and grackles, gradually replacing the great flocks of waterfowl, herons, and shorebirds of yesteryear. One of the largest "blackbird roosts" was located on the Kingsland tract on the westerly edge of the Hackensack meadows, just east of Lyndhurst

AVIAN INVADERS

The garrulous and aggressive starling (Sturnus vulgaris) is native to temperate Eurasia and North Africa but has been introduced in many other places throughout the world. The first North American starlings were liberated in New York's Central Park in 1875, and within about 30 years the species had reached the West Coast. The starling is abundant virtually everywhere in the Meadowlands, where it often assembles in large roosting aggregations in phragmites or on buildings, bridges, and other structures.

The much smaller but equally problematic house, or English, sparrow (Passer domesticus) also hails from temperate Eurasia and North Africa and it has also been widely introduced all over the world. The first successful release of house sparrows took place in Brooklyn's Greenwood Cemetery in 1870; the species is now found throughout North and South America. This drab but highly adaptable little bird is most common near human habitations, industrial buildings, highway verges, and other altered habitats. It is much less seen in extensive areas of marshland.

center. In 1939 Clarence D. Brown, a member of the then-fledgling (Charles A.) Urner Ornithological Club of the Newark Museum, vividly described this roost and the character of the surrounding meadows, which changed with astonishing swiftness:

> In Colonial days the Kingsland tract, with several thousand adjoining acres, as now bordered by the Erie Railroad, the

Hackensack River, Harrison and the highland, was mostly forested, all above high-tide level and drained by winding cedar water streams, similar perhaps to parts of Manahawkin Swamp [in Ocean County] today.

The old Belleville Road from New York was cut through a thick forest, which during Revolutionary times furnished wood for the people of New York. Settlers of these parts, many from Holland, looked upon this "waste swamp" and determined to reclaim it, and there began one of the most intensive drainage projects this area has known. Ditches were dug, many of them navigable at high tide, commencing at the Hackensack River and Berry's Creek, bringing tidewater up to the highland. Tide gates were installed at the river, and effective drainage began. The land was cleared and cultivated or pastured, and old plantations extended over what is now a wet meadow. For a time this drainage was effective, but shrinkage or subsidence of the soil soon followed, until it dropped to low-tide level, becoming saturated and useless for agriculture. East of Harrison, near the turnpike, on a tract of marsh which was embanked by New Jersey Land Reclaiming Company about 1867, the marsh had subsided in 1887 to three and a half feet below its normal level.

Within my recollection [since 1895] the Kingsland Tract was still under partial control of abandoned tide gates, and some of the old live cedar trees remained. Hundreds of acres were growing hay. Wagon roads meandered through the meadow. Planked bridges crossed the creeks and ditches, and old, rough-leg hay poles, or haystacks, dotted the landscape. Marsh mallow, wild rice, cat-tails and tall grasses bordered the waterways. Extensive beds of cat-tails were unusual, and the foxtail [phragmites] was actually rare, occurring only in beds of a few acres, and it was slow getting established.

But changes continued. Rotting away during the '80s and '90s, the tide gates finally disappeared, and the shrunken land, being below high-tide level, again became flooded, forming what in those times local gunners knew as the Duck Ponds—a place of breeding rails and gallinules, and many muskrats. The flooding was gradual, and from a pond of an acre or two, it extended in time over several hundred acres, while solid beds of cat-tails developed in favored spots. Conditions were attractive to marsh and water birds of many species, and duck boats were poled through

oozy bogs and floating islands, where as boys we had rid-
den the hay ricks through the cut fields.

   With time this sunken land, now saturated or submerged, began to level up through sedimentation until year
after year it filled; the Duck Ponds disappeared–foxtails
spread everywhere–and the starlings came.

   Nature does indeed abhor a vacuum. Where the pristine and complex *Spartina* marsh ecosystem yielded to the single-species plumegrass
"meadowlands" (or to the open weedy plains of closed or abandoned
landfills), tough and hardy floral and faunal immigrants, the so-called
urban-adaptable species, soon moved in to occupy the suddenly available ecological niches.

   By 1939, Brown speaks of the Kingsland marsh as already dominated by phragmites, or "foxtails–hundreds of acres of foxtails–as far
as the eye can see. All this time, for as far back as my recollection runs,
the Blackbirds and Swallows have flocked here, shifting locally as
woods and vegetation changed, but coming each evening to roost in
the reeds. . . . and while the drastic ecological changes mentioned here
have compelled the birds to shift somewhat, their general location today is the same as when first known."

   Among these birds, the starling (*Sturnus vulgaris*) was particularly
successful in making itself at home. Following its arrival in the New
World from Europe in 1890–the two initial introductions in New York's
Central Park totaled no more than one hundred birds–the species
swept across the length and breadth of the land, reaching the West
Coast and southern Canada less than forty years later. The starling is
now one of the more abundant and noticeable birds of the Meadowlands, though it is not wetland-specific in habits and requirements.
Although the species underwent a huge population expansion in the
thirty or forty years following its establishment here, its numbers, like
those of the equally foreign and bothersome house sparrow, have lev-
eled off. Today, the starling is a grudgingly accepted member of the
North American avifauna, though it has retained its quasi-dependence
on humankind for the disturbed natural habitats it favors, and thus
is never found far from cities, farms, or industrialized areas like the
Meadowlands.

   Brown notes that the Kingsland blackbird roost was virtually de-
serted in December and January, with the first arrivals, usually male
redwings seeking to establish their territories, coming in from the south.
But with the advent of spring there was a rapid peak and decline: "on
March 17 [1938], 5,000 birds were occupying the area, mostly grackles;
on March 27 at least 27,000 birds came in during the evening flight
from the north, and the total of all birds observed the same morning

was estimated at 38,000. The roost peaks and declines as fast: 50,000 birds was the spring maximum; by April only 20,000 were known to be present and by April 17 but 5,000 remained, most having passed to the north or being occupied in nesting activities."

Birds of a feather have always flocked together in the meadows, and the Kingsland roost's nocturnal population has long included several other "blackbird" species in addition to starlings. The redwing (*Aegelaius phoeniceus*), the brown-headed cowbird (*Molothrus ater*), the rusty blackbird (*Euphagus carolinus*), and the common, or purple, grackle (*Quiscalus quiscula*), along with a smattering of robins (*Turdus migratorius*), often gather in winter roosting assemblies along with starlings. Indeed, in many roosts these native species may outnumber the European interloper by a considerable margin.

The common grackle possesses every bit of the sagacity attributed to blackbirds, crows, and jays and is as adept as any starling at exploiting every possible source of food. It also has a predatory side to its nature, unusual among perching birds, that makes it a hunter of nearly equal ability to that of a shrike. I once saw a big glossy male zip in out of nowhere and scatter a flock of house sparrows feeding on the ground near the edge of the Overpeck meadows. The sparrows fled in all directions, but the grackle singled out one, chased it down, and battered it to the grass with repeated blows of its bill and wings. It dispatched the sparrow with a few powerful jabs of its bill and then sat there panting, mantling its prey with outstretched wings like a tiny hawk. In an instinctive reaction to the horrifying assault, I had sprinted up to try to "save" the sparrow from its fate; the grackle stood its ground, glaring defiantly at me with bright yellow eye, bill wide open. Then, when I

*The common crow (*Corvus brachyrhynchos*) is a conspicuous, "streetwise" bird found throughout much of North America, from central Canada to Texas and Baja California. Much more abundant near farms, cities, and towns, it may be seen throughout the Meadowlands district, mostly in edge habitats and upland situations. The similar but smaller fish crow (*C. ossifragus*, not illustrated) is a sporadic visitor in the Meadowlands; the best field mark is its voice, a higher-pitched* kwok! *or* cah-hah! *that is very different from the familiar* caw caw! *of the common crow.*

hesitated, it quickly plucked up the still-twitching sparrow in its bill and flew off over the reeds. I was amazed at the speed and ferocity of the attack and kill, never having thought a familiar lawn and garden "songbird" capable of such brutal conduct!

Apparently, our forebears witnessed such reprehensible behavior on the part of these vaguely crowlike birds and determined that they, like the despised crows, were prime candidates for extermination. Brown writes:

> The Grackles were in primitive times birds of the marsh and waterside in forested regions, but as settlements and clearings took the place of the primeval, those birds found a new food supply in the corn crop of the settlers and multiplied. [Edward Howe] Forbush relates: "In Colonial days bounties were placed on their heads, and in some Cape Cod towns a young man was forbidden by law to marry until he had turned in to the town clerk a certain number of Blackbird heads." Surely many of our young men must still have matrimony first in mind, and knowing the Blackbirds' lines of flight, are there in the fall along the Lackawanna tracks, or on the Jersey City Pipe Line, or strung out along the meadows' edge below Rutherford and Carlstadt, banging away into the sable masses as they pass. Intensive shooting has gone on here from earliest recollection, and still persists [in 1939] with no apparent diminution in the number of any of our Blackbirds. While this could be outlawed by a little pressure on the local communities, possibly reasonable killing is desirable, as both Starlings and Grackles hold a potential menace. Surely there is a limit to the numbers the surrounding country can sustain, and it would not be well to hear too loud and too persistent cries from the farmers of Blackbirds damaging their crops.

Although the site of the former Kingsland roost has undergone great change and no longer attracts significant concentrations of blackbirds, the action and vitality of birds in general are still one of the natural attractions of the Meadowlands. Masses of redwings, grackles, and starlings flow over the marshes in fall and gather in roosting aggregations that, while still impressive in density, do not match those of Clarence Brown's era. The geographical location of the Meadowlands, astride converging lines of flight on the Atlantic flyway, has long made them a crucial fall stopping point for avian travelers winging their way down the continent from the Great Lakes, the eastern Canadian Arctic, and the Maritimes. Even in their much reduced state, the meadows pro-

*The red-winged blackbird (*Agelaius phoe- niceus*) is extremely widespread, occurring throughout North America south to the West Indies and Costa Rica. It is usually found near water and marshes—in both phragmites and* Spartina *marshes, for example, through- out the Meadowlands. This is a highly visible and audible bird: black, red-shouldered males may be seen defending territories at regular intervals along the New Jersey Turnpike.*

vide these birds the fundamental food and safety they need during their perilous flight from the northern winter. As late as 1955 *The Record* of Hackensack, in a series of feature articles on the Meadowlands, noted that "although factories have arisen and towns have grown all around, suburban civilization has ended where the swamp muck begins. The Hackensack River still flows undisturbed through a lonely, green flat- land from Bergen to Newark Bay."

For a short while longer, that lonely strip of green was all the wil- derness needed—not only to support the migrating birds, but also to support the local sportsmen.

SUBURBAN HAWKEYES

Firearms have figured prominently in meadows history from the very first days of European colonization. Virtually everyone carried a mus- ket or rifle, from the Dutch and English farmers and soldiers to the Lenape warriors, who acquired the weapons from their new overlords through barter or theft. For three centuries, generations of waterfowl and rail hunters continued to gun the meadows, and as late as the mid-1960s the guns of autumn were as characteristic of that season as was the annual Thanksgiving Day gridiron donnybrook between the

*The meadows of yesteryear, view from the Barrows House, Orient Way,
Rutherford. From a photo entitled "Overlooking New York, 1907," courtesy the
Meadowlands Museum, Rutherford.*

Village of Ridgefield Park and the neighboring borough of Bogota.
Shotguns and ammunition were sold in local hardware stores, and high
school classrooms emptied of all outdoors-oriented youths on the first
day of pheasant season.

Carl Vercelli, a high school classmate of mine and a member of the
football squad, told me that he and a few other boys would bring their
guns to football practice, leaving them in the field house until a flight of
geese or teal appeared over the meadows; scrimmage was then suspended for an hour while the eager party of suburban Hawkeyes made
their way out to the creek and banged away at the birds. "This happened all the time," Vercelli told me. "Surrounded by the meadows like
we were here, there was still a strong hunting tradition here in town in
those days."

With the filling of the Overpeck meadows in the 1960s for the
county marine park and the construction of Interstate 95, though,

hunting as a way of life among the village youth quickly faded from the cultural scene. In a rapidly urbanizing environment, the average citizen soon came to regard firearms more as an agent of crime than as a means to secure a meal or engage in recreation. Tolerance for the noise and violence of sport hunting declined, and the staccato sounds of gunshots over the autumn marshes were silenced for good. But along with hunting, other traditional forms of outdoor recreation also declined.

Voices

CHARLES A. VAN WINKLE, RUTHERFORD:
RECALLING THE 1890s

"The children in my day had more to do than they had time for. The Jersey meadows were one vast playground. About opposite where Bonnie

Dell Farms now are, there used to be a ditch called Little Bend where we learned to swim. Then, once we could swim Little Bend, we graduated to Big Bend, and then to Berrys Creek.

"The meadows were full of crabs, fish, snapping turtles, muskrats, birds; and along where the meadows reached the uplands were quail and woodcock. The meadows had been partially drained by the early Dutch settlers, who had dug a series of ditches and installed iron sluice gates which automatically let the water out at low tide. In those days, the meadow hay was especially cherished by the Dutch, who cut it as bedding for the horses and cows. It was salt hay, and the animals would not eat it.

"As boys, we put set lines across Berrys Creek. That is, a stake on either side of the creek with a line strung taut between them. To the taut line at regular intervals were tied fishing lines which we baited every morning. After school we would go down to the creek, take the fish off, and sell them.

"We used to fasten a hook to an old broom handle and search for snapping turtles with it. We would poke the broom handle down a muskrat hole, and when we hit something hard, we knew we had a turtle. The hook would then catch between the upper and lower shells of the turtle, which on snapping turtles do not come together, and we could pull them up to the surface. Then we would have the turtle bite on a piece of wire which we then fastened to his shell like a horse's bit so he could not bite us. When we had caught two or three, we would row them in our rowboat up Berrys Creek to the Paterson Plank Road, where there was a hotel which featured snapping turtle soup on its menu. We would get fifty [cents] apiece for our catch.

"There was a big cedar swamp between Paterson Plank Road and the Erie railroad which was full of rabbits and cranberries. We used to pick cranberries and sell them. There was also a big cedar swamp opposite the copper mines in what is now Lyndhurst. Copper had been mined for over a century from tunnels in the side of the hill which are now abandoned. Several of us were down by the mines shooting reed- and railbirds one day when a rabbit ran in front of us and into one of the tunnels. Mr. Ellsworth Elliott, who lived on Chestnut Street, was the first one into the mine after the rabbit. The tunnels were only waist high so that we had to stoop down and creep along. Mr. Schneider was the second, and I followed him. We were all carrying our shotguns. Schneider stumbled; his gun went off and hit Elliott in the back of the head, killing him instantly. That was the only shooting fatality in the meadows that I can remember, which in retrospect seems remarkable since we all had guns."

THE MEADOWSMEN

For many boys growing up in the meadows towns of the 1940s and 1950s, the swamps were synonymous with muskrats. In the Ridgefield Park of my youth there were four or five professional trappers—men who actually made something of a living at it—and perhaps twenty-five or thirty amateurs. The latter were mostly boys of high school age who trapped the meadows for a little spending money or simply because they were attracted to the adventure offered by the wilderness at the end of their streets.

Many of my own friends were "recreational" trappers. Richie Johnson, Dorsie Kerlin, and Herbie Prince all beefed up their savings accounts through their trapping activities. And then there was Pete Poirier. Pete was regarded as one of the best trappers and hunters in town. He had begun exploring the meadows at about the same age I had, though his turf was at the south end of town, near the Route 46 bridge. In his time he trapped, skinned, and sold hundreds of muskrats before giving it up in his senior year of high school.

Like most of the other young trappers of the 1950s, Pete Poirier has long since left the village, but I tracked him down using the address list for our class's upcoming fortieth reunion. Today, he lives in Connecticut and is manager of facilities for Chesebrough-Ponds in Trumbull. He was surprised to hear from me after all these years, but he agreeably recalled his life as a 'rat trapper, with wistful clarity:

Voices ⌒

PETE POIRIER

"I started 'playing,' as you'd actually call it, in the swamps of the Overpeck area when I was about eight years old. We'd find boats adrift and bring 'em back off the main creek to a dock we had on the little creek near the foot of Christie Street. We'd use 'em for crabbing in the summertime; the blue claw crabs would come up the creek and we'd catch a bushel in an afternoon if the tide was right.

"An older trapper, Connie Kuiken, gave me a trap and showed me how to use it. It was an old trap; didn't have much strength to it. He took me out and showed me what a muskrat hole was, and we put the trap in there. Next day I come back and, lo and behold, I have a muskrat in the trap!

"But I can't see him; I can see the trap, and [see] the trap move. I started pulling the trap out and he's fighting like crazy. The trap is old and it had only caught him by a toenail. When I yanked it out, that's what I got—a toenail. So my first try at trapping, I caught something but lost it.

"I would say the biggest years I made maybe two or three hundred dollars from trapping. We used to get two dollars for a pelt; if it was a real big one you might get two-fifty, three dollars. The baby ones, called 'kits,' you'd get fifty cents for. . . . Naturally, you didn't want to catch a kit, but if you caught 'em they'd drown anyway.

"Most of the time the muskrats were drowned when the tide came in; sometimes when I had sets that were not drowning, I would use a trap called the 'stop-loss.' It had a big spring that would come down on the animal and hold him away from the trap. Because what they would do, a 'rat would chew his foot off to escape. Sometimes you'd get a muskrat with only one leg left; they'd already chewed off the other three legs in traps.

"I'd have, at any one time in my house, maybe twenty, thirty pelts in various stages of preparation. You'd take the 'rats home and skin them, throw the carcass in the garbage, and I'd have pelts inside-out drying on stretchers. I wonder now about the smell, and I can't imagine parents today letting their kids do that, just because of the smell. Or any parents today letting their kids go out into the swamps, trapping or hunting; today, they feel like they have to take 'em to the bus stop in the morning.

"I couldn't wait 'til I was seventeen and got my driver's license. If I got a car I could do so much more trapping, 'cause I could go all over and it'd be easier to get to the traps; I could run more lines. But when I turned seventeen, got a car, girls came into the picture and I no longer was crazy about it. I [had] always kinda wondered why the older guys with cars didn't do any more trapping. That's pretty much how it happened."

Pete Poirier, with all his experience in the meadows, pursued the muskrat part-time, as recreation. There were others whose whole existence centered on the land and its wildlife.

Twenty-five years ago I enjoyed a brief but wonderful correspondence with a man named Jerry Komarek, who lived in the meadows town of Little Ferry. In fact, his family went back generations in the town, and both he and his brother, Rudy, were well known as outdoorsmen. Rudy Komarek is an inveterate urban troubadour and collector of rattlesnakes whose exploits with the venomous reptiles still earn him occasional notice in the press. Jerry Komarek was a self-taught naturalist, a member of that vanishing cadre of rugged individualists in the manner of the legendary trapper Jake Kraft of East Rutherford, who probably spent more of his time in the swamps than out of them.

I never met Jerry in person, but our lives did intersect fleetingly in 1970. Over a two-month period near the end of that year we exchanged two letters and a phone call. The things he told me then, the little wisdoms and insights he shared with me about his beloved meadows, stuck in my mind over the ensuing years.

Komarek was a poet as well, in both philosophy and in practice. His efforts, while lacking the abstract intricacies and clever lyrics of a laureate, had a direct honesty, inspired by an absolute clarity of purpose and passion. They spoke to the heart and the conscience, of the environmental variety. Most of his poems concern nature and what we are doing to it, especially in the Meadowlands. Komarek mourned the accelerating loss of a place he knew and loved, and he expressed his outrage and grief in prose of childlike simplicity but flawless logic; his poetry was a form of folk art. Komarek's modest legacy—his expression of love for the earth—was in large part the initial inspiration for this book, which came to me ten years after I had received his letters.

Jerry Komarek died early in 1995. I learned of his death through a friend, a former trapper himself, who had seen the obituary in *The Record*. Even though I had never met the man, I felt an oddly profound sense of loss, for I realized that I had forever lost the opportunity to record a part of meadows history as it had been lived by one of the last of the true "meadowsmen." All that survived of our brief encounter were two faded letters and the echoes of a late December phone conversation, a quarter-century in the past.

In his first letter, Komarek told me a little about himself. He wrote that he had been born and raised in Little Ferry and had known the surrounding meadows since early childhood. "I learned to swim in the Hackensack. Over the years I trapped muskrats and hunted waterfowl throughout the meadows. It was a wonderful place to grow up near." As a child he worked as a farmhand when there were still farms in the Little Ferry and Moonachie area, and he developed a lifelong interest in the Lenape occupancy of the region. He wrote of collecting American Indian artifacts and of his close friendship with Ridgefield Park's Frank Morrison, a respected authority on the subject. As of 1970, he was still a Meadowlands hunter: "I still catch snapper turtles during the winter months," he wrote. "I make soup, using the turtle meat." Craig Claiborne, the *New York Times* food writer, heard about Jerry's talents as a snapper soup chef and wrote an article about him.

But it was on matters of nature that Jerry Komarek truly waxed

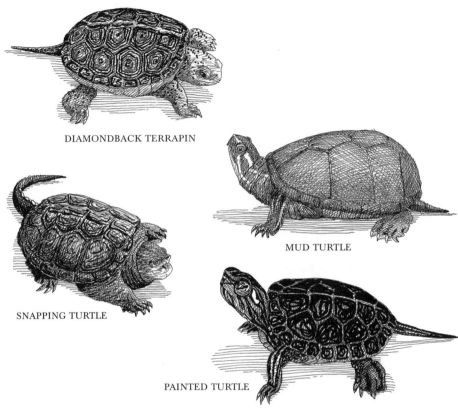

DIAMONDBACK TERRAPIN

MUD TURTLE

SNAPPING TURTLE

PAINTED TURTLE

TURTLES

*The diamondback terrapin (*Malaclemys terrapin) *occurs in saltmarsh estuaries, tidal flats, and lagoons from Cape Cod to Texas. Once nearly extirpated from the Meadowlands, this animal is now effecting a considerable comeback here. One of the few terrapins able to tolerate salt water, the diamondback appears to be most abundant in the 1,100-acre Sawmill Creek Wildlife Management Area, where many may be observed basking or at the water's surface during the warmer months.*

*The mud turtle (*Kinosternon subrubrum) *is found from Long Island and northern New Jersey west to southwestern Indiana and south to the Gulf states; the Meadowlands are near the northern extent of its range. This turtle has been reported in the Bellmans and Berrys Creek areas, as well as Kearny Marsh.*

*The familiar painted turtle (*Chrysemys picta) *exists in two subspecies (the eastern and midland) and occurs from Nova Scotia south to Georgia. It is common in freshwater and brackish habitats in the Meadowlands and has been reported in Berrys, Bellmans, and Overpeck Creeks, Kearny Marsh, and the Saw Mill Creek area.*

*The snapping turtle (*Chelydra serpentina) *is a large aquatic species occurring from southern Alberta to Nova Scotia and south to the Gulf of Mexico. It may be found in both freshwater and brackish habitats. In the Meadowlands the snapper occurs throughout the district, inhabiting freshwater impoundments such as Overpeck Creek and Kearny Marsh as well as the middle and upper Hackensack River. In the past the snapper was actively hunted in the Meadowlands and sold to local restaurants as an ingredient for stews and snapper soup.*

eloquent. "I am sad that some people just can't wait to destroy the works of nature," he told me in our last phone conversation. "I hunted and trapped in the meadows for many years. I took a lot from them, and they gave me a lot, so I try to give something back in my poetry."

Jerry's poetry revolved almost entirely around ecological themes and often speculated on the ultimate effects of overpopulation and industrialization. One of those he sent me, however, expressed his melancholy at the demise of the Meadowlands he saw occurring within his own lifetime. He called it "The Ecology of the Hackensack Meadows," and its final four stanzas surely contain some great truths, perceived by all who love the land and decry its abuse.

> *Sandy beaches and streams with water clean and pure,*
> *Have been converted into little more than an open sewer.*
> *And this is something that should concern us all—*
> *Wildlife now has its back against the wall.*
> *Rather than concern for any individual's personal prosperity,*
> *We should retain a portion of its natural state for posterity.*
> *While with money much can be done, it's been reiterated,*
> *The work of nature, by man, can never be duplicated.*

Later in 1995, the same year I learned that Jerry Komarek had died, I came to learn something about the life and times of another hardy Little Ferry frontiersman who had known the meadows of yesteryear on an even more intimate basis. Willy Royka, like Jerry Komarek, was a trapper and hunter, a lifelong resident of Little Ferry, and a meadows wayfarer until his death in 1984 at the age of sixty-five. Though lacking Komarek's literary bent, Royka was still some kind of poet. His rigorous daily pilgrimage into the wide open spaces of the meadows was a poem in itself—one lived rather than written.

Willy knew the meadows with a familiarity based on need, which far surpassed the casual focus of the town-bound naturalist. To be sure, the meadows were his inspiration and place of solitude and contemplation, but they were also his coal mine and assembly line—his place of employment. It can be next to impossible for most of the rest of us, accustomed to working out our lives inside heated buildings, to imagine what it must have been like to walk into the reeds on a below-zero morning with the idea of doing a day's work there. Because you had to. Because, natural beauty aside, you were going to feed a large and trusting family on what your half-frozen hands might manage to wrest from the brine-ice and subterranean muskrat tunnels of the winter marshes. And you were going to do this for virtually your entire life.

Steve Royka is one person who can not only imagine the hardships of such a lifestyle; he can remember it. He is Willy's youngest son, and

Willy Royka, veteran muskrat trapper and meadowsman. This 1970s scene shows Royka, holding a trapped 'rat, looking southeastward over his domain toward the skyline of New York City. From a photo courtesy the Meadowlands Regional Chamber of Commerce.

he is the source of information about Willy that I sought out in 1995. In his childhood Steve often accompanied his father as he endured in a difficult trade that Steve saw as entirely logical—simply because his father pursued it, and the family was fed and kept warm because of it. "They were hard times, but they were good times, too," Steve told me. "Even as a kid, I knew that what my father did for a living was a vanishing way of life. And it was a unique life. People always found it fascinating to hear about what he did."

Steve, when I met him, was twenty-nine, a slender, nervous man with restless pale blue eyes and an eager, almost childlike enthusiasm; he was openly friendly, spoke hurriedly, and smiled a lot. His face, the back of his neck, and his arms were sun-browned in the "farmer's tan" of a man who earned his living outdoors, with his thinning blond hair bleached even further by the sun. He was, indeed, still working out-doors, but not at his father's trade. Steve had a "regular job" with the Little Ferry Department of Public Works and had not ventured out into the marshes in many years.

I met Steve Royka in front of the family home on Washington Avenue in Little Ferry. He and his brother Lennie are the sole remaining Roykas living in the ninety-five-year-old house his Czech grandfather bought in 1917, when the meadows came right up to the backyard. The place, a modest frame and brick building, looks somewhat timeworn among its much younger, more ostentatious garden apartment and ranch house neighbors. As we talked by the front stoop, a black, battle-scarred tomcat sat on the top step and watched me speculatively with narrowed eyes while another cat dozed on a second-floor windowsill, its white-mittened forepaws dangling languidly over the edge. The Royka home, as though in memorial to its deceased patriarch, is still surrounded by an imposing collection of assorted auto parts, sheet metal, and other scrap. Steve's older-model Chevy pickup sits by the side of the house, in about the same place his father's battered old truck rested between its labors, back in the fifties and sixties. On the ground-level front porch there is an old kitchen chair and a plastic milk crate filled with empty, hand-crushed soda cans. "I'm always out here on summer evenings," Steve says, "just enjoying and taking in the passing scene."

Voices ॐ

STEVE ROYKA

"When I was a kid I used to explore and collect scrap in the big cedar swamp where the Sports Complex is now. . . . A dirt road went through there; that's all there was. That wasn't all that long ago. You're talkin' a lotta changes out there."

As he speaks he gestures over his shoulder, in the general direction of East Rutherford and the recently renamed Continental Airlines Arena. "My brother and me, we'd play catch out there, sometimes in thirty-below weather; there wasn't a house in sight then," he says.

Steve began to accompany his father on trapping and scrap collecting forays into the meadows "oh, when I was three, maybe four years old. . . . I guess he liked what he was doin'; he stuck with it all those years. He was real independent; he liked bein' his own boss. He was tough, too. He would walk from the Mill Creek Mall to Little Ferry—about three miles—with a hundred pounds of 'rats and traps on his back.

"He used to say, 'they're killin' more muskrats when they fill in the land than the trappers ever could in their whole lives.'

"He used to shoot ducks right out our back window years ago, when the meadows came right up behind the house. Him and a couple other guys, they'd go upstairs, load the rifles, open the windows and shoot the ducks. The meadows were right here, there were no factories, there was nothing. It was all open in those days.

"He used to mostly hunt the ducks. He'd only hunt what we'd eat. He wouldn't kill something just for the heck of it. If he wouldn't eat it, he wouldn't hunt.

Snapping turtle "periscoping" in Saw Mill Creek. One of the Meadowlands' many railroad bridges over the Hackensack River is visible in the background.

"My father used to pull in the snapping turtles but he used to just chop the heads off 'cause he never liked those. They eat the ducks, they eat the muskrats. They'd still walk around without the heads, an eerie-looking sight, but they do. I've seen 'em do it, many times.

"I went out there with him lotsa times when I was a kid; we'd walk out across the ponds. He'd know when the ice was thick enough. He'd chop a hole in the ice, put in his hand, and pull up the trap. Hopefully there would be a 'rat in it.

"There was no one out there to be afraid of. Even the crooks couldn't tolerate it; I couldn't see them out there in the middle of nowhere for a couple of days, twenty below zero and all that!

"That kind of lifestyle, the kind he lived, you don't get holidays or weekends . . . you have to be out there 365 days a year. You don't check the traps, either the dump rats'll get 'em [the trapped muskrats] or somebody else'll steal 'em. He used to put the traps up on the roof of the house and let 'em get rusty so they couldn't be seen in the water and get stolen. . . . We'd be out there Christmas, we'd be out there Thanksgiving, New Year's—we'd be out there. It didn't matter. Every day of the year. Trapping's four months of the year, from November fifteenth to March fifteenth, but the scrap collecting went on all year.

"Trapping's disappearing now; the old-timers are almost all gone. It goes up and down, like the stock market. Now it's about fifty cents, a dollar a pelt. All these animal rights activists, with this fake fur—there's not much demand for real fur anymore. If you're going to trap something and you're going to use it, that's one thing. If you're going to trap and just leave it, that's a waste. But if you're going to use it, what's the big deal?

"With the prices going up and down you have to catch a hell of a lot in four months to live on it for the other eight months. Most trappers couldn't do it. It was good for kids, it was spending money. But then when it got to be work, most of 'em gave it up.

"My father started slowing down as he got older. My brother Willy would get twelve hundred 'rats a year, while my father'd get eight hundred. He was slowing down a bit; he was getting older. My brother was only in his twenties. After my brother died, he [my father] lost the will; he died the next year, in 1984. They were trapping partners. My brother started going out with him in 'seventy-one, and they were partners ever since.

"Most of the others are gone, too. Pete Mavis, he was a trapper. This was way back. He and my father were partners back in the forties and fifties. They were two of the best trappers around. They used to bring in stuff no one else could catch. There was Louie Crecco; he was a trapper. He died. There was Petrick; he was a trapper. He died. There was the guy with the mink farm; he died. Most of 'em are gone now.

"There was an old guy, Newt; he used to set traps all around a muskrat house and then jump on it to chase the 'rats out into the traps. We used to tell him you can't do that! It's against the law, for one thing. The game warden'll pull your license in a minute. For another, that's not sportsmanship; that's stupidity. But he'd always do it. He's gone now, too."

Steve Royka grows pensive, reflecting. His older brother, Willy, is gone, dead of an aneurysm in 1983 at the age of twenty-nine, his own age; his mother died in 1991. One sister lives in Hackensack, another in Manchester in central Jersey. Steve and his brother Lennie, a bank messenger, are the only family members left in the weathered house that was once "right next to the swamps." Though he admires the persistence and hardiness that saw his father through decades of subsistence trapping and metal scavenging in the meadows, Steve Royka clearly has no desire to follow in those footsteps—even if he thought he had a fair chance of making a decent living at it, in this expensive age. Hence the full-time job that pays his bills and keeps the roof of the family homestead over his head.

"Years ago," he continues, "you couldn't give the meadows away. It was a dollar an acre. Nobody wanted it. They used to try to give it away in card games; they used to play poker and try to give it away, but nobody wanted it. Now it's one of the most valuable pieces of real estate in the country.

"That lifestyle has gone now. It's called progress, I guess. I kind

Herring gulls loafing on winter ice at the Kingsland Impoundment. The Hartz Mountain Corporation's huge Harmon Cove residential and commercial complex rises in the distance.

of liked the meadows, you know? I liked the freedom. I remember
when half the town was meadows, and I know people who remember
ber when 90 percent of the town was meadows. Now it's gotten all built
up—no more elbow room anymore. It's a shame.

"Show 'em a picture of him [Willy Royka] out in the meadows, and
they'll say where the heck is that? And you say right here, right were
you're standing, right where your house is!"

Toward the end of his long career as a meadowsman, Willy Royka
had become something of a legend. In 1971 the CBS television show
60 Minutes aired an eight-minute segment on the Roykas; correspondent
dent Morley Safer called the grizzled trapper and metal scavenger
"a remarkable fellow." *The Record* of Hackensack did a profile on Willy
in one of its Sunday editions the following year. Reporter Tom Toolen
wrote with compassion and sensitivity of the beleaguered but fiercely
proud Royka family, noting that its head could be found "rain or shine,
winter or summer . . . searching through the meadows, eking out what
can only be called an existence" for an income that often amounted to
three or four dollars a day.

In 1972 ten-year-old Karen Royka composed an affectionate ditty
in tribute to her father, and recited it singsong fashion to a newspaper
reporter:

> *My Daddy is happy when he is free;*
> *He likes all the dumps and the meadows, you see.*
> *Ohhh, my big brother Willy is with him too;*
> *They're always together 'cause they're their own boss.*
>
> *Ohhh, I have a nice mother who's good to me.*
> *When my Daddy finds junk, he sells it each day.*
> *Ohhh, he's glad he can be his own boss that way;*
> *To be in the meadows is where he is free.*

Those childish words, borne away on the winds of change, faded
in the din of the commerce and industry that had already overtaken
the Hackensack meadows. They are more than a wistful paean to one
man; they are an epitaph to the passing of a frontier, from wilderness
to megalopolis in a mere eye-blink of geologic time.

Today

This is the ultimate technological landscape. Here is where you come to see the twentieth century.

ANGUS GILLESPIE AND MICHAEL ROCKLAND,
Looking for America on the New Jersey Turnpike

All changed, changed utterly:
A terrible beauty is born.
WILLIAM BUTLER YEATS, *Easter, 1916*

For many centuries the river offered the only route of passage through the forbidding marshes of the Hackensack estuary. Until the early eighteenth century, in fact, not a terrestrial roadway bisected the rippling expanse of reeds from Little Ferry to Newark Bay. The transport of goods and people was effected over water alone. But roads have come to dominate the Meadowlands of the late twentieth century, and one road stands alone as virtually synonymous with the Meadowlands: the New Jersey Turnpike.

It is from the shoulders of the Turnpike that the majority of residents of the urban Northeast now form their impressions of the Hackensack River and estuary. Little do they know, then, how much the water itself has changed—how much of it now lies impounded behind Oradell Dam.

Of all the recent construction projects affecting the meadows, perhaps none have had more lasting impact than the Turnpike and the dam. Both are large-scale engineering feats, hailed as monuments to the march of progress, that permanently altered the ecological integrity of the Hackensack valley. The superhighway and the dam, both seen as vital to the continued economic health of the urban Northeast, were built when the eventual reclamation and total development of the Meadowlands was accepted as a desirable given. They were simply two more large-scale accomplishments of humankind, in its steady ascent from the primeval "noble savages" of the Stone Age to tomorrow's godlike wanderers among the stars.

John Locke, the leading philosopher of the eighteenth-century European Enlightenment, would have loved both the Turnpike and the dam, for he and most of his contemporaries firmly believed that "the negation of nature is the way to happiness." If Locke's ideas and those of the Enlightenment as a whole can be said to contain even a kernel of truth, then the 18 million residents of the Great Eastern Megalopolis are surely intoxicated by the elixir of happiness. For in few other places on this planet can the "negation of nature" be experienced on a grander scale.

THE VIEW FROM THE TURNPIKE

Egypt has its pyramids, China the Great Wall, and New York City its famous Manhattan skyline. And yet, while many cities, states, and nations boast human constructions—artifacts, if you will—of noteworthy size and awesome splendor, none but New Jersey has the Turnpike. The *New Jersey* Turnpike.

Although this world-renowned traffic artery has virtually come to symbolize modern motorized humankind, not to mention the state of New Jersey itself, it is not, in fact, the first New Jersey Turnpike. Nor was it the first toll road, though it came close. The honor of being the very first New Jersey roadway to collect a fee for passage belongs to the Morris Turnpike. That road, chartered in 1801, was a meadows highway at least in part, running from "Elizabeth-Town" in the east to Morristown and Newton in the west. By 1829 New Jersey lawmakers had chartered fifty-one turnpike-building companies, though only about half of them ever constructed so much as a mile of road. By that period, however, there were some 550 miles of "improved highways" in the state; New Jersey had evolved from a provincial wilderness transected by rutted wagon trails and Indian pathways to the beginnings of an orderly and civilized modern entity.

The *original* New Jersey Turnpike was chartered in 1802, the year following the genesis of the Morris Pike. It was an east-west road designed to link the then-rural municipalities of New Brunswick and Phillipsburg, and it survives today—in part—as the venerable but rather pedestrian State Route 22. But the *real* New Jersey Turnpike, completed

Common or great egret, Kingsland Impoundment, DeKorte Park. The New Jersey Turnpike's western spur and the Conrail suspension rail bridge are seen in the background.

from end to end in 1955, is another matter altogether. This 136-mile-long (including the Newark Bay extension) monster road, running north-south through most of the state, is surely the archetypal modern traffic artery, and very close to the busiest—anywhere in the world.

Annually transporting nearly 150 million motor vehicles and their passengers, the New Jersey Turnpike has its equal virtually nowhere else on the planet. Not even the world-famous autobahns of Germany or the serpentine Los Angeles freeways transport such an unrelenting volume of passenger and commercial traffic, and through such a thoroughly urbanized landscape.

The Turnpike is also a symbol, a larger-than-life monument to technology—one of the more conspicuous end results of the immense energy and muscle unleashed at the start of the Industrial Revolution 250 years ago. As the greatest and most critical artery servicing the New York City environs, as well as a central part of the longer Interstate 95 linking all the major metropolitan areas on the eastern seaboard from Maine to Miami, the New Jersey Turnpike offers a journey through the very heart of the eastern urban experience—a trip that often defies description, let alone definition. If, however, you accept industrial society as a legitimate presence on Earth, as James Lovelock suggests, then the Turnpike requires no explanation or defense; it simply exists. And it is never at rest.

Occasionally, while traveling between the cities and suburbs this great road serves, motorists will notice the land it bestrides. So the New Jersey Turnpike is also, inextricably, a large part of the popular image of the Meadowlands—but only the Turnpike's northernmost section. The southern section, by contrast—the one hundred or so miles between its juncture with the Garden State Parkway at Woodbridge and the Delaware Bay Bridge at Deepwater, New Jersey—is virtually indistinguishable from many other limited-access superhighways anywhere in the country. At times it passes through a countryside reminiscent of rural Maryland, Virginia, or even California. Traffic at least *seems* somewhat lighter on the southern section, and the drivers are more civil, or so it would appear. Deer may be spotted browsing along the green verges in Cumberland or Salem Counties, and the horizon is a rather benign mélange of forests, farmhouses, and the occasional corporate park.

But it is the nine miles of the Turnpike between the Pulaski Skyway and the exit ramp for the Vince Lombardi Service Area in the borough of Ridgefield that dominates the popular imagination. This is *the* Turnpike, the world-famous, industrialized, every-man-for-himself civilian racetrack of the Hackensack Meadowlands. Somehow this monster evolved from earlier roads that served the metropolis, plied by such lightning-bolt conveyances as the stagecoach, popularly known as the Flying Machine:

> *Historical Note: The Flying Machine.* That plies between Hackensack and Hoebuck, intends to set off on Mondays, Tuesdays and Saturdays, from Hackensack at 7 o'clock in the

*The roly-poly woodchuck (*Marmota monax*) is found from central Yukon, James Bay, and southern Labrador south to Virginia, Tennessee, Oklahoma, and British Columbia, but is absent on Newfoundland and Cape Breton Island. This familiar small mammal is not a marsh creature but is nonetheless present in the Meadowlands in suitable habitats, namely, the human-created edge habitats of landfills, park lawns, and highway verges. Adventurous individuals are frequently observed grazing on the shoulders of the New Jersey Turnpike's eastern spur near the Vince Lombardi Service Area.*

Morning; and to set off from Hoebuck the same Days, at
2 o'Clock in the Afternoon, for this Season. The Subscriber
humbly thanks the Public for their past favours, and hopes
a Continuance of the same. Passengers carried at Three
Shilling each, and Baggage at a reasonable Rate.

(Andrew Van Buskirk, New York Gazette and
Weekly Mercury, *June 24, 1776)*

Even two centuries ago New Jersey roads were designed for speed.
Most of the first highways followed the well-walked trails of the Lenape, graduating from sylvan paths to graveled lanes to an intricate
system of plank roads, in which three-by-twelve-inch cedar planks were
laid down to form an eight- or nine-foot-wide roadbed. The wooden
highways were considered so durable that the state was afflicted by a
"Plank Road Fever." "When kept up," a highway engineer once noted,
"plank roads were the smoothest highways built in the country prior to
the modern asphalt and concrete arteries of the twentieth century." The
venerable Paterson Plank Road was constructed in part from the primeval white cedar forests that once covered extensive sections of the
Meadowlands.

The old plank roads were soon replaced by macadam surfaces
and finally by concrete and the petroleum-based asphalt of today. The
new road-building technology came just in time to meet the demand
for new construction that descended on the nation in the wake of
World War II. For the duration of the war, road construction in the
United States had come to a virtual standstill. New Jersey's antiquated
roads and highways, designed to handle 1920s traffic loads, were woe-
fully inadequate for the huge surge in traffic that occurred by the early
1950s. Despite the growing swarm of passenger cars and trucks chug-
ging around the Garden State, a mere eighty miles of new roads were
constructed between the war's end and 1950.

Thus the perceived need for the New Jersey Turnpike and its sister
superhighway, the 173-mile-long Garden State Parkway. The Turnpike—
the modern one—had its genesis in the creation in 1948 of the New
Jersey Turnpike Authority by the state legislature. The authority was
empowered to build the road between the proposed northern New Jersey terminus at the Village of Ridgefield Park and the Delaware Bay
port of Deepwater—a distance of 117.5 miles.

Construction was begun in September of 1949. The route was divided into seven sections, and contracts awarded in that year for grading, drainage, and bridge substructures in eight of the ten counties that
would ultimately be involved amounted to $19,046, with a total con-
struction cost estimated at $230 million. The Turnpike also became
functional in sections, beginning on November 5, 1951, when the first

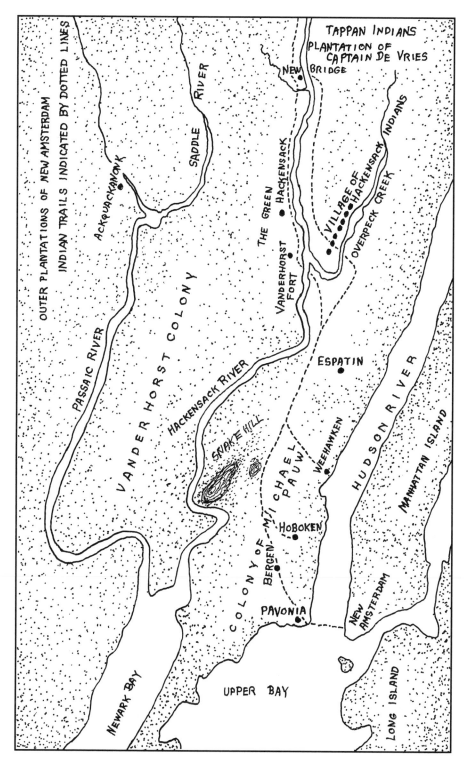

Major Lenape trails in the eastern Meadowlands area, ca. 1640. Adapted from Koehler, 1940.

Aspens and chain-link fence, near the New Jersey Turnpike, Lyndhurst.

56 miles, between Deepwater and Bordentown, opened to traffic. Fifteen days later the ribbon was cut on the next section—the 40 miles between Bordentown and Woodbridge—and by December 2 the road was open all the way to Interchange 14 in Newark. The final leg, the nine meadows miles of the Turnpike's eastern spur between Newark and the road's terminus in Ridgefield Park, opened on January 15, 1952. The eight-mile Newark Bay extension opened to traffic in 1956, and the Turnpike's parallel western spur, which arced through the heart of the extensive meadows acreage west of the Hackensack River, was completed in 1971.

When the costs of construction, including the later extensions but minus the western spur, were finally tallied in 1962, it was found that nearly double the original cost estimate had been spent in building the Turnpike: $450 million. As for materials, the road had consumed more than 5 million square yards of asphalt and 12 million square yards of topsoil and grass seed.

Right from the start the Turnpike was an indisputable success, by standard economic measures. In 1952, its first full year of operation, it carried nearly 18 million vehicles and reported toll receipts in excess of $16 million. In 1962, 55 million vehicles traveled 1.5 billion vehicle-miles and anted up $39 million in tolls. Statistics for that year reveal that ten thousand motorists ran out of gas on the Turnpike, fourteen thousand had flat tires, and nearly eighteen thousand were busted for speeding.

Today, the Turnpike is still, quite literally, a roaring success; it has its own radio station, "1610 on your AM dial," that offers motorists up-to-the-minute advisories on potential trouble spots and personal safety: "Don't forget to buckle your seat belt and observe all posted signs. Thank you for driving the New Jersey Turnpike, and have a safe trip." The road also carries a far higher volume of traffic than ever before. In 1994, some 140 million cars and trucks coursed the Turnpike, logging 3.4 billion vehicle-miles. Nearly 3 million vehicles use the Turnpike on an average weekend, and about $1 million in tolls are collected on an average day at the road's twenty-one toll plazas. But the true toll actually runs higher:

> Americans love automobiles. No doubt about it. What we *don't* love is the price we pay for our affection. We don't love 47,000 fatalities per year. We don't love pollution, noise, loss of open space, sprawl and global warming. We don't love wars to preserve energy security. We don't love 200 million discarded tires each year, plus 8.75 million junked cars, 138,000 tons of lead from old car batteries, millions of gallons of oil spilled on lands and in waterways, and more

than 100,000 leaking underground gasoline storage tanks. We don't love traffic jams. And we certainly don't love what Lewis Mumford described as "the tomb of concrete roads and ramps covering the dead corpse of the city."

(*David G. Burwell,* Earth Issues*)*

The Turnpike's heaviest daily traffic volume has usually been reported on the northernmost section of the highway—where it passes through the Meadowlands. A drive on this section offers an object lesson in the root causes behind the accelerating disintegration of the planet's living biosphere. The landscape through which the highway directs its speeding vehicular throngs long ago yielded to the machine. Writer John McPhee sums up the Meadowlands region as "one great compression of industrial shapes, industrial sounds, industrial air, and thousands and thousands of houses webbing over the spaces between the factories."

It is a graphic and overwhelming portent of the ultimate industrial

Northbound on the New Jersey Turnpike at dawn. The ubiquitous rock doves, or street pigeons, find the Turnpike's many bridges and overpasses a source of secure shelter and nesting sites.

state. This brave new world might, perhaps perversely, have been unintentionally prophesied in the promotional blitz for Turnpike Man, a Nordic-type superhero wearing purple and blue tights and sporting a tire on his left arm and a hubcap on his right. His credo, emblazoned on plastic cups and other trinkets sold at Turnpike rest stops, announces: "I was born on Planet Asphalt, a world with no rest stops! When I escaped to Planet Earth in my super-colossal, souped-up big rig, I vowed no traveler would ever go hungry or thirsty again!" Turnpike Man, accompanied by sidekicks Quality Man and Ultra-Val(ue), is the brainchild of the Marriott Corporation. He will soon take up residence in rest areas on toll roads from New Jersey to Florida.

The Turnpike Man promotion is perhaps symptomatic of our society's accelerating retreat from its roots in the nurturing soil of the planet. Increasingly, our spaces become the manufactured, the artificial, while the genuine lies neglected and ignored, just beyond the barren verges of the highway. Or worse, the once-green vistas and winding tidal waterways may actually be feared:

> The roadway is rising up under the Pulaski Skyway now. The swamps are spread out in every direction. But these aren't swamps like any Jim Bob has known before. The chrome-colored water looks lethal. Rusting factories, surrounded by mud and reeds, stand around on blasted islands of high ground.
>
> The vistas [the Turnpike] provides . . . are at best boring, at worst horrible. They lack even a hint of charm. Few of the wildflowers and ornamental trees that grow alongside other major highways flourish beside the Turnpike. The Turnpike seems intentionally designed to exclude the esthetic.
>
> (*Gillespie and Rockland,* Looking for America on the New Jersey Turnpike, *1989)*

One perceives, in fact, while driving north into the southern edge of the meadows, an industrial landscape so intimidating and forbidding that the mournful words of nineteenth-century landscape painter Thomas Cole seem not only appropriate but necessary. Hurrying past Newark Airport and ducking beneath the grim colossus of the Pulaski Skyway, all the while surrounded by the flying forms of our fellows anonymous within their huge trucks and low-slung cars, we may feel certain that

> *Our doom is near; behold from east to west*
> *The skies are darkened by ascending smoke;*

> *Each hill and every valley is become*
> *An altar unto Mammon, and the gods*
> *Of man's idolatry—the victims we. . . .*
>   *(Lament of the Forest)*

Cole lived in a time when smoke was primarily of one color and texture—a defect we have since improved with more sophisticated varieties. A Manhattan-bound commuter crossing the meadows in 1966 described the scene as befouled by "plumes of black, brown and tan smoke from power plants; yellow and purple smoke from chemical plants; palls of tan and white smoke from Meadowlands fires; black greasy smudges from city dumps, incinerators and oil refineries; and black smog from diesel trucks."

There is also, we may be sure, a constant updraft of carbon dioxide, an invisible "greenhouse" gas that raises the risk of global warming, and perhaps of catastrophic climate change. Environmental writer Jonathan Weiner warns that "each human being on the planet loads the dice with more than one ton of carbon each year. In the United States, unless one is very poor, it is almost impossible not to help load the dice in a big way. The average American car contributes its weight in carbon dioxide to the atmosphere each year." Indeed, some 66 million gallons of gasoline are burned daily worldwide, the bulk of it in motor vehicles.

Such grim and foreboding statistics seem to have special import here, on the New Jersey Turnpike and in the surrounding Meadowlands. A thin pall of exhaust drifts above the roadway, even on the clearest days, and one knows that the blackish, toxic streamings of the big rigs that ply the turnpike drift lazily across the verges and then descend, to infiltrate the sediments of the wide green marshes that lie just beyond the guardrails.

Journal

SUMMER 1990: LIFE IN THE FAST LANE

I can clearly recall the thrill of fear that coursed through me when I realized, as the steering wheel of my van pulled sharply to the right, that I had a flat tire. Now, under most circumstances a flat is an inconvenience, a minor irritation, unless you are an elderly or disabled motorist.

I was fully capable of changing a tire, but as it turned out, my "minor irritation" had chosen just about the worst possible place on this

Southern "gateway" to the Meadowlands, the Pulaski Skyway elevated span, viewed from the northbound New Jersey Turnpike. The birds are starlings.

country's thousands of miles of limited access highways to occur. Traveling north, I had just passed beneath the girdered span of the Pulaski Skyway and was ascending the Turnpike's first major bridge, over the Passaic River at Kearny Point. I was on the road's western spur, in the center lane, in the midst of heavy speeding rush-hour traffic. The shoulders on this bridge are slim to nonexistent, but I had to get over, nonetheless, to whatever safe haven they offered.

Struggling to control the vehicle, I saw an opening in the traffic— to my left—and managed to bring the van to a halt hard by the concrete divider. The right side of the van, the side with the flat, was mere inches from the lane of travel—the fast lane.

As I grappled with the tire change, buffeted by passing traffic, my glance fell on a strange sight. About ten feet up the divider I saw the lush green of a living plant. It was sprouting from a crack in the barrier and clinging as precariously as I to this narrow sanctuary in the roaring insanity of the superhighway. In spite of the extreme urgency of my own situation, I could not resist a closer look at this tiny scrap of nature tucked among the concrete seams of the city.

The plant was a goldenrod, surprisingly robust and sporting three lovely blooms. Its roots must have found some meager sustenance here in the accumulated grit of the median, and I marveled at this demonstration of sheer survival. I saw, too, that the goldenrod had a few visitors. Wind-flogged though they were on this bridge, the blossoms were being tapped by a couple of shiny green insects that resembled gnats, and a black-and-yellow syrphid fly that looked something like a honey bee. I was amazed: somehow these tiny insects had found the plant, high atop a bridge amidst a stampede of speeding cars and trucks, and here they fed on it as though it were growing in the middle of a Vermont pasture.

As I watched the industrious activity of these intrepid little flies and studied the minute perfection of the bright yellow flowers they probed, I found my tension draining away. In the face of such innocent determination it was easier to place my predicament in its proper perspective. If the bugs could carry out their small duties here with such unconcern and presumably depart the place with life and limb intact, then so could I, surely a creature of much greater intellect and resourcefulness!

Whistling a quavery tune and glancing at the wind-whipped weed from time to time, I finished changing the tire, tossed the jack and iron into the van, and edged back out into traffic. Accelerating up and over the bridge, I glanced in the rearview mirror and watched the goldenrod with its tiny occupants recede and then vanish from sight over the curve of the roadway. As the grille of a huge tractor-trailer supplanted the weed in my mirror, I marveled not at the forbidding Turnpike but at the wonderful tenacity of life on this planet.

Architect Ada Louise Huxtable sees the inexorably spreading metropolitan complexes of North America as clear indication of a planet "relentlessly on its way to *ecumenopolis,* or a totally urbanized world." She further predicts that this ultimate fate "may take a little while, but we'll get there." Huxtable's *ecumenopolis* may lie decades or even centuries in the future, but the genesis of such a world-machine may be glimpsed here, in the New Jersey Meadowlands of the late twentieth century. It is a relief, then, to learn that "totally urbanized" does not necessarily mean totally apart from nature, at least not yet. Even here, the Turn-pike has an edge. In the Meadowlands, another world lies not a stone's throw from the road's guardrailed shoulders.

Journal ⟣

THE TEAL
Richard Kane, director of conservation for the New Jersey Audubon Society, is a man on the late-summer side of middle age. He has birded the Meadowlands for many years, and he has testified at numerous state and federal hearings on the fate of this estuary.

Kane's roots in nature run deep, back to his 1940s boyhood in a Bronx that was more lushly vegetated and populous with indigenous wildlife than it is today. He has been associated with the New Jersey Audubon Society since 1973, when he assumed the directorship of the society's Scherman Wildlife Sanctuary. But his affinity for birds precedes that staff appointment by many years. "I remember walking along the stream in Van Cortlandt Swamp in the spring of 1949," he once wrote, "and finding a male wood duck snared in a muskrat trap. One leg was mangled beyond use, and a game warden released it, giv-ing it once again the freedom of an uncertain future. The incredible beauty of the bird and the insanity of the rusted metal are etched in-delibly on my mind."

Rich Kane recalled that painful incident in an Audubon biogra-phy written more than twenty years ago. And though wood ducks are uncommon in the Meadowlands today, and relatively few muskrat traps wait in rusty ambush here as compared to the 1940s, Kane's love of avian folk has survived the test of time; much of his energy is ex-pended in the defense of their habitats here in the marshes.

Kane's view on the question of further development in the Mead-owlands, even if well planned, has long been consistent: he is ada-mantly opposed to the controversial proposals of the HMDC's Special Area Management Plan (SAMP), a compromise that would allow fur-ther development in exchange for what he considers questionable marsh restoration in a few areas. "The remaining district wetlands need to be protected," Kane insists with blunt finality.

We are squinting into the sunlight on Bellmans Creek—a Hacken-sack River tributary that nowadays probably rises somewhere among the storm drains in the borough of Ridgefield—motoring up the narrow channel at no-wake speed on a bright and windy summer day, having just slipped beneath the six-lane overpass of the Turnpike's eastern spur.

Richard Kane, director of conservation for the New Jersey Audubon Society,
scanning a mitigated marsh for avian rarities.

Kane is taking a bird survey as part of the New Jersey Audubon
Society's comprehensive habitat study of the entire Hackensack River
system, from the New York State line to Newark Bay. He wears khaki
trousers, a well-washed plaid shirt, and a sturdy windbreaker, all topped
by a faded and frayed peaked cap that looks as though it has overseen
many a bird count. The weathered and lined face beneath its bill has
the look of an outdoorsman, though somehow not a hunter—a forest
ranger, or a yachtsman, maybe.

There are five of us on the river today, including our boat skipper,
Bill Sheehan, a conservation advocate who cofounded the Hackensack
Estuary and River Tenders environmental group. As we taxi slowly up
the marshy creek in Sheehan's "eco-cruise" pontoon boat, the *Queen
Mary E*, Kane calls out the species as they make their appearance and
then enters them on a clipboard: "There's killdeer, over there, on the
flats; yellow-crowned night heron—that's a good bird, good to see it
here; plenty of spotties [sandpipers] today, and yellowlegs. . . ."

The waterway gradually narrows and curves to the right. At the
bend in the creek a nondescript little duck suddenly launches itself off
the half-tide mud bank and skids awkwardly into the coffee-brown

water ahead; it swims rapidly and rather erratically ahead of us, rowing with its wings, and then abruptly dives out of sight. We identify it as a green-winged teal, a drake. Kane at first speculates that the bird is attempting to distract us from a nearby nest, but a hasty onboard discussion of bird behavior determines that the drakes of most waterfowl species don't assist the hen with domestic duties, and this causes him to revise his call: "It's injured, I think; something's not right with it."

We chug on up the narrowing creek, all eyes searching the riffled water ahead for any sign of the bird. It seems to have vanished into thin air. Minutes go by. Then it reappears, just ahead and very close to the boat. We all marvel at the bird's nearly successful effort to escape notice: it is less than ten feet away, close to the bank; yet a casual sweep of the eye would easily miss it. "Will you look at that," one of us whispers. Indeed, all that is visible of the duck is the tip of its black bill, the

The marsh wren (Cistothorus palustris*) occurs from southern Canada to Mexico in freshwater cattail marshes and estuarine habitats. Formerly called the long-billed marsh wren, this bird is effecting a comeback in the Meadowlands after a long period of decline. It breeds in some abundance in the Saw Mill Creek Wildlife Management Area. The similar sedge* wren *(C.* platensis*), formerly known as the short-billed marsh wren, is also found from southern Canada to Mexico. It occurs rather locally in grassy freshwater and brackish marshes; biologists consider it a declining species. The sedge wren seems to be returning as a breeder in the Saw Mill Creek area and is also present in Kearny Marsh.*

crown of its bright green-and-chestnut head, and a sprig of its dark tail. The rest of the duck's body is submerged and invisible in the murky water, and its small webbed feet work mechanically but deliberately to propel it along at precisely the speed of the wind-driven riffles. "Talk about keeping a low profile," Kane offers.

The teal dives again but soon reappears just ahead; it seems to be tiring, but still it swims flattened out and with a tense, grim determination. The bird's antics and peculiar posture appear almost comical, but no one jokes about it. Indeed, one is struck with pity, and with admiration, at this unfortunate creature's determination to save itself, though apparently injured and unable to fly. Our own behavior is that of casual though sympathetic curiosity, but the teal's is earnest, disciplined terror, for it instinctively "knows" it will die, in earnest, if its ruse fails.

Though nobody articulates this, we all wonder whether we should rescue the bird, and try to rehabilitate it. We glance at the big landing net that Sheehan keeps in the bow of the boat. But this little drama is part of the overall play of life, not only here but anywhere we intrude on things natural and then decide it's not right to interfere any further. We all know the teal is best left to its own, yet undetermined, destiny.

Sheehan throttles up, and we move ahead. The teal dives once more but surfaces quickly, swimming now in the opposite direction. As we round the next bend, all we see of this bird is an oddly ragged little riffle, barely distinguishable from the many on the sun-sparkled creek behind us. Then it is gone.

Later that morning, as we exit Bellmans Creek on our way toward the Turnpike bridge and the main stem of the river, we scan the spot again. But the duck is nowhere to be seen. No one says so, but we all wish it well. Gradually, the silences of the reedy channel give way to the muted roar of the roadway. The only bird sounds we can hear above the traffic noise are the rich, clear cries of yellowlegs as they course swiftly over the highway and descend into the marshes beyond.

Rich Kane has resumed his commentary, now on the district's so-called mitigated marshlands, which combine limited industrial development with ambitious attempts to restore damaged ecosystems: "When they talk about 'better,' that's very misleading," he is shouting, above the growing din of traffic. "Because nobody knows what 'better' is when you talk about marshes. What you're talking about is 'different.'" We pass under the bridge, and the hollow thunder and bump of the traffic just over our heads nearly drowns him out. "It's a kind of 'Frankenmarsh' that's been created there . . ." he trails off; then smiling and shaking his head, he gives up.

We reenter the sunlight and contemplate the wide river in front of us—the Hackensack. Its water appears blue, a reflection of the sky, and the green wall of reeds on the opposite bank gives the scene the look of a tropical river, like the broad Amazon, or the Ganges. We relax and inhale deeply of the fresh breeze; the wind, out of the west, smells clean and good, like mountains and marshes and ancient rivers.

We move south on the river, parallel to the Turnpike, reveling in the beauty of the day. Somewhere behind us, beyond the bridge, beyond the Turnpike, in a world ages away from the industrial machinations of the Meadowlands District and the often acrimonious debate over the SAMP, I imagine a male green-winged teal riding high in the water. Its fright has been forgotten, but it remains alert to everything around it. The bird sticks closely to the protective cover of the reeds and the tentative new stands of *Spartina* in the mitigated marsh, its bright green-and-chestnut head held high, its dark eyes scanning its surroundings for the slightest sign of peril.

The duck moves through its circumscribed world of wind, water, and reeds like a tiny mote of life on a liquid lens. It knows nothing of events beyond its immediate ken as, isolated from its fellows that fly unfettered and free overhead, it awaits without emotion whatever fate may have in store.

☙ ❧

The New Jersey Turnpike has had a profound effect on the ecology of the meadows. The massive berms of its eastern and western spurs interrupted the tidal action of the original estuary, and the traffic that thunders over the 'pike today sheds multiple tons of debris and airborne automobile dust—pollutants such as copper, rubber, and brake-lining materials—into the watershed yearly. The full effect of this toxic fallout on the chemical balance of the estuary has yet to be determined, much less understood, biologists say, but one may be fairly certain that it cannot be positive.

Andrew Willner is director of the American Littoral Society's New York–New Jersey Baykeeper program, which monitors the health of the Hudson River region. Willner is emphatic in his appraisal of the Turnpike's negative effect on the estuary. During a recent cruise on the Hackensack River, within earshot of the Turnpike, he stated that the highway "was a major intrusion—it changed the entire hydrology of the Meadowlands by dividing the marsh up and only allowing the water to run under the bridges. It changed a lot of things"—more, probably, than the railroads. "If we're going to abandon rail transportation," he says, "we're always going to have roads like the Turnpike."

MALLARD

BLACK DUCK

PINTAIL

GREEN-WINGED TEAL

GADWALL

SMALLER WATERFOWL

Ducks of many species are present as both residents and migrants in the Meadowlands. Once hunted here extensively, they are still hunted, and protected, during regular hunting seasons.

The abundant and familiar mallard (Anas platyrhynchos) is circumpolar in distribution in the northern parts of the Northern Hemisphere; it occurs throughout central Canada and the western United States. A growing population of resident, generally nonmigratory birds now inhabits the Atlantic seaboard as well, supposedly descendants of escaped domestic stock. The mallard is abundant throughout the district, with a large breeding population

in the Kearny Marsh, Kingsland Creek, and Saw Mill Creek areas. It also breeds in the Overpeck Creek area.

The closely related black duck (A. rubripes) is also found throughout the district, though it nests primarily in the Saw Mill Creek and Kearny Marsh areas.

Anther common waterfowl species, the gadwall (A. strepera), has a viable and growing nesting population in the Saw Mill Creek area. The gadwall now equals the mallard in nesting frequency and success in this part of the meadows.

The pintail (A. acuta) is a regular transient throughout the district in fall and winter. The pint-size green-winged teal (A. crecca) is

BLUE-WINGED TEAL

CANVASBACK

AMERICAN WIGEON

BUFFLEHEAD

RUDDY DUCK

WOOD DUCK

an abundant fall and winter duck through-out the Meadowlands, though it may sporadi-cally breed here. The related blue-winged teal (A. discors) is a regular summer breeder in the Meadowlands, primarily in freshwater wet-land habitats. I have found the nests of this duck concealed in vegetation in a wide variety of meadows habitats, from dump edges and the verges of service roads to extensive and isolated wetland areas.

The noisy and conspicuous American wi-geon, or baldpate (A. americana), may breed in scattered locations in the estuary; it is a fairly common winter duck. The gorgeous wood duck (Aix sponsa) is a regrettably uncommon resident and migrant, possibly breeding in small

numbers in Kearny Marsh and the Losen Slote Creek area.

The canvasback (Aythya valliseneria) was formerly much more abundant in the re-gion. It is today a fairly common winter duck, sometimes rafting in sizable flocks on the Hack-ensack River. The pert little bufflehead (Bu-cephala albeola) is a regular winter visitor, usually observed in the Kingsland Impound-ment, in Kearny Marsh, and along the main stem of the Hackensack River.

Ruddy ducks (Oxyura jamaicensis) are common during the warmer months, breeding in small numbers in the Kingsland Impound-ment and in Kearny Marsh.

Ruddy ducks in the Kingsland Creek area.

But he is willing to concede one incidental, yet perhaps significant, benefit of the Turnpike's presence. Though he insists that nearly
all its impacts on the environment have been negative, he does admit
that the Turnpike has served as something of an unintentional aid to
environmental education. "At least now, many, many people do see

it [the estuary] every day; at least now they know what they're looking at, and maybe that'll help in its preservation. If you build it, they
will come."

THE ORADELL DAM
AND A CHANGING RIVER

James and Margaret Cawley, in their marvelous and oft-reprinted classic, *Exploring the Little Rivers of New Jersey*, knew the Hackensack River
in a very different age. They dismissed the lower Hackensack as "not a
particularly attractive river" at the time of the book's first printing in
1942, but they were especially partial to the upper reaches of this "river
of many bends." They also knew, to their chagrin, that before the
construction of the Oradell Dam, the Hackensack had been canoeable
"from Old Tappan all the way to Newark Bay." The Cawleys, nevertheless, were able to paddle their wood and canvas canoes over rivers not
yet assaulted by fleets of powerboats or hemmed in by high-speed motor traffic. They camped overnight on isolated wooded shorelines free
of 1990s-style apprehensions; nowhere in the pages of *Little Rivers* did
they feel compelled to warn readers of the threat of assault or robbery.

The two gentle adventurers spoke of an upper Hackensack River
that will never be again: "We recently met a very charming old lady
who told us interesting tales of the Hackensack before the reservoir was
built and motor traffic intruded upon the scene. With a sparkle in her
eyes she told us of the old Kinderkamac Canoe Club, which was organized by a group of her friends, and of the good times they used to
have at their club house above Oradell, the site of which is now under
the impounded waters."

"That Mardi Gras parade of the canoes," wrote another paddler of
the old Hackensack, "all lighted up by Japanese lanterns, against the
background of the river bank where all the boathouses were similarly
illuminated and decorated with bright festoons of bunting, that was
one of the prettiest sights I ever saw."

Historian J. Irving Crump, in *Biography of a Borough: Oradell*, noted
that the construction of the dam profoundly affected not only the ancient flow of the river but the character of the town itself. "The building
of the dam and reservoir was by all means the largest and most difficult
construction project ever undertaken in Oradell, and, as large under-
takings of this type always do, it changed a great many features of the

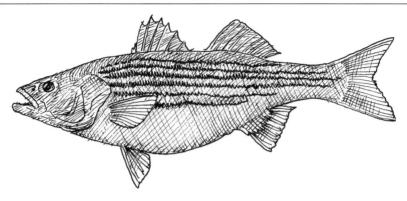

*The striped bass (*Morone saxatilis*) is native to the coastal marine waters of the Atlantic from the Gulf of Saint Lawrence to Florida; it is most abundant from Cape Cod to Cape May. The striper, also called linesides and rockfish, is fairly common in the Hackensack River and tribu- taries. The young venture far upstream, well above the city of Hackensack, where they may be found in nearly freshwater habitats. Large individuals are occasionally caught in the river, though their consumption as food is advised against.*

area, wiping out dwellings and farms, altering the contour of the land, and changing the river completely."

The Oradell Dam and reservoir were built, according to Crump, in "a fairly well-populated area with quite a number of farms and dwell- ings," and thus the cultural and social impacts of this huge engineering project were considerable. Unlike the large-scale landfilling and build- ing in the meadows to the south, which took place on extensive tracts of uninhabited wetlands, the dam and reservoir, deemed vital to the common good, required the purchase and demolition of many dwell- ings and the felling of the lush forests that once lined the upper Hack- ensack. Woodcutters came in to clear the land in a large area on both sides of the river channel.

With the completion of the dam in 1921 the centuries-long flow of fresh water that had nourished the Hackensack's freshwater ecosystem was reduced by two-thirds—up to 80 percent, some hydrologists have claimed—and the river's transformation into a brackish estuary began. The flow of fresh water into the lower river was so reduced that in dry summers the Hackensack actually flows in reverse as far north as River Edge. Experimental dyes introduced into the river at the Bergen County Utilities Authority's sewage treatment plant at Little Ferry have taken as long as a month to reach Newark Bay.

With the intrusion of salt water far up the river, plants dependent on freshwater habitats were quickly eliminated. By the late 1920s the

FROGS

The green frog (Rana clamitans*) occurs from the Maritime Provinces south to North Carolina and west to Minnesota and Oklahoma; it has been introduced in Newfoundland and, in the West, British Columbia, Washington State, and Utah. Formerly much more abundant in the Meadowlands, it is now found in freshwater ponds, impoundments, and creek headwaters beyond tidal influence. It may be encountered in Kearny Marsh and Losen Slote Creek.*

*The leopard frog (*R. pipiens*) is very widely distributed in two species (the northern and southern) from southern Canada to the central and southeastern United States. It is fairly common in suitable habitats within its range but reported as declining in the Meadowlands' fresh and mildly brackish creeks and impoundments, in particular the Kearny Marsh, Overpeck Creek, and Saw Mill Creek areas. The closely related pickerel frog (*R. palustris, not illustrated*) has been reported at Kearny Marsh.*

few remaining cedar stands of the Meadowlands were a memory; all we can now see of this once-thriving and historically important coastal forest are the gnarled, muddy root systems that line the low-tide banks of Berrys Creek and other Hackensack River tributaries.

The increasingly brackish character of the estuary, combined with the diking and draining activities of the early developers, tipped the balance in favor of plants adapted to a saline environment. Cattails, once widespread throughout the Meadowlands, retreated as the tide extended its influence far above historical levels. Today these plants, the source of the familiar dried "smokin' punks" of yesterday's schoolchildren, are limited to Meadowlands areas under impoundment and beyond the reach of the tide.

The nature of canoe trips, of course, has also changed. The Hackensack River is, amazingly, still canoeable from its source in New York's Rockland County to Newark Bay—if you stretch the definition of "canoeable" to the utmost. The would-be adventurer must "portage" a craft, *by car*, around the first reservoir, Lake Tappan, and through the streets of several towns to circumvent "the largest and most difficult construction project ever undertaken in Oradell."

Although I have canoed the upper Hackensack countless times and have found the experience unique and rewarding, to truly experience this river—to place a finger on its still vibrant natural pulse—it is much the better course to venture out on its wide, southern expanses.

Journal ⌖

JULY 1994: ON THE RIVER WITH DON SMITH

We appear to be adrift at the center of a vast, flat bowl, suspended somewhere between a heaven of white sky and an earth empty of all but water and reeds. There is no breeze whatever. The sound of the outboard motor—a low, throaty roar—is all that ties our minds to the activity we are engaged in: a boat trip on the lower Hackensack River.

Early in the day, the heat has already become oppressive, the eastern sky bleached, bone-white. The blazing sun has slid behind a scrim of cloud, which appears completely wrung dry of moisture due to a persistent heat wave that has crawled with glacial inertia across the continent.

It is quiet here, but not entirely so; the distant, soaring spans of two great roads loom in the haze, dominating the river. Far and away, the muted roar of a hundred thousand moving vehicles drifts down to the water's mirrored surface.

The boat, a nine-passenger pontoon craft of utilitarian but comfortable design, plows south with the outgoing tide; a gangly black cormorant passes overhead, hurrying west, toward the Meadowlands Sports Complex. Don Smith, chief naturalist and resource specialist for the HMDC, stands at the boat's helm. He touches the wheel with the light hand of experience, leaning forward slightly against the boat's motion, watching from behind mirrored sunglasses the flat river unfolding before us. He is a tall, strapping man and has the weathered look of a Grizzly Adams, or a Gloucester long-liner. Or maybe an old-time meadows muskrat trapper, which he in fact once was. He is impassive, vaguely taciturn, but it is obvious that the eyes concealed behind the reflecting lenses are restless, ever-moving.

Don Smith, a native-born meadowsman, naturalist, and environmental educator.

A grim, rust-and-black railroad bridge lies low across the river ahead, the very image of stark utility. At this tide we have but a scant six feet of passage beneath the suspended track bed. Smith gradually throttles down and folds the boat's collapsible sunroof as we approach and then glide under the span. We all duck as the flaking, grime-coated girders pass by just inches overhead.

Furtive rustling sounds—something's moving up there. A light shower of falling grit. Suddenly the air is filled with the fleet, angular forms of barn swallows; their lumpy mud nests are everywhere here, up among the dim steel supports, well out of reach of all human disturbance save the occasional bridge maintenance crew. The birds zip by so closely that the wind pressure of their passage can be felt on the face. They are incredibly swift, streaking back and forth beneath the bridge and out into the empty white sky above the river, where they soar in effortless, sweeping acrobatics. But the swallows return to the bridge as though tethered by invisible rubber bands, chippering in annoyance and dismay; they are not often threatened here and clearly resent the intrusion.

Beyond the bridge, Smith raises the canopy and throttles up the

Barn swallows, lower Hackensack River. Barn swallows are common breeding birds along the river; the numerous bridges, no matter how utilitarian and ugly, provide secure nesting anchorages for the swallows' unique mud nests. From a photo by Steve Auchard, by permission.

big Evinrude; nothing but open water and a distant, hazy shoreline of reeds, industrial buildings, and the skeletal transmission towers of the Kearny skyline lie ahead. The twin hulls lift easily against the water, and we are suddenly blessed with the manufactured breeze of our passage. The river here is empty of other boats. Although a single pleasure craft buzzed by earlier in the trip, there is none of the commercial traffic the Hackensack was famous for earlier in the century. And given the tangle of highway and rail lift bridges spanning the river to the south, one suspects the logistics of hauling cargo today would be considerable.

You can tell the man loves the place, warts and all. Smith becomes defensive if critics suggest that his position with the state agency in any way compromises his commitment to preserving the wetlands. "All of this was destined to be filled with garbage," he says flatly, adding that "no other entity [than the HMDC] has saved more of this ecosystem

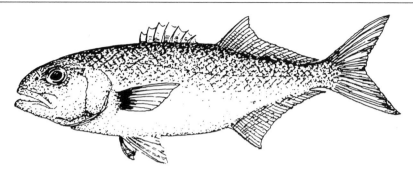

*The formidable bluefish (*Pomatomus saltatrix*) is a widespread marine species, occurring throughout the temperate and tropical Atlantic and Indian Oceans. In our area this aggressive predator is most abundant during the warmer months from southern Maine to Virginia, where it supports a large recreational fishery. It enters the Hackensack River via Newark Bay, where it is a fairly regular resident in the warmer months. Big blues are called choppers or alligators, while the smaller juveniles are locally called snappers.*

for the future. That's why all of this is here today." Listening to Smith plead the meadows' cause with quiet passion, I recall how Thoreau insisted that "if a man is rich and strong anywhere, it must be on his native soil."

That Smith knows his native soil is beyond doubt; it would appear that the meadows know him as well. We have throttled down and are gliding into the glassy serenity of the eleven-hundred-acre Saw Mill Creek Wildlife Management Area. "Hee-yaah! Hy-yaah!" Smith shouts into the heavy, motionless air, trying to put up a few ducks. The sky remains empty of wings. "Ah, they're probably saying 'It's just him again,'" Smith laughs.

But then, just ahead, off to the right and close to the wall of reeds flanking the channel, we see a nondescript duck escorting a brood of about a half-dozen tiny ducklings. They move through the water smoothly and swiftly, heads up, clearly nervous, following every curve in the reed bank, low in the water, trying to outrun the boat. They are gadwalls, a waterfowl species that Smith says is showing an encouraging increase as breeders in the meadows, especially in the Saw Mill. As we draw near, the hen breaks into a flopping, skittering flight over the water, wings rowing, quacking loudly; her brood scatters, like fluffy little windup toys, vanishing into the reeds. "You provide the habitats and the critters will come to them," Smith says. His mood seems expansive; he even has a good word for the ubiquitous phragmites, which offer little in the way of food for wildlife. The dense stands do provide

Waterfowl in a mitigated marsh, Secaucus. Pencil drawing.

waterfowl with secure nesting havens, he says. "Not even a raccoon can penetrate them."

Later, we approach the trim-looking Turnpike overpass on the channel leading into the Hartz mitigated marsh. On a high, landfilled bank a huge sign, emblazoned with the image of a pair of hands tenderly holding planet Earth, delivers a message to passing motorists. Erected by the Hartz Mountain Corporation, the billboard proclaims: "A Five Million-Dollar Wetlands Improvement Project. Because We Care About the Environment."

Slipping beneath the bridge at near high tide, we all duck as another nesting congregation of barn swallows sweeps back and forth, complaining all around us in the green gloom, their rich yet strident voices all but negated by the constant thump and boom of traffic passing on the span just above our heads. "If I go through here too often the Turnpike'll see us and put a toll booth in," Smith shouts above the noise. Then the bridge is behind us, and we move out into a spacious open area of land and water.

This is a mitigated wetland—a place of startling contrast. The "natural" aspect is pleasing, a carefully groomed landscape of low islands and shallow tidal lagoons; waterfowl and shorebirds seem to be everywhere, and muskrats patrol the graded shorelines. Though it has obviously been extensively altered by machinery and manipulated until it

Gadwall and brood, Saw Mill Creek Wildlife Management Area.

Trio of glossy ibis, Hartz mitigated marsh, North Bergen area.

bears little resemblance to the salt marsh of its distant past, this wetland looks and smells like the real thing. In its own peculiar way, it is beautiful. But flanking the marsh and crowding nearly up to its banks are utilitarian warehouses and rather spartan corporate structures, one of them an immense low-lying egg crate of a building bearing the name Liz Claiborne. These modernistic buildings, which seem poised to overwhelm the place, form the backdrop for a small flock of green-winged teal that tacks and wheels in tight and orderly precision over the manufactured wetland.

It is among these shrubby and obviously artificial islets, and the banks of saltwater-loving *Spartina*, that Don Smith becomes insistent on the validity of the HMDC's role in the Meadowlands. He has been near the center of nearly every debate over Meadowlands ecology and protection, and is usually the HMDC's spokesperson on things natural here.

"The reality today is that without some compromise between preservation and economic pressures, all of this marsh would eventually be lost to filling and development," Smith says, gesturing out over the passing hummocks, gravelly beaches, and vibrant green grass beds. "It was because of the legal decisions made, creating the HMDC, that this is all here today—without it, the haphazard dumping and filling would still be going on, throughout the meadows." He says that wetland mitigation, which may cost up to fifty thousand dollars per acre, is required to oust the invasive phragmites and restore a functioning saltmarsh habitat, something like the original version. "The phrags build up peat very quickly and convert invaded wetlands into dry lands," he says. "Unlike cordgrass, the tough stalks don't readily decompose and con-

MUTE SWAN

CANADA GOOSE

TUNDRA SWAN

LARGE WATERFOWL

Ducks, geese, and swans have made the Meadowlands home for thousands of years. Following years of decline due to habitat degradation and hunting, many have undergone a recovery and are once again seen in the Hackensack estuary.

*Among the larger species, the introduced mute swan (*Cygnus olor*) is a fairly common resident of the district. Native to temperate Eurasia, this attractive swan has been widely introduced all over the world, including North America in the mid-Atlantic states and in the Great Lakes region. It has gradually expanded its range in the Northeast since a number of individuals were released or escaped from large private estates on Long Island early in this century. Though not reliably reported as breeding in the Meadowlands, adult swans and their fledged young are often seen here.*

*The native tundra swan (*Olor columbianus*) breeds in arctic Alaska and eastern Canada. It is an occasional migrant in the Meadowlands; most individuals proceed farther south along the coast to Currituck Sound and Chesapeake Bay, where large assemblages gather for the winter.*

*The Canada goose (*Branta canadensis*) needs no introduction to most people who live in New Jersey. Its large and growing feral populations have become a nuisance for many municipalities in the region. This impressive wild goose occurs in several distinct races from Alaska and arctic Canada south to the central United States. An increasing nonmigratory feral population breeds on the Atlantic seaboard, including (over the past 20 years) most of the Meadowlands. Adults and young can often be seen grazing on the grassy verges of the Turnpike's eastern spur.*

vert into nutrients as in a healthy salt marsh; they form dense layers of peat that raise the level of the wetland and dry it out after a few years."

Conservationists like Bill Sheehan of the River Tenders and Andy Willner of the Baykeeper have disagreed, insisting that mitigation is a costly exercise in futility and that, given a chance, nature is the best

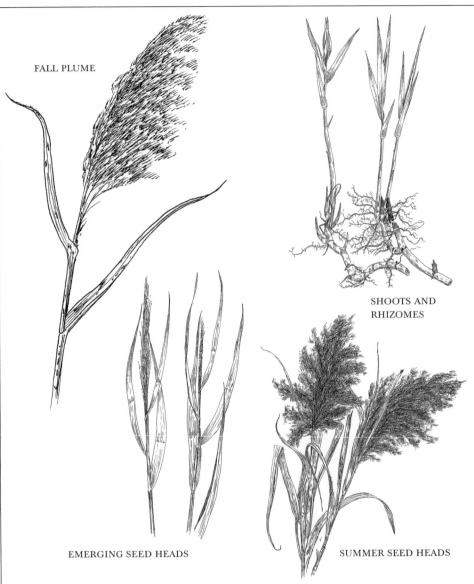

FALL PLUME

SHOOTS AND
RHIZOMES

EMERGING SEED HEADS

SUMMER SEED HEADS

*The common reed (*Phragmites australis*) is native to temperate Eurasia, Japan, and North America. It has been introduced worldwide in such widely separated places as Mexico, the West Indies, South America, Africa, and Australia as an ornamental plant and erosion control agent. The generic name stems from* phragma, *the Greek word for fence, assigned because of the dense, fencelike stands the plant forms along streams. It is often called plume-grass, foxtail, and phragmites, or simply phrags. By 1920 this highly adaptable and invasive reed had outcompeted the cattail (*Typha*) of the former freshwater ecology and dominated what had become a saline environment. It is now the most widespread and visible plant in the Meadowlands, occurring in vast swards throughout most of the undeveloped acreage.*

healer of the environmental ills that afflict the Meadowlands. They have pointed out that a storm-caused, 1950 breach of tide gates on the Saw Mill Creek opened a degraded, 720-acre tract to the tides, which drowned the phragmites and created extensive mudflats that, over the years, provided a seedbed for the natural *Spartina* marshes that eventually reclaimed it. "Nature—and pollution control—is the best healer in the meadows," Sheehan insists.

Now, as if continuing that debate internally, Smith concedes that time and the tides have effected something of a recovery in the Saw Mill. But he counters that what worked there may not work elsewhere in the meadows, where many of the most degraded areas are beyond strong tidal influence and thus subject to invasion by phragmites. Smith is no fan of this aggressive interloper. "The phragmites is an opportunistic plant. . . . It's nature's way of not leaving a vacuum," he says, adding that the graceful-looking reed, showy and exotic though it is, will completely dominate a degraded wetland, turning it into "nothing more than a single-species lawn" instead of a productive marsh. "As the reeds expand, the biodiversity and productivity of the wetland decreases," Smith explains, pointing out first a nearby dense stand of the bamboolike plant and then a distant bank of bright green *Spartina* in the process of reoccupying one of the artificial islands. He points out, again, that the tough, fibrous invader, rather than offering edible seeds and leaves for wildlife, instead provides only protective cover. In addition, spreading via rhizomes and tenacious underground runners, the

*Spike grass (*Distichlis spicata*) is found near seacoasts from Prince Edward Island to Texas. It is common to abundant in many areas of the Meadowlands, including the Saw Mill Creek area and higher elevations of the marsh removed from the Hackensack River.*

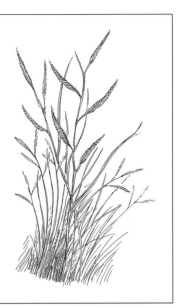

*Salt hay (*Spartina patens*) occurs in salt marshes and on wet beaches from Quebec to central Florida, and from Florida to Texas on the Gulf Coast. In the Meadowlands it is much diminished in abundance; sizable stands persist in the higher and drier marshes, especially along tributaries such as Berrys and Bellmans Creeks and near Saw Mill Creek.*

plant can colonize vast acreages of once-productive salt marsh in a very short time. "In the long run, phragmites won't just go away; it has to be removed so that a marsh can recover."

It is shortly after noon; high-heat time on the river. We are moving south, toward Secaucus and the pontoon boat's berth at the Red Roof Inn marina. A welcome breeze has come up; it has cleared the air and seems to blunt the power of the sun.

As we pass the shoreline of Secaucus, a collection of sooty black cormorants poses stolidly on greasy pilings, the remains of an old river barge dock. A few of them, with heads pointed skyward and wings spread against the sun to dry, look as though they are consciously striking an "American eagle" pose for our benefit. They are doing no such thing, of course; they are fairly stupid, as birds go, but few seafowl look more dramatic, up close, than a cormorant. Another one surfaces a few yards ahead of us, ducks below, and resurfaces again farther away, paddling furiously, head twisting back and forth in an agony of indecision. It splatters noisily across the smooth water, rises powerfully against the wind, and turns north toward the Carlstadt shoreline.

Watching it go, Don Smith reflects on this place and his sense of attachment to it, and on his impatience with those who may see things differently where it comes to protecting the Meadowlands. "I grew up here, in the meadows. I've hunted and trapped the meadows all my life, since I was a young kid, so no one has a greater stake in it or a love for them than I do," he says. "No one."

He has known virtually all the legendary muskrat trappers of Little Ferry and Moonachie, seen their day come and go, and he understands that way of life. He has been on the staff of the HMDC very nearly since its inception twenty-seven years ago, parlaying his love of a place into a livelihood, and over that time he has spoken to thousands of people—the young and the not so young—who have come here looking for the "real" Meadowlands.

As we cruise in toward the dock, across what today seems a placid and benevolent riverscape, Smith recalls the time when these marshes and landfills were decidedly inhospitable. He challenges those whose commitment he perceives as being of recent origin, asking, "Where were they all these years when the old battles were going on?" It's a rhetorical question. "I've been fighting for years on behalf of these meadows; I can recall times when I'd walk into a trailer in a landfill, to check on permits, and they were pretty unfriendly. The guy'd lay a .45 on the table and say, 'Now, what can we do for you?' . . . I've put my life on the line for these meadows; how many others can say that?"

And yet, whatever decisions others may make in the interest of preserving, or developing, this estuary, one senses that Don Smith somehow stands detached from the conflict and the acrimony. For when you watch him, standing at the helm of his boat on the Hackensack River, you have the distinct impression that you are observing a part of its natural fauna. He has become an almost mythical figure in the manner of Daniel Boone or Natty Bumppo. The news media seek his opinions, for nearly all his predecessors are gone now. Countless generations of hunters, fishermen, market gunners, trappers, and gleaners of discards and ersatz treasure have taken their livelihood from the

Cormorant on derelict pier, lower Hackensack River. From a photo by Steve Auchard, by permission.

*Cormorants on dock pilings, Hackensack River. The eastbound bridge
of State Route 3 is seen in the background.*

swamps since prehistory. More than a few of them lost their lives out
there. And Don Smith is pretty close to the sole inheritor of that long
tradition. He has killed countless muskrats and waterfowl in the meadows he is now fighting to save, and he offers no apologies for his skills
with trap or gun. None are required, for judgments passed in the cities
have never held much water on the frontier.

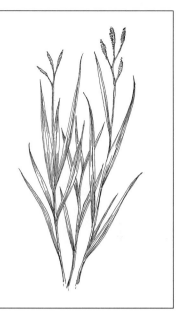

*Saltmarsh cordgrass (*Spartina alterni-flora*) is found in coastal salt marshes from Quebec to central Florida, and west to Texas on the Gulf of Mexico. In a healthy salt marsh this is the dominant estuarine plant. Long since extirpated from much of the Meadowlands and replaced by the common reed, cordgrass is effecting an encouraging recovery, most notably in the Saw Mill Creek area and, in smaller, tentative stands, in the mitigated marshes east of the Hackensack River.*

In the end Don Smith, along with men like Willy Royka of Little Ferry, Jake Kraft of East Rutherford, and other leathernecked swamp runners, may well represent the passing of an America that did not depend on the shopping mall, Hollywood, or "virtual reality" for its adventure and meaning; it had plenty of the real thing. Don Smith, at ease in his flannel shirt, shooter's pants, and heavy rubber boots—and steeped in centuries of meadows lore—may be precisely what many of his admirers have said he is: the last of the real meadowsmen.

In the early 1980s I spent a year in the newsroom of *The Record*, one of the largest daily newspapers in the country. At that time I was the police reporter for "South Closeup," the section of the paper that focused on the ten South Bergen County communities that lie within or near the Meadowlands District. Although my reportorial duties did not include coverage of the district and its political doings, I did produce a human interest feature on the Hackensack River, in partnership with another reporter who had an interest in canoeing.

Joe Donnelly was an outdoorsman and a good man to have in the bow of a canoe when both the wind and the tide were working against you on this wide and sometimes unpredictable river. Joe and I decided to "do" the river in a south-to-north paddle, from Droyer's Point on the industrialized Jersey City waterfront on Newark Bay to as close as we

Public Service Electric & Gas power plant in Ridgefield.

could get to the dam at Oradell, a distance of some thirty-five miles. We figured it would take us, loafing along and camping, the better part of three days. We in fact were ordered out of the river by a Hackensack Water Company security officer about a hundred yards downriver from the dam, shortly after noon on the third day. So we were close.

The intent of the cruise was to get a hands-on overview of the river itself, talk to whomever we could buttonhole along the shoreline, and then speculate on the validity of the touted recovery of the Hackensack and its Meadowlands. I'm not sure that we were ultimately successful in cramming so much history and shoreside pontificating into one all-too-short feature story, but we did our best. We came out of the river on that third day exhausted and suburned, with barely the energy to haul our old aluminum canoe up the weedy, littered bank. But we each agreed that the adventure had left us with a refreshed and optimistic perspective on our world and on our relationship with it; we had not felt so alive in a long, long time.

Among our observations on that trip were the revelation that shorelines that had been grassy or wooded in the past

> are now lined with refineries, sewage treatment plants, generating stations, warehouses. The cries of the bald eagles, osprey and peregrine falcons that once nested in fair numbers along the river have been replaced by the roar of jets taking off from Newark International Airport across the bay.
>
> From the shore of Newark Bay, near the outlet of the Hackensack River at Droyer's Point in Jersey City, there are few reminders of the wilderness encountered by Indians in their bark canoes and Dutch explorers in their skiffs. The gray waters of the river and bay glint in some places with oil slicks turning in the flow.
>
> Yet despite the sights and sounds, the sulphur smell, and the chemical taste in the wind, the river is coming back. The process isn't always visible, but those who use the river for work or play say it is getting cleaner and that some stretches are teeming with life.

The memory of that river journey, made more than fifteen years ago, remains with me to this day. Our water-borne communication with the river was far from unique, of course. Countless adventurers, as well as generations of common laborers of the waterways, had set sail upon its broad face before us.

Today, relatively few recreational paddlers ply the lower Hackensack and explore its aesthetic attributes, though the river's environmental boosters hope to rectify that regrettable state of affairs through public education. But I have kept coming back. Page upon page of my journals reflect impressions I have collected in the course of canoe passages over the face of this river, some in the company of others, many in solitude.

The perspective gained from a canoe is bittersweet. The place speaks to you, in the winds that furrow the green reeds of summer, in the soft drop of brine ice on a January creek, in the airy music of terns wheeling high overhead, above a picturesque river that mirrors a wonderfully blue sky. But there is an easily unmasked deception here. The water's color depends on your angle of view. A look over the gunwale at the "blue" water inches below tells you that this river is in pain; it is still suffering. There is a healing going on in the Meadowlands, but full recovery will take decades more. Maybe centuries.

The water my bow divides is the color of café au lait, and so turbid that objects a few inches below the surface cannot be seen. One hesitates

COMMON TERN

LEAST TERN

FORSTER'S TERN

BLACK TERN

TERNS

Several species of terns make their home in or near the Meadowlands. The common tern (Sterna hirundo) is circumpolar in distribution in the temperate areas of the Northern Hemisphere. This graceful "sea swallow" is fairly common in the Meadowlands, most often seen on the Hackensack River. It breeds along the coast in suitable undisturbed beach habitats.

The smaller least tern (S. albifrons) occurs along temperate and tropical coasts and oceans worldwide. In the United States it breeds from the southern Maine to Texas coasts, and inland along larger rivers. The pint-size "leastie" is fairly common on the Hackensack

River during the warmer months; a few breed on the coast in the area of Sandy Hook.

Forster's tern (S. forsteri), difficult to distinguish from the common tern, is a regular transient in the Meadowlands in summer, seen most often along the Hackensack River and near Newark Bay.

The enigmatic, slate-gray black tern (Chlidonias nigra) frequents freshwater marshes during the breeding season, moving to the coasts in winter. This bird probably formerly bred in freshwater habitats in the district, but it is now observed primarily as a late-summer and fall transient. It is most often seen at Kearny Marsh and in the Saw Mill Creek area.

Mockingbird on discarded shopping cart, upper Hackensack River at River Edge.

to dip a finger in it, here, in this basically beautiful place, so painful is the paradox. In all my many canoe trips on the Hackensack, over the course of thirty years, I have never seen its water in any other condition. The sight has always provided me with a mournful counterpoint to this river's wonderful clarity of two generations past. A water-logged seat cushion; a plastic shopping bag; a deflated, algae-encrusted

Common egret near Saw Mill Creek. The sight of these beautiful birds in the industrialized Meadowlands never fails to elicit awe on the part of the average unsuspecting observer.

volleyball—these make their way north on the incoming tide; a quartet of terns take their leisure on a creosoted plank drifting at midriver.

But amid the flotsam, life abounds. As I approach the bank, I watch the water erupt with what looks like a flood of raindrops. The shallows are alive with killifish, millions of them, and although their color so closely matches that of the water itself that they are virtually invisible, their vitality, and thus that of the river, is obvious and uncontainable. Tiny shrimp skim beneath the surface. They are nearly translucent, with only their pinpoint black eyes readily visible. Up ahead, where the mud slips easily into the river's flow, an egret leans forward in eager slow motion, a portrait of intense concentration. It studies the erratic actions of fish that scurry about in the murk, selects a target, and strikes in a flash, like a snake. Egrets are peerless anglers, and this one straightens up with a tiny, silvery fish that bobbles like a pendant at the tip of its bill. It flips the fish in the air and swallows it effortlessly; then it freezes and abruptly jumps into the air, flying south along the reed bank, toward the open water.

I am suddenly aware of an engine's roar; I look up and watch a seaplane flash by over the reeds, so close the pilot is a discernible face in the cockpit. The plane's bellowing passage empties the plank of its terns and puts up a raft of ring-billed gulls resting on the river. It rises rapidly against the wind, banks to the southeast, and heads toward the Jersey City skyline. Watching the plane shrink in size, I find myself thinking that while a canoe allows you ingress to the heart of the Meadowlands, it is only through the agency of wings that you see the entire corporal body, in all its extent and variety.

FLIGHT

In the summer of 1960 three North Bergen High School students in search of grist for a geology class project came across an unusual find at the edge of the Hackensack Meadowlands. In an exposed seam of ancient shale outcrop, its face scrawled with modern graffiti and coated with industrial soot, they found the fossilized remains of the first known vertebrate capable of flying under its own power. Scientists later described the creature and dubbed it *Icarosaurus seifkeri*, the genus named for Icarus, the mythological Greek who attempted flight using wings made of bird feathers, and the species name bestowed in honor of Robert Seifker, the youth who actually spotted the fossilized bones of the flying lizard. The site was not two hundred yards from the noise and stench of busy Tonnelle Avenue, a grimly modern industrial truck route.

Millions of springs have passed since that reptile glided through Triassic skies. Today, the skies are still filled with flying creatures—the birds—which evolved from lizardlike ancestors. But then, very recently, a rather heavy, slow-footed primate got the hang of it too.

The gold-and-white Cessna Skyhawk seaplane taxis out into the broad Hackensack River at Little Ferry, swinging into a brisk southeast wind. The plane is compact and sturdy—a truly beautiful flying machine—but to a passenger its quick and sensitive response to the wind and waves makes the experience rather like a ride on an amphibious kite.

Floatplane on the middle Hackensack River, swinging into the wind in preparation for takeoff. The sight of these aircraft is not as common an occurrence as it once was.

Roger Urban, a slim, suntanned man amiable in nature and economical with words, is chief pilot of Waterfront Airways, a combination floatplane and helicopter terminal that lies at the juncture of the river and its tributary, Overpeck Creek. He has sun-blond hair and crow's-feet at his eyes and wears jeans, a plaid sport shirt, and a bulky bomber jacket. Urban is in fact a bush pilot of sorts—of the smoky skies over the metropolitan Serengeti known as the Meadowlands. He took his first flying lesson at the age of eight and soloed at sixteen. He has a thing about seaplanes. "You can fly 'em anywhere you can fly anything else," he says, noting that a floatplane in trouble can be brought down safely on a plowed field—across the furrows—something no wheeled craft could ever accomplish.

Today, as we prepare for takeoff, Urban squints through the plane's Plexiglas windshield into the bright afternoon sun; he studies the wind-driven riffles moving on the river, reading the watery runway that lies ahead. A sizable flock of gulls, perhaps two hundred, appears as a multitude of tiny silhouettes adrift on a glistening expanse of water that looks clean from the vantage point of the passenger's seat. The breeze freshens and lightly rocks the plane; outside the cabin the wind thrums through the guy wires of the wings, and a small bow wave shushes up and away from the starboard pontoon. Urban, following a brief, static-crackling conversation over the radio, eases the throttle forward. The aircraft picks up speed, surging ahead, down the open, empty river, with curls of sparkling spray flying off to the sides.

The gulls prudently yield to the bigger bird, as the pilot knows they will. The birds rise easily from the water ahead, slip to the side, and then flash by the windows as the plane catches the wind, bounces once, and then lifts off. We climb swiftly and bank to the west, over the meadows. Soon we are sailing high above the reeds, landfills, industrial plants, roadways, and river that comprise the modern Meadowlands.

Gazing at the sight unfolding below us, I can see that the Hackensack River's floodplain today is but a phantom of its past, very little of it surviving intact from what existed even a short century ago. As the grim, smoke-obscured landscape slides by, now far below, birds are everywhere. In spite of a steadily diminishing sanctuary, somehow they adapt; they occupy the airy spaces and still-expansive tracts of reeds that sprawl, checkerboard fashion, among the confusion of highways, industrial complexes, and garbage dumps.

Platoons of waterfowl cruise the gray-brown waters below, appearing as darkish, grainy smudges against the blast of sun-reflection on the river and its tidal embayments. There are the familiar mallards, the wary black ducks, shovelers, gadwalls, and a host of other lesser-known species, still hanging on.

Turkey vultures above the landfill at Lyndhurst near DeKorte Park.

To the west, near the township of Lyndhurst, swarms of gulls crown the working landfills, and a solitary marsh hawk sails just above the reedy plains, a tiny avian glider far below, tilting and rocking in its flight, sailing on and on over the marshes, watching for rats.

Other aircraft move above and below in the near and far distance, glittering in the sunlight, silent against the wind and the bellowing roar of the seaplane's engine. They all gradually slip downward through the haze toward Newark International or Teterboro Airports. The sky here is truly the province of the fliers today.

And below all, a unified-looking city—Ada Huxtable's *ecumenopolis?*—sprawls to the very limit of vision, appearing, in the words of naturalist John Hay, "a smoking heap of civilization . . . embodied all around us as cars, planes, miles of glass, countless lights; a huge fantasy-filled horizon spewing out poverty and grime on its fringes and belching tons of waste into the atmosphere."

But in the face of all that, or perhaps in spite of it, spring has faithfully returned to this river. Lost in the tangle of last year's dried and desiccated reeds, fresh, tender green shoots of phragmites emerge tentatively from the oily muck. In a few weeks they will transform this place into the vibrant green industrialized grasslands that motorists on the New Jersey Turnpike cross without seeing.

The seaplane swings into a long, sweeping arc to the east, and the skyscrapers of Newark, nearly submerged in a sea of photochemical smog, slide by below. The mean streets of New Jersey's largest city cannot be seen beneath the pall of industrial prosperity. The cityscape reminds me of the aftermath of an aerial bombardment–Dresden or Hiroshima or perhaps Coventry come to mind; the place looks that incendiary.

Urban is unfailingly enthusiastic about his plane. On my fourth, totally innocent reference to the grace and handleability of the "seaplane," he can contain himself no longer. "They're floatplanes, *not* seaplanes," he snaps. "Three- to four-foot waves like you'd find on the sea and you've got a problem." Over the solid roar of the engine, he rattles off a few stats on the craft: The Skyhawk is powered by a three-hundred-horsepower Lycoming engine that will lift the 1,720-pound aircraft into the sky with a six-hundred-foot run into the wind, at the seemingly terrestrial speed of fifty-five knots. New, such a plane costs "anywhere from forty thousand to a hundred thousand dollars, depending on the options," he says. Looking down at a landscape that

Low-tide mudflat, Ridgefield meadows. This area, just south of Bergen Turnpike, illustrates the unsightly combination of mud, industry, and discarded refuse that has unfortunately come to characterize, for many, the modern Meadowlands.

seems singularly bereft of places to land with any hope of survival in mind, I ask him how much fuel a small plane like this one carries. "I've got an eighty-gallon tank, good for about eight hundred miles," he replies. He glances at a gauge and grins: "Don't worry; it's nearly full."

We are pulling away from Newark, moving east toward the bay. I notice that the plane seems tight and solid, no in-cabin rattles make themselves known, and all wing guy wires are as tight as guitar strings. I ask Urban about the projected lifetime of the Cessna; how long can you expect it to keep flying? "With care, ninety-nine years," he says, adding that an airplane "is like any other machine: if you baby it, take good care of it, it will last forever." Urban religiously cleans and waxes his plane; it's more than a matter of cosmetics. "If you simply keep an aircraft like this cleaned and waxed, it'll increase its airspeed by an average five miles an hour and reduce the stress on the engine."

Urban directs the plane east-northeast, then due north, dropping down to eight hundred feet above the river; we are close enough to the water so that it slides by below us at a considerable clip. It is silvered, corrugated by wind, very beautiful. We now have a tailwind, and the engine's pitch suddenly changes with the assist; one senses that the stress on the machine, as with people, is less when nature is unintentionally cooperative. The pilot slides open the side window, and a rush of wind fills the cockpit, booming and rumbling in my ears. Up here it is clean and smells like the sea. From these heights the smoke and grime of the city are mere visual impressions, like a museum exhibit on the Industrial Revolution.

To the northeast the sky is a rich pewter blue, and the steel, stone, and glass spires of Manhattan glisten with the burnished light of the late afternoon sun. A faint, unearthly roar, or is it a whisper, seems to emanate from this immense urb at the edge of the sea. It is a cityscape unlike that of any other in the world: it seems to rise directly from the sea itself. It is at once monstrous, intrusive, brawling, beautiful—clearly the very center of, the end result of, something. Civilization itself, probably.

A crowd of gulls, brilliant as sparks in the warm light, ride an updraft in great lazy circles ahead of the plane. In all, it is an impressive, almost mystical sight. Urban has seen it many times before, under many different weather circumstances in his years over the river, but he feels moved to comment on the view while taking it all in—the birds, the winding silvered river, the broad brown marshes, and the great city beyond. "It's really beautiful, isn't it? When you really—I mean *really*, look at it," he says.

Tomorrow

The Jersey meadows, the aromatic stretch of real estate between Newark and Jersey City, once considered only a ghastly eyesore, are now recognized as a vital asset for the future of northeastern New Jersey.

JOHN T. CUNNINGHAM, *New Jersey: America's Main Road*

The big 747 banks smoothly in the late afternoon sun—east-southeast, southeast, south-southeast, then due south—on its approach to Newark International Airport. Brilliant sky light flares off the wing as the plane sways gently, throttles down, and begins its descent; a muted rumble-thump somewhere underneath must be the landing gear, reaching for the world below. Folded uncomfortably into a tourist-class window seat, I am returning home on the final leg of a journey to the West Coast to see my new grandson for the first time. It is early December 1992.

"Yep, this indeed is the 'Back East' you've heard all about," I was saying to my aisle-side seatmate. "There it is, in all its glory." My fellow traveler had been commenting on the vast, hazy cityscape sliding by far below us, gaping in awe at the sprawling, unrelieved urban panorama, overseen on the eastern horizon by the sun-jeweled towers of Manhattan. A midwesterner, he had never been this far east before.

Our flight is making its final approach to Newark International from the north, and its path takes us almost directly over the Meadowlands. This seemingly out-of-place feature in the otherwise urban landscape below us is of definite interest to my acquaintance, for it seems vaguely familiar. The broad, grassy expanse reminds him, he says, of the windy and empty high plains of Nebraska, or the Dakotas. He

Impression of the Meadowlands and surrounding New York metropolitan area of today. Urbanization has all but overwhelmed this primeval glacial estuary. Drawing not to scale.

asks me what these "plains" are, and I tell him. He gazes in silence at the acres and acres of dun-colored grass, then asks me how such an "empty natural area" could possibly have survived "in the middle of all that . . . ," trailing off and finally gesturing at the riot of constructions, roadways, and traffic below.

I reply that it's a long story, "about three hundred years' worth, give or take a decade."

More than a decade ago, when the idea for this book first came to mind, I had a long talk with an energetic fellow named Chester P. Mattson, a man who knew the Meadowlands well. His perception of the meadows and that of my travel acquaintance eleven years later, who had neither seen nor heard of them before, were of a remarkably similar slant. Mattson recognized these urban marshes as the degraded and unattractive landscape they had become, but was impressed by them anyway.

At that time, in 1981, Mattson was in his late thirties, and bearded. He was the first director of planning and environment at the Hackensack Meadowlands Development Commission—charged with much of the responsibility for determining the future of the meadows. He was also, along with meadowsman Don Smith, one of the earliest staff naturalists at the HMDC. A transplanted New Englander who in his youth had hand-built and lived in a spartan cabin deep in New Hampshire's White Mountains, Mattson appreciated the "natural" aspects of life. He came to know New Jersey's premier urban marsh complex intimately, and he became one of its most ardent defenders, outlander though he was. "You learn to love a place, you know?" he told me then.

Mattson saw the question of development in the ecosystem as "a collision of two histories." He used a hill-and-plain metaphor to describe two historical forces pushing to dominate this area: "People, power, and castles on the hill; swamps, mosquitoes, and industry on the plain." Neither force had won the contest, and he saw fragments of their collision everywhere. Mattson viewed the surviving meadows as, first, "a marsh intersected by a transportation network; and, second, a transportation network intersected by a marsh." As a result, the meadows' natural essence today, he said, is that of "a form of salt marsh, given over to *Phragmites communis*, the common reed."

Today, Mattson is director of the Bergen County Department of Planning and Economic Development. As such, he must grapple daily with the county's near crisis-level growth and transportation woes. It is, he says, "an exercise in controlling migration—of men, goods, services, dollars, and ideas. Getting a handle on all of these as they waft across the landscape is what this is all about." Though charged with somehow controlling the future economic growth of the area, Mattson still speaks of the importance of habitat preservation. "The belief was strong from 1960 to 1990," he was quoted as saying in a 1995 Hackensack *Record* article, "that the more development you have, the better off your tax base would be. But we have found that the emperor sometimes doesn't wear any clothes." If you develop something to death, that is, your tax base is going to be zero.

Mattson was commenting, in that article, on open space preservation. By that time, undeveloped space had shrunk to about 5 percent of all property in Bergen County. Although he had changed employers, one thing, at least, had remained fairly constant for Mattson—and for the land he was still charged with developing/protecting. "It's plenteously easy to do the right thing; it's *knowing* the right thing that's difficult," he told me in 1981. Surely, the need for such intelligent action today, in the Meadowlands—finding the "right" balance, whatever it may be, among competing historical forces—is nothing if not far more critical.

Attitudes toward the living landscape were much more prosaic and exploitative in the distant past, when such reflection was essentially a nonissue. A century ago, a meeting of an East Texas cattlemen's association, probably after hearing pleas for prudent range management, concluded with the following declaration: "Resolved, that none of us know, or care to know, anything about grasses, native or otherwise, outside the fact that for the present there are lots of them, the best on record, and we are after getting the most out of them while they last." It is probable that the early dikers, ditchers, and developers of the Meadowlands regarded these marshy East Coast "prairies" with much the same speculative and mercenary eye.

The Texas prairies had great value in and of themselves as the vast, grassy ocean of terrain that was crucial to the profitable production of beef. The land was thus of high value; the grass itself, existing in apparently limitless quantity, was as gold to the nineteenth-century cattlemen. But do the meadows of New Jersey have a comparable intrinsic hard-cash value simply as wetlands? Ecologists J. Gosselink and Eugene Odum once sought the answer to that question—concerning similar tidal marshes on the southeastern United States coast—and determined that indeed they do. The purpose of their study was to establish a monetary value based on tangible resources or services that marshlands provide. Aesthetic values—estimated at about $5,000 per acre per year by the American Littoral Society—were therefore not considered. The resources and services that Gosselink and Odum studied included the action of tidal marshes in removing pollutants from coastal waters (a kind of tertiary sewage treatment), sport and food fish production (the marshes serve as a nursery for young fish), the potential for commercial aquaculture, and an assortment of other hard-to-quantify functions. They calculated the ultimate dollar value to be $82,940 per acre, a sum reasonably close to the per-acre value of undeveloped Meadowlands real estate today.

Despite a heightened public awareness of the critical value of wetlands in recent years, we are still losing them to development, throughout the United States, at the rate of 290,000 acres annually (as of 1992). Indeed, they are still viewed in some quarters as intrinsically worthless, little more than a barrier to urban expansion. Less than a generation

Common egret on a sunken 50-gallon drum, Bellmans Creek, Ridgefield.

ago a grand plan to subjugate the Hackensack meadows in finality, to transform them from a "mosquito-breeding, garbage-dumping waste-land" into "a billion-dollar dream come true" was set in motion. The above phrases, reflecting two utilitarian views of the meadows—as a wasteland good for nothing but dumping, or as potential new land for airports, roadways, industry, and housing—appeared in newspaper accounts published in the mid-1950s. The latter view expressed an exuberant optimism based entirely on physical reclamation and economic development. A third option, preserving the meadows in their natural state, was never seriously considered.

That remained the environmental state of affairs in the Meadowlands until the late 1960s: either way, as industrial sites or landfills, the natural meadows would be doomed. A victim of the conventional wisdom that "marshland" was synonymous with "wasteland," the meadows were fast approaching ecological catatonia, a state of total biological collapse. For nearly a century they had been subjected to the combined assaults of draining, haphazard landfilling, and unplanned development in a relentless process that can only be described as land "wrecklamation."

Then, in the late 1960s, the Hackensack Meadowlands Development Commission appeared on the scene. Better known to both friend and foe by its acronym—HMDC—this regulatory body was created in 1968 by the state legislature as part of the Hackensack Meadowlands Reclamation and Development Act. It was signed into law in April of the following year in order to, according to New Jersey's Division of State and Regional Planning, "create a single agency to reclaim and develop the Meadowlands in cooperation with the United States Army Corps of Engineers." Subsequently, the HMDC's mandate became somewhat more environmentally correct: "To protect the delicate balance of nature; to provide for orderly development; to provide facilities for the disposal of solid waste."

It was clear, even in 1969, that this task would be far from easy. By that time the Meadowlands District had become the repository of one-third of all New Jersey's solid waste; thirteen active sewage plants discharged their effluents into the Hackensack River, and several huge power plants contributed thermal pollution and lowered dissolved oxygen levels in the beleaguered estuary. Only one-third of the total land area of the river and estuary remained in the form of natural, relatively intact wetlands. The Jersey meadows of old had indeed deteriorated into the "wasteland" its modern detractors labeled it.

Still, as Chet Mattson has pointed out, this new agency was expected to "do the right thing"—find a workable balance among historical forces competing to dominate the meadows. The balance has shifted from time to time, as the HMDC has gone through three executive directors in its twenty-seven-year history. The current holder of the chair is a former mayor of Lyndhurst (a meadows town) and state senator named Anthony Scardino, Jr.

Scardino, a soft-spoken, rather courtly man, has helped chart the course of the HMDC's land use policies for the past fifteen years. Being a veteran of both the local and state political arenas, he knows when to listen as well as when to stump. The job involves pacifying, browbeating, guiding, and advising a lot of people with, to put it mildly, differing perspectives on the issue of economic growth versus environmental protection in the meadows—people like biologists, environmentalists, industrial developers, highway builders, real estate operatives, state Environmental Protection Agency bureaucrats, and the Army Corps of Engineers.

Tony Scardino is not a big man, though he can be imposing without intimidation. He dresses well and speaks carefully, rather like the CEO of a Fortune 500 corporation. He is generally regarded with suspicion by environmental activists, dismissed as "a typical bureaucrat and a political animal" much more in league with the development side of the Meadowlands debate than with those who favor ecological enhancement. Yet the true man lies somewhere between those extremes, as it usually does in attempts to stereotype.

As I talked with Tony Scardino I noted that he, like the chief executive of any large organization involved in decisions concerning real estate, development, and high-stakes finance, is prudent in his verbiage. I sensed that he knows he cannot answer every question with complete candor or offer careless, off-the-cuff opinions. And I could not fault him for his caution; this sprawling, fragmented wetland environment lies close to the heart of the eastern megalopolis, and fortunes—in the billions of dollars—do stand to be made or lost here. But Scardino was willing enough to recount his own journey from the urban streets of Hoboken to the executive director's chair from which he presides over the projected future of the Hackensack meadows.

Voices

ANTHONY SCARDINO, JR.

"I moved to Lyndhurst from Hoboken at age eleven, in 1947. This was the country, the open spaces, so to speak, compared to where I had come from. Not only was the scenery and the activities different, so were the smells. In some instances you could smell the swamps, as they were called in those days; at other times, when the meadows cooked and steamed on a hot summer day, a combination of swamps and garbage. Or just the smell of garbage.

"After making some friends, I learned that one of their favorite pastimes was, in the early evening, to go down to the dumps and, with large sticks, hunt rats. I did this once or twice, out of peer pressure, but I absolutely hated it. It was my initial experience in learning that I could not destroy anything that had life.

"I also discovered the meaningful natural side of this invitingly strange new place. The awareness grew out of another swamp activity that I loved passionately. I would take my bicycle and ride along the Jersey City sewer pipeline, through the marshes, or punk weeds, as we used to call them, to the Hackensack River, where I spent many a wonderful summer day crabbing. The smells, the sounds, and the serenity of it all are still with me.

"What is it about these meadows that gave me a sense of peacefulness and awe at the same time? This was a question that, at the time, I could not answer or explain, and frankly I had no inclination to try; I just absorbed and enjoyed all of it.

"When it was time for me to move from the phase of adolescence and playing to that of participating in the working world, what I missed more than anything were my excursions into the 'swamps.' It would be many years later, when I was grown and participating in the world of civic affairs and looking toward elective office, that I reintroduced myself to this natural, earthy, marshy area we began to call the Meadowlands in the 1960s."

Scardino admits that his opposition to the "dumping of raw garbage into valuable wetlands" in the 1960s was not, for the most part, based on environmental considerations. "My sense of the 'value' [of the Meadowlands] was not from an ecological standpoint, but from an economic development viewpoint," he says. But he insists that he did experience something of an epiphany when he entered the reeds for the first time since childhood and saw for himself the havoc that unregulated trash disposal had wrought there: "What I saw twenty-five years ago were bulldozers pushing and shoving garbage into the waters, dispersing and destroying vegetation in its path. What stuck with me more painfully was seeing various species of birds with chicks, running with fright out of the path of those monsters destroying their habitat. I knew at that moment that I wanted to do all that I could to preserve as much of the remaining wetlands as possible. I never dreamed that one day I would be in a position . . . to do my best to achieve that objective."

GRAND PLAN FOR THE MEADOWLANDS

At the heart of the struggle is the question: How can the
Meadowlands be developed and saved at the same time?
(Tom Topousis, The Record*)*

Anthony Scardino's vision for the Meadowlands—his view of what
constitutes an acceptable degree of preservation—is often at odds with
the views of environmentalists. Though clearly dismayed by the environmental destruction he has witnessed, Scardino is, in the final analysis, a businessman. But he is only one player in the Meadowlands
drama, his role rather like that of the conductor of an orchestra, attempting to bring unity and cohesion to what might otherwise degen-
erate into a discordant bedlam of environment-versus-development
angst.

There are, in fact, many other demons, aside from trash disposal,
that will determine the shape of things to come for the meadows. Some
are so all-encompassing and implacable that one wonders whether

Crows and power transmission towers, DeKorte Park, Lyndhurst.

Incoming jet and Canada geese near the New Jersey Turnpike's Hackensack River bridge, western spur. The view is westward, from just south of the Turnpike's Vince Lombardi Service Area.

they will ever be brought under control and reconciled with any workable plan for the meadows. Like the region's horrific traffic woes, for example.

In the past, the basically unplanned expansion of road and rail arteries had a powerful disruptive effect on the district's ecology. As for the future, the Port Authority of New York & New Jersey does not wax optimistic—expansion is still, basically, unplanned. In the December–January 1995 issue of *Omnibus*, the agency's house publication, the Port Authority warns that "without major investment in the interstate network [in the Meadowlands District] the scenario for mobility throughout the region by 2015 is not promising." Among the transportation nightmares in store for the residents of this already overcrowded part of the world are even greater "congested conditions with extensive delays throughout weekday commuting periods; chronic 'stop and go' traffic conditions in both directions" in and out of New York City; vastly increased emissions of "unhealthy carbon monoxide, ozone precursors and nitrogen" generated at clogged toll plazas and in monster traffic jams; and "higher costs to business and consumers due to delays in truck deliveries."

The PA's Interstate Transportation Department warns us that inaction in the face of this looming specter of regional gridlock will result in "economic stagnation" that will irreversibly and permanently harm the region. Economics notwithstanding, the effect on the already tenuous ecology of the meadows will be equally devastating.

In response to this looming crisis, the HMDC and a host of other contributing state and federal agencies in 1988 began formulating a comprehensive program for the development of the meadows under the "no net loss of wetlands" banner. This new management approach, designed to update and replace the district's current development plan promulgated in 1980, is embodied in a four-thousand-page document: the Special Area Management Plan (SAMP).

Called "a unique vision" for the Meadowlands, the approved and implemented SAMP would be "the result of a true meshing of the interests of economy and environment forged by the coming together of parties, not unlike those who gather for group therapy, who didn't necessarily get along in the past." So editorializes the Meadowlands Regional Chamber of Commerce, an obvious champion of the SAMP's controversial agenda.

ADEQUATE BLUEPRINT FOR THE FUTURE?

As currently written, the SAMP would provide for:

Incorporation of the Federal Clean Water Act into the master plan for the region.

Preparation of an environmental impact statement (EIS) in cooperation with the Army Corps of Engineers and US Environmental Protection Agency.

Utilization of public and private sector resources to implement a long-term environmental program that will include the management of the approximately 6,000 acres of intact wetlands.

Financing of the $875 million environmental cleanup through tipping fees charged garbage haulers and fees paid by developers for the right, under the plan, to develop their properties.

Improvement of the region's transportation infrastructure.

Fulfillment of regional higher-density housing goals, impacting approximately 500 acres of wetlands.

Assurance that development in the Meadowlands District over the life of the SAMP will be calibrated to ensure the maintenance of no net loss of wetlands and net environmental benefit.

The SAMP is the first major land development and restoration project in the nation to be formulated under the requirements of the 1964 federal Clean Water Act, its designers say. The preliminary SAMP environmental impact statement, unveiled in the summer of 1995 and at this writing still undergoing amendment, identifies those sectors of the Meadowlands District where further development will be permitted and offers an $875 million environmental cleanup of existing degraded wetlands and riverine habitats.

This new environmental impact statement has been endorsed by the four "partner agencies" involved in the SAMP: the Army Corps of Engineers, the National Oceanic and Atmospheric Administration, the US Environmental Protection Agency, and New Jersey's Department of Environmental Protection. But the US Department of the Interior has come out in strong opposition to the SAMP's wetlands-filling provision. "It is the view of the department that the Hackensack Meadowlands need immediate, permanent protection, not more wetland fill," the Interior Department has found.

Under the original provisions of the SAMP, new development would be permitted on 2,200 acres of the Meadowlands, including 841 acres of marsh that would have to be filled. The remaining wetlands—

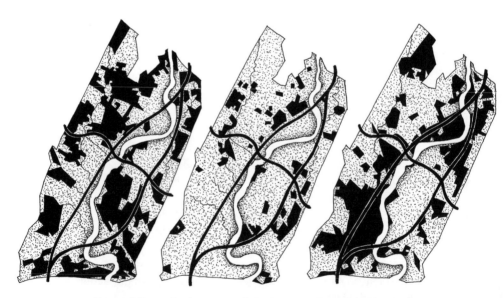

Proposed future development and preservation of marsh habitats in the Meadowlands District. Adapted from the SAMP proposal, Hackensack Meadowlands Development Commission. Left to right: areas already developed; areas slated for further development; wetland areas slated for preservation or mitigation.

about 7,700 acres—would be earmarked for preservation as open space and crucial riverine habitat. Of the open space, about 3,400 acres are considered degraded wetlands that will require improvement, or mitigation, to restore them to ecological health.

The earlier HMDC Master Plan, drawn up more than fifteen years ago, allowed for up to 1,800 acres to be earmarked for development. The current SAMP allows for more, which is one reason many oppose it. They say that further development, even if countered by mitigation somewhere else, will not yield "no net loss"—because so much damage has already been done. The Interior Department, for example, has stressed that further loss of wetlands in the district—more than 10 percent of those remaining—should be taken in context with the total loss over time. From the original 20,000 untouched acres of colonial times, more than 12,000 have since been altered or destroyed through draining, filling, and development. If you add those 12,000 acres lost to the 2,200 proposed for further development, the preservation of 7,700 less-than-pristine acres seems pathetic, even if 3,400 will be "mitigated."

Anthony Scardino admits, moreover, that the SAMP will create winners and losers among investors and developers with meadows holdings. Property owners who are permitted to develop their sites will be required to reimburse owners of marshland that is off limits to development. But for landowners given the green light, approvals for development, under the plan, will become much more streamlined. Regulatory agencies will review proposals in unison, so that a permit issuing process that once required up to eight years can be completed in less than one. In defense of this part of the plan, Robert Shinn, chief of New Jersey's Department of Environmental Protection, said the SAMP's system for compensating out-of-luck landowners follows valid legal precedents; it is similar to that used to protect the state's unique Pine Barrens and rapidly vanishing agricultural lands.

More controversial, in many quarters, is the "no net loss" provision. The key word here is *net.* Part of the dictionary definition runs: "excluding all nonessential or extraneous considerations." Environmentalists such as Andy Willner of the Baykeeper and Richard Kane of the New Jersey Audubon Society have contended that no nonessential or extraneous wetlands remain in the modern Meadowlands. "The Meadowlands has already lost two-thirds of its wetlands," says Kane. "It's too late to talk of balance between conservation and development."

Willner is even more emphatic in his condemnation of the SAMP: Instead of protecting "natural resources," the plan "would destroy over 840 acres of wetlands, have an impact on nearly 2,000 more, and still leave the balance of the wetlands in the district vulnerable to development," he warns. Willner further charges that the SAMP is a plan "designed to accommodate only the needs of the largest landowners and development companies" in the Meadowlands.

Others recognize the need for the affordable housing and jobs proffered by the plan's proponents but disagree as to where the need for that development is most critical. "What they are doing is steering development away from the inner cities, where it is needed, into the remaining wetlands of the Meadowlands, where it is not," says Margaret Utzinger of the Hackensack River Coalition, a River Edge–based environmental advocacy group.

In the view of the Meadowlands Regional Chamber of Commerce, which refers to the Hackensack meadows as "a still-in-a-state-of-becoming" region, economic growth has been "stymied by a regulatory process" that has impeded "balanced, prudent development." The Chamber, not surprisingly, has tendered an unqualified endorsement of the plan. "Because of this SAMP effort, years of wandering and wondering may now give way to a healthy and vibrant future for a region that may well have withered without it," a recent editorial in *Meadowlands USA* proclaims. The publication calls the SAMP "the second wave of what was once referred to as the Meadowlands Miracle," explaining that the proposed development would bring with it "the creation of 100,000 new jobs . . . sorely needed mass transit . . . affordable housing . . . and a vital and dynamic future."

The specifics of the SAMP are not likely to be approved as drawn up by the HMDC. But under the initial SAMP proposal, new construction in the Meadowlands would have included the Transportation Center3–Allied Junction in Secaucus, the 14,000-housing unit Meadowlands Town Center in Carlstadt, and a 2,000-unit Hartz Mountain Industries townhouse development on Mill Creek in Secaucus. These huge projects would join other, less ambitious ventures that would ultimately expand the existing residential, commercial, and transportation infrastructure in the Meadowlands by an additional 17.8 million square feet of office space; approximately 16,000 new residential units; approximately 15.3 million square feet of manufacturing and warehousing space; approximately 2.7 million square feet of commercial space; and mass transit, highway, and secondary roadway improvements. And all this would create, as the Chamber pointed out, those promised 100,000 new jobs.

In the past, the promise of such a volume of development in the "wasteland" of the meadows, with all the attendant employment opportunities and tax benefits, was almost universally anticipated with a breathless sense of euphoria by the South Bergen citizenry and its elected officials. But this is no longer necessarily the case. In an April

1995 televised call-in "Town Meeting" in which Bergen County residents got an opportunity to voice their concerns to those who govern them, Carlstadt mayor Dominick Presto responded to a resident's fears of the potential social and environmental impact of the mammoth $2.5 billion Meadowlands Town Center planned for the borough. Presto, who had come out in favor of the SAMP in principle, now complained that the proposed "minicity" in the meadows would be a "development over which we [the borough] have absolutely no control because it is within the [Hackensack Meadowlands] District." Presto said that Carlstadt residents had "overwhelmingly objected" to the size of the development in a nonbinding referendum. Apparently, they felt they would *be* overwhelmed. For Carlstadt, with a current population of 5,500, the projected 14,000 new residential units within its borders would result in a tripling of the borough's population.

That the SAMP as it is now conceived will survive hostile public scrutiny and legislative resistance, however, is doubtful. In late February of 1996, the HMDC announced that the size of the Carlstadt "minicity" would likely be scaled down by as much as 50 percent. Although the agency's spokespersons denied any connection, the move came two weeks after a state Senate committee voted in support of a resolution that would virtually scuttle the SAMP in its present form. "Right now, we're looking at reducing the residential units," Tony Scardino said. "They could be reduced by 30 percent, by 50 percent, by 60 percent. At this point we can't commit to any numbers."

Indeed, in response to growing pressure to reduce the scope of development allowed under the SAMP, the HMDC in March of 1996 announced the establishment of a Meadowlands conservancy that would better manage and preserve the remaining natural habitats. Tony Scardino noted that this new body, modeled on California's State Coastal Conservancy, which works with the California Coastal Commission, would give the HMDC's more vocal critics a stronger voice in discussions of the Meadowlands' future. If implemented, the conditions that establish the conservancy would require the HMDC to obtain the approval of all fourteen Meadowlands District towns before any development or wetlands-filling project could be carried out. The conservancy "makes [environmentalists] a part of the process," Scardino said, adding that "this is something positive." It "adds a greater dimension" to the dialogue on the SAMP.

The new provisions would, in fact, not only give environmentalists a stronger voice; they would give the meadows towns an unprecedented power to veto any proposed development. The concerns of local residents would thus play a far greater role in decisions about the

Female marsh hawk, Moonachie area. This species, unlike most raptors, has sexes distinctly different in color: the male is primarily pale gray; the female is brownish, heavily streaked on the breast and underside. Both sexes display the characteristic white rump, visible at a considerable distance.

Meadowlands, whether or not those concerns happened to coincide with environmentalists' views.

Voices ~

GEORGE FOSDICK, MAYOR OF RIDGEFIELD PARK

"People don't understand: *any* development out there [in the Meadowlands] has an impact in places where you don't think it will. And I never really thought about this until it occurred to me that, since I was first elected commissioner in 1978, we've had, here in Ridgefield Park, three of what the Department of the Interior calls 'hundred-year floods'–in the south end of town, near the meadows.

"When they built the Meadowlands Sports Complex–and there's a lot of positive and good things to say about that, but remember, it was all swamp there–in order to get a foundation there, they had to put in six hundred million cubic yards of sand. Now, the water that used to go there, to be absorbed by the marsh, is still there, that water. But now, it backs up. In the past we never had, in Ridgefield Park, the frequency and severity of floods like we've had in the past several years. To me, they're filling in all the places where the water used to run off and be absorbed; it now just backs up.

"The water is still there. They've now displaced [the flood plain] with various things, structures, that have economic benefits, other benefits. I don't say you can't have any of these things, but I think we've done it to the extent where we don't realize what we've done."

THE HEART OF THE MEADOWLANDS

> You protect a river because it's a river. For its own sake.
> Because it has a right to exist by itself.
> *(Dave Foreman, Earth First!)*

Bill Sheehan of Secaucus, cofounder of the Hackensack Estuary and River Tenders (HEART), brings to mind some of the more determined and fractious environmentalists of our time. His unswerving dedication resembles, for example, that of Dave Foreman–one of the founders of the radical Earth First! organization. Foreman has done jail time as a consequence of his actions on behalf of the planet; he insists

Environmental activists on the Hackensack River. From left: *Andrew Willner of the New York–New Jersey Baykeeper; Captain Bill Sheehan of the Hackensack Estuary and River Tenders; Steve Barnes of the Baykeeper.*

*The meadow vole (*Microtus pennsylvanicus*) occupies a vast range, stretching from the Arctic Ocean and Northwest Territories east to Hudson Bay and Labrador, south to North Carolina, Arizona, and Washington State. An abundant though seldom-seen small mammal in all but the wettest parts of the Meadowlands, it is found in abandoned landfills, fallow fields, and meadow-edge habitats. The vole is an important item in the diet of raptors, especially the rough-legged hawk.*

on "wilderness for its own sake, without any need to justify it for human benefit." And some of Sheehan's pronouncements appear to echo the late Edward Abbey, a radical environmentalist whose rollicking yet fiercely eloquent novel about eco-sabotage, *The Monkeywrench Gang*, was the inspiration for the Earth First! organization. "The only purpose of highway building, river-damming, pro-development rezoning, and opposition to wilderness preservation," Abbey fumed, "is to make possible, encourage, and create the runaway growth that enriches a few and gradually impoverishes the rest of us." These are the kind of passionate utterances that have placed environmentalists and business leaders at regrettable loggerheads for decades; fortunately, Bill Sheehan voices them at a more moderate pitch.

Sheehan is a mustachioed and amiable guy. He holds down a day job as a dispatcher for a Hudson County cab company. But his alter—and no doubt dominant—ego defines him as a fisherman, a naturalist, a man of the river: the Hackensack River, or, as he affectionately calls it, "the Hack." Captain Bill, as he prefers to be known, is a self-proclaimed "river rat" with a penchant for duds better suited to fishing and cutting bait; though no unschooled rustic, he would look out of place wearing a three-piece suit in an expensive office. When I first met him—on the river at the helm of his pontoon boat, the *Queen Mary E*—the first personage that popped into my mind was Big Mike Fink, the gruff but heart-of-gold "King of the River" in a popular Walt Disney television series of the 1950s. In presenting such a distinctive image, Sheehan is a lot like Don Smith, the HMDC's chief naturalist, and very much his grassroots, political-activist counterpart—a self-described environmental gadfly of the old school and a member of his hometown's environmental commission. Both are dyed-in-the-wool, uncompromisingly committed ombudsmen for the Meadowlands, unafraid of debate on

*The white-footed mouse (*Peromyscus leucopus*) occurs from North Dakota and northern New England south to the Carolinas, New Mexico, and into Mexico and Central America. It is very abundant wherever it can find food and shelter; in the Meadowlands it is most common on abandoned landfills and other places where there may be heavy weed growth and plenty of sheltering rubble.*

behalf of their "client"—this ecosystem they both deeply love. The two in fact respect one another, albeit somewhat warily.

The group that Sheehan cofounded in 1993, the Hackensack Estuary and River Tenders, is a nonprofit environmental organization geared toward educating the public on the virtues of the river and its priceless marshes. It has maintained a consistently high profile in the press—with the colorful, extroverted, eloquent, and well-informed Sheehan its usual spokesman. He and cofounder Troy Noble have kept the HMDC's feet to the fire whenever and wherever the issue of development versus preservation in the Meadowlands has gone public. The group was, of course, an especially vocal contributor to the public input on the proposed SAMP.

Bill Sheehan refers to the ancient, meandering Hackensack and its surrounding meadows as "my river, my estuary." He does not, of course, mean that to exclude other legitimate claims. "These are *our* natural resources, meaning, *we*, the people," he qualifies. "Whether they be wetlands in the Hackensack estuary or the Great Lakes or the Mississippi River, they belong to all of us equally, because we are citizens of the United States." But Sheehan does in fact hold something of a possessive view—in perhaps the spiritual sense—of the river, and its meadows.

"This is my little piece of the universe, you know; I feel like Huck Finn when I'm out here." Sheehan laughs as he says this. We are moving up the river against a brisk northwest wind in his pontoon boat, near the mouth of Berrys Creek. It's a fine day, brisk and bright, and although Manhattan looms to the east with startling clarity, and the jackhammering din of seemingly interminable construction drifts toward us from the nearby Berrys Creek bridge, it would require only a small stretch of the imagination to conjure up the lonely majesty of Mark Twain's nineteenth-century Mississippi.

Our destination today is the Hartz mitigated marsh on the east side of the New Jersey Turnpike's eastern spur. On the way, the electronic fish finder in Sheehan's boat emits fitful beeps as we pass above large fishes or schools of bait fish invisible in the opaque, muddy water below. "Might be a big carp down there, or a striper, or maybe a weakfish," Captain Bill speculates. "The big ones have been coming back to the estuary in recent years, though you still can't eat them with any degree of safety."

Cruising a mitigated marsh in the Meadowlands is a study in contrasts. This is clearly a natural area of sorts, and I have never seen so many spotted sandpipers in one place. The lively little shorebirds are everywhere, dozens of them, in high activity on every bank and mudflat. They fly over the water on stiff, vibrating wings, essaying their bright, cheery *wheet wheet wheet!* from every shoreline of every mitigated island. A trio of glossy ibis sails overhead; killdeer patrol the expanses of low-tide mud—and there, lifting up and over a reed bank and flying hurriedly off, a yellow-crowned night heron, a rare bird in these parts. Canada geese, mallards, and gadwalls are everywhere, a sign that at least the more human-tolerant waterfowl species find the place acceptable.

But despite its action and vitality, the Hartz Corporation's mitigated marsh has been overhauled too recently to have the look of a truly viable ecosystem; it has the vague appearance, instead, of the vast land-groomings that are carried out in preparation for a theme park. It looks freshly "sculpted," the carefully situated islands clothed in upland shrubs and trees—some supported by stakes—that have clearly been planted there by people. Shorelines, for the most part, lie exposed to the sun, naked and without plant cover, awaiting the return of the extirpated *Spartina* grasses—the "salt hay" of yore—that will hopefully, over a five-year period, recolonize these brutalized wetlands.

Opinions on the effectiveness of marsh mitigation are strongly divided. Many biologists caution that the process, a relatively new environmental art, offers a false sense of security, as if preservation had gained the upper hand. But mitigation may in fact stimulate further development in unsuitable areas. It may "encourage developers to push for moving rare plants out of the way of subdivisions, shopping centers, and other development," resulting in a series of plantings and

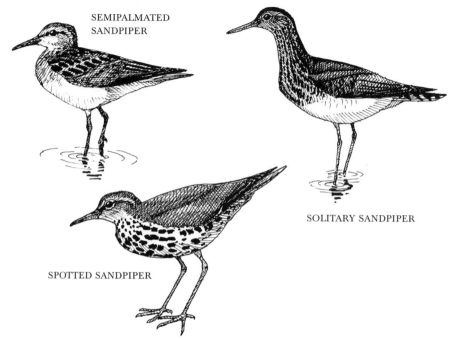

SEMIPALMATED SANDPIPER

SOLITARY SANDPIPER

SPOTTED SANDPIPER

SHOREBIRDS

Various shorebird species are common and highly noticeable residents or transients in the Meadowlands, depending on the time of year.

*The semipalmated sandpiper (*Calidris pusilla*) breeds throughout the North American Arctic, on tundra, wintering on the coast of northern South America. This migrant bird is one of the commonest "mud peeps" of the Meadowlands, assembling in large feeding aggregations on the exposed mudflats of the Hackensack River and surrounding marshes in late summer and early fall.*

*The spotted sandpiper (*Actitis macularias*) has a very broad range, breeding from*

Alaska and northern Canada to the southern United States. The little "spottie," or "teeter tail," is probably the commonest breeding shorebird throughout the district, exceeding even the noisy and conspicuous killdeer in numbers. This bold and active sandpiper may be observed along nearly all creeks and tributaries of the Hackensack River and is an abundant breeder on the artificial islands in the Saw Mill Creek and the Hartz mitigated marsh areas.

*The solitary sandpiper (*Tringa solitaria*) breeds in boreal Alaska and Canada, wintering to the Gulf of Mexico and Argentina. It is a regular migrant in the Meadowlands in fall and spring, usually seen singly or in small*

replantings—"a kind of domino effect of natural habitat destruction," in the words of one botanist. The weight of scientific opinion leans toward a generally negative view of wetlands mitigation—some biologists go so far as to call it a "Faustian bargain"—and this skepticism is nowhere more evident than where the practice is applied to the Hackensack meadows.

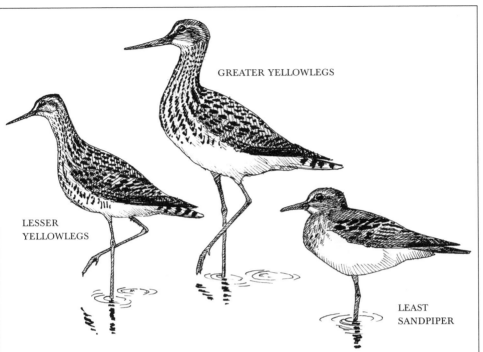

GREATER YELLOWLEGS

LESSER
YELLOWLEGS

LEAST
SANDPIPER

groups of two to four individuals, all of whom forage independently.

Two species of so-called yellowlegs sandpipers frequent the Meadowlands. The greater yellowlegs (T. melanoleuca) nests in trees in muskeg bogs and boreal forests. It is a common spring and fall migrant in the Hackensack estuary. This conspicuous and noisy shorebird often associates with the smaller lesser yellowlegs (T. flavipes) and other smaller shorebirds. The lesser yellowlegs breeds throughout boreal Alaska and Canada in open taiga forests, wintering in the southern United States and farther south to Argentina. It, too, is a common and conspicuous wader in suitable marsh and mudflat habitats throughout the Meadowlands.

Although it is much more abundant as a migrant in fall, winter, and spring, stray individuals often remain in the district throughout the summer as nonbreeders.

The smallest sandpiper visiting the Meadowlands is the tiny least sandpiper (Calidris minutilla). This sparrow-size bird breeds from the Aleutians and Alaska throughout arctic Canada, wintering from the southern United States to central South America. This species is one of the commonest fall and spring mud peeps of the Meadowlands, often seen feeding on the low-tide mudflats or wheeling about in tightly coordinated flocks. It is commonly observed in the Kingsland Impoundment at DeKorte Park.

One of the major points of Meadowlands management both Sheehan and officials of the New York–New Jersey Baykeeper program take issue with is indeed that of the extensive marsh restoration, or mitigation, that has been carried out by the Hartz Corporation and the HMDC. The dictionary defines mitigation as any activity that serves "to mollify or abate" something, to make a situation or circumstance

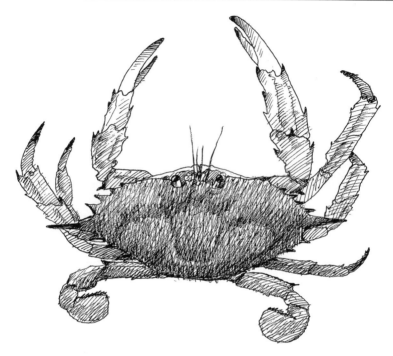

*The blue crab (*Callinectes sapidus*) of culinary renown occurs in brackish bays and estuaries from Nova Scotia to Florida and Texas; it is also found in Bermuda, the West Indies, and south to Uruguay. It is common throughout the Meadowlands in all waters under tidal influence. It is also present in the impounded Overpeck Creek. Consumption of the "blue claw" as food is currently prohibited throughout the Newark Bay and Raritan Bay estuary system due to high concentrations of dioxin in the animals' tissues.*

*The brackish mud crab (*Neopanope texana*) occurs from Prince Edward Island and southern New England south to Florida in brackish waters with muddy bottoms and oyster beds. It is fairly common throughout the Meadowlands. Collections made near the mouth of Sawmill Creek have revealed an average population density of one crab per square meter of substrate.*

"less severe, violent, cruel, intense, painful." Virtually all these adjectives have been employed by environmentalists to describe the effect industrial humankind has had on the world in general and on the Meadowlands in particular, so perhaps the term *mitigation* is in fact apt when applied here, among these artificial islands and placid lagoons.

With Sheehan and me in the pontoon boat today are Andy Willner, the outspoken head of the New York–New Jersey Baykeeper; his associate Steve Barnes; and Richard Kane, one of the state's preeminent birders and the New Jersey Audubon Society's director of conservation. Earlier on this trip we saw an injured teal, a reminder of these meadows' perilous condition today. Now Sheehan and the other passengers are looking toward the future. All have been speaking–shouting, really–above the insistent roar of the boat's motor, on the pros and cons of mitigation.

Voices ·°∂

ON THE RIVER WITH **HEART**

"It's a shame," says Andy Willner, "when you get in here and see the devastation that mitigation has caused." Willner grimly surveys the scene as Bill Sheehan throttles down the pontoon boat; we drift in silence into a flat, marshy landscape punctuated by low, shrubby islands.

When it comes to criticizing what is actually going on in the name of restoration in the Meadowlands, Willner is the most verbal and articulate. "The land has been bulldozed down to a certain hydrologic level so that the tide would inundate it, but there are certain missing factors," he points out. "It's not enough just to take the land down and replant it with something that may not have existed here. It's very expensive to make it work. It has to be fertilized; herbicides have to be used to get rid of unwanted species.

"The concept of mitigation *can* work, but it has to be done almost in a hothouse environment, almost total stewardship. What happens here, where they do it to compensate for development–once the developers do the original work, they walk away from it. There's nobody left to mandate it, to make sure it's gardened every year. Rather than compensating for the loss of a certain amount of wetlands by finding uplands to turn into wetlands, they do what is called 'enhancement mitigation.' They lose wetlands. This was all wetlands, and what they did is they took wetlands after they filled some and compensated for it by bulldozing out functioning wetlands and turning them into a biological desert. These are 'vegetated islands.' Essentially a biological desert. There is algae growing here and there's some biological value to algae.

Rubble and backfilled shoreline overgrown by weeds and ailanthus trees, north bank of Overpeck Creek near its juncture with the Hackensack River. This scene is typical of roughly handled waterways throughout the Meadowlands.

But the *Spartina* is much more successful in coming back through *natural* means, along the main stem of the river.

"We should *at least* eliminate this site as an example as to how restoration can occur in the estuary." In fact, Willner implies, it's an example of how true restoration can be thwarted—quite the opposite message from the one Don Smith, of the HMDC, delivered when he showed me this same site in July 1994.

Sheehan guides the boat up a narrow channel between banks covered by a lush growth of cordgrass, the *Spartina alterniflora* that ecologists and botanists would like to see reoccupy this wetland. Unlike the dominant phragmites, which has an exotic, alien look, like an Asian bamboo thicket, you can tell that cordgrass is a botanical native. It

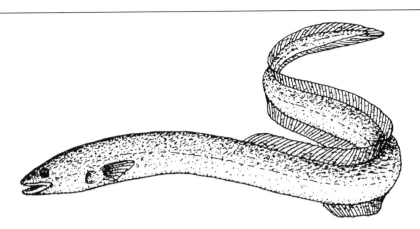

The American eel (Anguilla americanus) *occurs from the Gulf of Saint Lawrence south to Brazil. The species spawns in an area of the open Atlantic south of Bermuda known as the Sargasso Sea; the elvers migrate landward, where they enter brackish and fresh waters. This snake-like fish is common to abundant throughout the Hackensack estuary, often growing to a large size in the river. It is caught in large numbers in the New York Bight area and the Hackensack estuary and readily consumed as food, despite advisories warning against the practice.*

looks "right"; it belongs here, along the muddy banks of this turbid little waterway.

Rich Kane, seeing both an intangible beauty and a very prosaic, fundamental value in this glossy, wind-whipped rank of grass, notes that wetlands do in fact have a value that can be measured in dollars and cents. He recites a few statistics: "One acre of wetland has five thousand dollars per year's worth of intrinsic value—the stuff it *doesn't* cost. At five thousand times one hundred years of destruction of the meadows by industry, that's five hundred thousand dollars out there that's owed to us—the people. They've convinced people that all of this is somehow not theirs, but they [developers] are simply holding it in trust for us, or they should be."

Willner agrees. His is an environmental viewpoint based on the time frames of geologists. He knows that the life span of this estuary, if its future is left to the will of time and nature, will extend over three or five millennia. Maybe longer. Yet given an individual human being's threescore and ten life prospects, we are not conditioned to thinking or acting on objectives—in particular environmental ones—that will not provide immediate benefit. "There is a huge gulf between the advocates of preservation and the advocates of power," he says. "Here in the Meadowlands it's the short-term versus the long-term. Everything

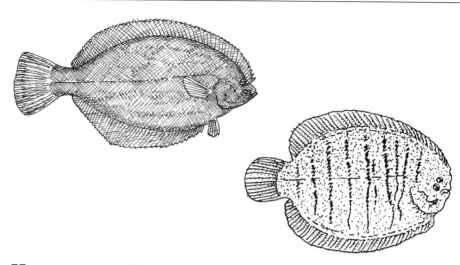

HACKENSACK RIVER FLATTIES

*The winter flounder (*Pseudopleuronectes americanus*), a popular food fish throughout its range, occurs in coastal waters from Labrador to Georgia. It has become fairly common in the Meadowlands due to habitat improvement and has been reported in the Saw Mill Creek area, Berrys Creek, and at many locations on the main stem of the Hackensack River. Juveniles are observed in smaller tributaries and brackish creeks.*

*The curious little hogchoker (*Achierus fasciatus*) is found in shallow coastal waters from Massachusetts to Virginia. The species is most abundant in brackish waters and may enter fresh water, moving for some distance up rivers. Hogchokers collected in the latter situations are often sold in pet shops as "freshwater flounders." This flatfish is found throughout the tidal brackish waters of the Meadowlands, especially in the Saw Mill Creek area, Berrys Creek, and the lower Hackensack River.*

has to be done now, in twenty years, for short-term gain. But saving this is not for now, it's forever. We need to think in terms of ecological time frames for the sake of our children, our grandchildren, and their grandchildren."

Willner is passionate about this. He, like many environmentalists, simply cannot understand why others so often fail to view the stewardship of their only home in the cosmos as a long-term investment. Indeed, the high passions of the Meadowlands debate are perhaps one of its most prominent features. Environmental activists like Bill Sheehan, Andy Willner, Steve Barnes, and others who canoe, fish, bird, and perhaps one day will swim this river are convinced that no amount of passion expended in its defense can possibly be in excess of the need.

They believe, probably rightly, that viable options for "the Hack" and its shrinking meadows are rapidly becoming fewer in number, and that once all the primal vestiges of this ancient estuary, those wind-and-water absolutes and esoterics that make it a unique and beautiful place, are gone, all the passion under heaven will not bring them back.

Captain Bill powers up the motor, and we move away from this hopeful yet somehow misbegotten aquatic garden. Our wake curls out behind us, a lacy curving frond the color of café au lait. Dragonflies course lightly over the water ahead; a jet slants in toward Newark Airport. The boat's fish finder squeaks tentatively as we pass by a greasy, partially submerged wreck of undefinable origin. "Twenty years"–the economic horizon–"is a geological wink," Rich Kane interjects suddenly, shouting above the motor's roar.

Willner, doubtless considering the paradox inherent here, between the patience of the glaciers that built this estuary over a span of twenty millennia and the dumps and industry–the people–that completely reshaped it within a century, grips the boat's handrail and glances sharply at us all in turn. "Not even a wink!" he hollers into the wide and windy sky.

TAKING CARE OF BUSINESS

Not long after my boat trip on the river, I sought a response from the other side in the development versus preservation debate. It would be unfair to dismiss the business view of the Meadowlands' future as invalid because it might be offered by a desk-bound executive rather than by a naturalist over a weathered boat transom. As Walt Whitman once wrote, "The work of man too is equally great . . . in these ingenuities, streets, goods, houses, ships"–words of a true New Yorker. But even James Lovelock, a natural scientist and author of the Gaia hypothesis, points out that nature produced humans, too, along with all their works. The debate comes down, perhaps, to the number of "ingenuities, streets, goods, houses, ships" the planet can comfortably accomodate–the size of our niche in the biosphere. And that is where the two sides of the Meadowlands debate part company, dramatically.

Richard Fritzky is executive director of the Meadowlands Regional Chamber of Commerce, which has seven hundred member corporations. As he earnestly explained to me recently, he appreciates "the natural beauty of the Meadowlands" as much as anyone, and has "personally been out there to see it many times." Yet the Chamber is, of

Dead end, Bergen Turnpike, Ridgefield Park. In the Meadowlands, most east-west roads must either cross the meadows or end at them. This spot, while it might never be mistaken for a stream bank in a national park, nonetheless offers the canoeist or kayaker ready access to the Hackensack River at the northern edge of the Meadowlands.

course, an enthusiastic cheerleader for the cause of continued planned development in the Meadowlands, and thus solidly behind the provisions of the SAMP. And Rich Fritzky logically defends this modern covenant between the busyness of humanity and the birds and fishes of the river. His are the words of a people-and-progress-oriented visionary, but they are decidedly not the rigid pronouncements of a myopic fanatic; instead, his musings on the future of the meadows are often those of the peacemaker, infused with the message of conciliation. He uses the word *rational* a lot.

The environmental-sociological personae of Rich Fritzky and Bill Sheehan may eye each other from distant summits, but in other areas the two men resemble each other. Like Sheehan, Fritzky is a mid-fortysomething, disarmingly friendly, down-to-earth fellow. He is physically robust and hirsute, with a full beard, often the lifestyle statement of male environmentalists and other suspected liberal types. Both Sheehan and Fritzky are decidedly conservative, however, where it comes to yielding riparian Meadowlands ground to the other side. Although Rich Fritzky seems more agreeable to compromise than Bill Sheehan, in the end maybe it's because he knows that in defeat developers stand to lose only potential dollars ("as well as opportunity and hope," he insists)—maybe a lot of them. Sheehan and other Meadowlands environmentalists believe that their side may well lose an ecosystem—for all time.

When I meet Rich Fritzky in his air-conditioned Rutherford office during the height of the record-setting 1995 heat wave, he receives me dressed in casual slacks and a colorful sports shirt. We shake hands over a huge desk cluttered with works in progress. We are both uncomfortably aware of the intense hazy-white heat outside, baking the wide parking lots and the nearby Meadowlands and radiating through the drawn blinds of the nearby window like a living force.

Rich Fritzky is, understandably, "very excited" about the future of the Meadowlands on the eve of ratification of the SAMP. He is pleased and optimistic because the future as outlined in that plan is gradually, and perhaps inevitably, taking shape according to his own vision for it. He is at ease and not at all defensive in speaking on both sides of the development versus environment issue in the Meadowlands as though, in the end, there really is no issue at all. "Economy and environment do not necessarily have to be at loggerheads," he says, insisting that "life in the [Meadowlands] District, both economically and environmentally, is much better today than it was ten or twenty years ago." This is standard "business" fare, and Fritzky knows this, but he readily acknowledges the "definitive tradeoffs" that will have to be made by all sides in this concluding chapter of the meadows story. He sees the compromises embodied in the SAMP as being the most reasonable solutions to what, twenty years ago, had seemed an insoluble dilemma.

I ask him about his view of the determined and growing grass-roots opposition to further development, on any scale, in the estuary. He answers with the confidence of one who knows that more houses, more highways, and more industry are all but a foregone conclusion on vacant land, no matter how wet it is, that lies within sight of New York City.

"I've long been troubled by those who say 'Leave it all alone.' In the best of all possible worlds—if we went back to the 1600s—you'd have a damned good argument," he says. "But the fact of the matter is there isn't one square foot of terrain here that wasn't ravaged or fouled or dumped on or exploited in some way in the past. So in order to nurture its capacity you've got to do things in new and different ways."

Fritzky got up and spoke at the sometimes contentious public hearings on the SAMP held in the summer of 1995. In his testimony he assured his listeners, many of them hostile to his position, that the changes portended by the SAMP would not take place overnight but, rather like those in a natural ecosystem, evolve over time. "SAMP is not about today, it's about tomorrow, about the future," he said. "It will take twenty years if and when and how. It's a plan, not a fait accompli."

But to environmentalists accustomed to thinking in terms of centuries, millennia, or even eons when they talk about a habitat, twenty years is indeed "overnight," and they are seldom pacified by such words of reassurance. In response to their peremptory, nature-based arguments, Rich Fritzky resorts to an analogy that perhaps strikes closest to the heart of the struggle for the Meadowlands of tomorrow—that of the economics at the root of the human presence on the planet: "I genuinely appreciate [environmentalists'] knowledge of the intricacies of life in an ecosystem, [but] please know that economy, too, has a life, a delicate ebb and flow that succumbs in bad times and rises in good times."

Voices ～

RICHARD FRITZKY

"The comprehensive Meadowlands environmental program drives the SAMP. Ultimately, rational people, from whatever passion drives them, will see that we can strike common denominators and a balance that would be effective. There are definite tradeoffs in the SAMP, but the tradeoffs both give up something and win something.

"I believe that the recovery of the Meadowlands will be enhanced by the SAMP. Yeah, we're going to fill some wetlands, and yes, we're going to do things for transit, but we've looked at development in the SAMP, we've defined where it should be, said there would be tradeoffs there: you're gonna pay for the right to develop here in extraordinary ways environmentally [including requirements for mitigation], [and] in the transfer of development rights [while compensating owners of land delcared off-limits to development].

"I've been out there in the past and had seen thousands of old tires along the Saw Mill; on a recent trip I saw one or two tires. The waterfowl just stared you in the face—jumped out at you. The turtles; just the living creatures that you saw everywhere. Life is thriving here again. I think that's encouraging!

"And I think mitigation *does* work, nature *does* reclaim itself. I look at all the phragmites—the common reed—on the one side, that eventually chokes off and limits life, and I look at all the low-level mossy grass and the other grasses that are growing on the Hartz mitigation side. That's functioning, and it's flowering.

"The SAMP is not going to make the whole world happy, but the economic community is being bold and proactive, going forward to find a way, in this 'urban wilderness' within the shadow of Manhattan in the most densely populated corner of the United States, to make it work.

"Give and take—there's no question that there will be a lot of giving, but you've got to be rational; and even in your passion, don't trade off the passion, but consider another road. Consider another path, consider another way to get there."

THE SEVENTEEN-ACRE DOT
IN THE SWAMPLANDS

We never seem to know what anything means till we have lost it . . . till in place of the bright, visible being, comes the awful and desolate shadow where nothing is—where we stretch out our hands in vain, and strain our eyes upon dark and dismal vacuity.

(Orville Dewey)

A sense of loss is precisely the emotion I experience whenever I stand on the tarmac in my hometown's contribution to the Overpeck County Park and gaze over the wide expanse of windblown weeds that used to be a tidal marsh. Within my lifetime this ancient river valley has changed, with a dispatch possible only in the twentieth century, from a viable wetland into a major transportation corridor and vast landfill. Although the view here is spacious and in some respects possesses an elemental beauty, I often look on it with a "dark and dismal vacuity."

While others debate the Meadowlands' future, for me one possible future has already arrived, right here on my own home ground. This is what the remaining meadows may become tomorrow, if nothing changes today—if all the forces unleashed in the past continue unabated.

Assorted flotsam, shoreline of Overpeck Creek, Overpeck County Park, Leonia.
Pencil drawing.

A 1955 *Record* editorial headlined "The 17-Acre Dot in the Swamp-lands" expounded on the positive aspects of marsh reclamation in the Overpeck drainage; it was the precursor of many such journalistic pro-nouncements that would follow over the next few years. Most of these writings would express the view that while the Meadowlands were beautiful in their unique but vaguely primitive way, their manifest des-tiny was to be a beneficiary of twentieth-century landfill technology and, ultimately, to develop into a productive landscape of human en-deavor. The paper acknowledged that the Overpeck meadows, "lovely in their green coating of fox grass, cattails and arrowhead," represented something of the vanished pastoral county in the midst of burgeoning suburbia but insisted that it was all "a deceptive picture of beauty." In-deed, the newspaper and presumably most of the citizenry of eastern Bergen County at the time saw the budding landfill on the north side of old Fort Lee Road as a godsend, holding the promise of "firm ground, feet above the surroundings, ideal for factory or playground."

The editorial was referring to the beginning of the end of that part of the "upper meadows" I came to know in my youth. Ornithologist

Ludlow Griscom had claimed in 1923 that "the best locality in the whole territory [the New York metropolitan area] for freshwater ducks, excepting Gardiner's Island, is to be found in the marshes of the Overpeck Creek." Griscom saw these "low, rich woodlands" as "the best place for warblers" as well, "excepting Central Park." Officials of the Regional Planning Association of the New York Metropolitan Area also paid a visit to Overpeck Creek in the 1920s. They declared the surrounding grasslands to be "one of the finest opportunities for preserving an open space of exceptional beauty in the metropolitan area."

Only three decades later the press, public officials, and presumably most of the electorate were of the conviction that the Overpeck meadows were in fact "a County liability," a foreboding environment and miasmic no-man's-land in which "gases ooze up in oily bubbles in hot weather," and yet something of a paradox. "County residents know well that the green growth hides only a quagmire and impassable terrain," noted the *Record*, alluding to the curious duality of a landscape very nearly as beautiful as it was considered worthless.

A limited amount of municipal and private dumping had nibbled away at the fringes of the Overpeck meadows for nearly a century, long before any thought was given to the prospect of large-scale reclamation. But in 1951, perhaps in anticipation of the unwanted industrial development that eventual filling would attract, towns surrounding the creek ceded riparian lands to the county for the creation of Overpeck Marine Park; those lands would revert back to the municipalites in 1956 if the county failed to develop the park by then. The Bergen County Park Commission expressed commitment to the expansive park, but as the 1956 deadline for development of the project approached without official action, real estate agents began eyeing the tract for residential and industrial development. The town of Ridgefield Park did, in fact, take back its section, leasing part of it to the Hartz Mountain Corporation and saving the rest (97 acres) as parkland. The other towns–Teaneck, Leonia, and Palisades Park–opted to give the county more time to finalize plans. Parts of the county park had already been built in Teaneck (a golf course) and Leonia.

But then, at the last minute, a highway intervened in the fate of the Overpeck. In the 1960s the State Highway Commission appropriated all lands below tide level (that is, future filled-in lands) for the construction of Interstates 80 and 95. The proposed parkland and the valley itself were thus fragmented into the right-of-way for I-95, the state's major north-south traffic artery, and an extensive recreational facility was virtually isolated from its prospective users on the west bank of the Overpeck. An engineer hired in 1963 drew up the master plan for the park; the Overpeck was dredged in 1966 and the spoils pumped ashore as landfill for the surrounding marshes as well as for the roadbed of the new superhighway.

Three decades later, the new highways were humming with traffic, but the county lands on the creek's west bank remained largely in limbo. Ridgefield Park's planning board noted in 1994: "It is . . . very much to the credit of the Village that the 97-acre Bergen County Overpeck park . . . was established as part of an overall redevelopment undertaken by the Village of the former landfill area east of Route I-95. A 21-acre section of this park . . . has presently been completed, including two soccer fields, two softball fields, a restroom building and a maintenance building. The County has now engaged engineering services to prepare site preparation plans for the remaining 76.4 acres in Ridgefield Park." Planning had also begun for the facilities: "it is anticipated that these will include, in addition to extending the access road and providing parking for 250 cars, the following: a 'Great Lawn' and Wildflower Meadow surrounded by a one-mile foot and jogging path; an amphitheater; two baseball and softball fields; a picnic area; an enlarged restroom and shelter building with a small restaurant; picnic and sitting areas; and a boathouse with a wood dock for rowboat or paddleboat rentals."

The development of most of these amenities has yet to be realized. Meanwhile the great, weedy, landfilled expanse that comprises the west bank of the creek has become a mecca for birds, and for birders, but Interstate 95 sees to it that few others visit the tract.

Commercial development, like highway construction, had also proceeded apace. At the south end of the unfinished park stand the steel-and-glass monoliths and sleek parking garages of the Hartz Mountain Corporation's Overpeck Centre. This sprawling, futuristic complex, with a multinational corporate headquarters and a multiplex movie theater, turned out to be a construction nightmare. As current village mayor George Fosdick explains, "When they began the Hartz Mountain project there, they thought they were going to be driving pilings, let's say, one hundred to two hundred feet. They drove piles three hundred to four hundred feet before they hit something solid that they could build on. I know that they were quite distressed because the firm underpinnings were substantially deeper than they had ever anticipated." The builders were, of course, contending with thousands of years of varved clays, laid down as the seasons of centuries passed and Glacial Lake Hackensack rose and fell, then finally drained seaward.

Today the scene in the Overpeck Creek valley is a curious blend of the pastoral and the commercial—a preview, perhaps, of the ever more checkered patterns to come in the Meadowlands. The sections of functioning county park in the borough of Leonia, the township of

Summer scene on Overpeck Creek, looking south. Pencil drawing.

Canada geese, striding through snow in Overpeck County Park, Ridgefield Park.

Black-backed gulls, Overpeck Creek, near a railroad bridge abutment.

Teaneck, and the Village of Ridgefield Park attract crowds of bikers, walkers, golfers, and other recreationists every day of the week, and more so on Sunday; the remaining empty acres of closed landfill, lying fallow under their lush cover of phragmites, goldenrod, ragweed, and panic grass, lend the place the aspect of a brooding Scottish heath. Over the years the extensive, weed-grown tract lying on the western side of the creek has "matured" and become something of an inadvertent wildlife refuge. The New Jersey Audubon Society's birding hotline lists the area as a reliable "hot spot." Among the more unusual or rare species reported there in recent years have been the clay-colored, white-crowned, grasshopper, and Lincolns sparrows, as well as the bobolink, dickcissel, and the elusive yellow rail. A European kestrel was spotted there in the summer of 1995.

The perpetual motion of the interstate prevents today's village youngsters from trekking out to the impounded watercourse in search of adventure, if they were inclined to do so. But there is another aspect of the original Overpeck that survives, perhaps the one remaining activity in this odd tomorrowland that is most evocative of its past. People still fish in the Overpeck's waters, and some of them converse in tongues other than English, as did the long-vanished Lenape and the early Dutch settlers. And they even, still, eat their catch—an act of some risk here today.

Bill Greene, a Bronx attorney and an ardent meadows angler, not long ago spent several hours fishing the Overpeck at the old Hendrick's Causeway bridge that spans the creek between the village and the borough of Ridgefield. He ended the day fishless, but noted that "apparently there are pockets containing carp—by far the stars of the scene there—and other spots barren of all but killies and small white perch."

Greene noted that "one Russian fellow had very good luck, about a dozen carp, among them a mirror carp of about seven pounds, and an eight-pound, four ounce, twenty-seven-inch regular carp. He got about ten others, two to four pounds, all caught in the trough. He knew

*The pumpkinseed sunfish (*Lepomis gibbosus*) (left) is native to the eastern United States and southern Canada but has been widely introduced elsewhere as a game fish. The little sunnie occurs in Meadowlands waters of lower salinity such as the mildly brackish headwaters of tidal creeks and in such impounded freshwater bodies as Losen Slote and Overpeck Creeks. The closely related bluegill (*L. macrochirus*) is common in fresh and mildly brackish water throughout the district; it is especially abundant in Losen Slote Creek, Kearny Marsh, and Overpeck Creek and tributaries. Both species are highly popular panfish.*

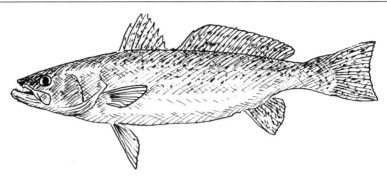

*The weakfish (*Cynoscion regalis*) is found from Maine south to the Carolinas in inshore waters, bays, and estuaries. It has been reported at many locations in the lower Hackensack River and Newark Bay. Captain Bill Sheehan of the River Tenders says that large weakfish have been caught in the Hackensack in recent years—a 7-pounder, for example, near Berrys Creek in 1994.*

and valued his carp; recognized the mirror carp and told me he caught them in Russia—Moldavia region is what I think he said."

Greene's real fish story, though, occurred on the Hackensack.

Voices ～

BILL GREENE: FISHING EXCITEMENT
ON THE HACKENSACK RIVER

"What to do when one's fishing alone, using two rods, and two good fish hit at the same time? Generally, when I fish with bait in the Hackensack or elsewhere, I use two rods to keep busy while waiting for a bite. Moving from rod to rod, checking and changing baits, passes away the time pleasantly.

"Saturday of the Memorial Day weekend, fishing the Hackensack began slowly for the first two hours. I could see some good carp in the water; they snuffled by my corn kernel bait [which usually works] without even a look. Occasionally a bullhead would take hold, keeping my hopes up.

"Switching to bread, I got an occasional nudge, hooked nothing, and figured it was the bullheads again. Leaving one rod propped up on a stick, with the line in the water, I walked about a hundred feet downriver with the other rod to try another spot.

"It was a deeper hole, loaded with snags, floating branches, and stalks. When the line started to move off after a weak nudge, I set the hook and found myself tied into the biggest carp I'd found in the river

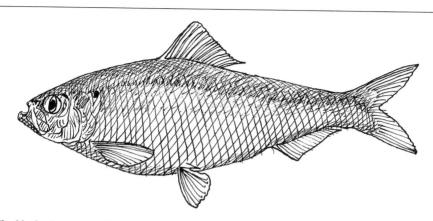

*The blueback herring (*Alosa aestivalis*) occurs in the North Atlantic, and can be found from Nova Scotia to Florida. Prior to the damming of the Hackensack River at Oradell, this species, also known as the glut herring, was an extremely abundant and supported an important fishery. In spring it migrates in vast numbers where access to spawning sites is not restricted by dams.*

so far. Happily, I was using a bait-casting rod with twelve-pound-test line; with my spinning rod I'd have been a goner.

"As I stumbled about on the muddy bank, trying to maneuver the fish away from snags, some movement caught the corner of my eye. It was my other rod, bent double over the prop stick and looking like it was about to go into the river with another fish! Luckily, I'd left the drag very loose, so the reel released line rather than following the fish into the water.

"This fish stopped in the weeds and stalks. I brought in the first carp, a fat fellow just shy of ten pounds, released him, and went back to the other rod. The second fish was still on, a carp of about five pounds. I worked this one out of the weeds, released it, and spent a moment resting or being thankful . . . maybe both!

"I caught one more carp, and one of my more unusual catches on the river: a fire-engine-red goldfish of about nine inches. I released it to swim free in the river with the others."

FLOWERS FROM GARBAGE

Scientist James Lovelock once described a peculiar collective myopia of urban humankind: "Because we are city dwellers, we are obsessed with human problems. Even environmentalists seem more concerned about the loss of a year or so of life expectation through cancer than they are about the degradation of the natural world by deforestation or greenhouse gases—something that could cause the death of our grand-children. We are so alienated from the world of nature that few of us can name the wildflowers and insects of our locality or notice the ra-pidity of their extinction."

Indeed, the development of floral identification skills is not high on the list of priorities for most residents of the New York metropolitan area, but maybe it should be. Flowers are among nature's most exquis-ite expressions of the inherent beauty of life on Earth; a virtual uni-verse of detail can be found in the magnification of a single dandelion petal. The visual exclamations of flowers come almost anywhere: in gardens and strawberry fields, certainly; beside a concrete divider on the New Jersey Turnpike, peeking bravely from a pavement crack; or lending a touch of color to a dump.

Brendan Riordan of North Bergen, a landscaper, came to his trade through a natural empathy for plants. He is a member in good standing of the New Jersey Native Plant Society, and a notable exception to Lovelock's diagnosis of general environmental myopia. In the summer of 1994 Riordan and several fellow Plant Society members made a trip to DeKorte Park, where once a foul and eminently toxic heap of garbage stood nearly as high as a Watchung foothill. That heap is now cultivated, and bursting with a variety of wildflowers and shrubs repre-senting a unique succession of habitats. Riordan was so impressed by what he found at DeKorte Park that he wrote at length about the expe-rience, and the plant society later conferred an award of merit on the HMDC for its singular accomplishment of big-league gardening there.

His account provides a vivid and comprehensive look at what wonders can be worked on the biological desert that constitutes the surface of an obsolete landfill:

> In our first stop, the Kingsland Overlook, we experienced the stages of plant succession and we viewed a Wildflower Butterfly Meadow, an Eastern Coastal Grassland Prairie, a Late Woody Shrub Field, a Young Woodland, and an Ever-green Forest. All of this on a mountain of garbage! I cannot list all of the plants seen at the Kingsland Overlook but I will highlight a few.
>
> The Wildflower Butterfly Meadow contained a colorful mix of Yarrow (*Achilles millefolium*), Common milkweed (*Asclepias syriaca*), Queen Anne's Lace (*Daucus carota*), Purple

*The narrow-leafed cattail (*Typha angusti-folia*) is a familiar freshwater marsh plant throughout temperate North and Central America. Though replaced over large areas by phragmites, it occurs throughout the Meadowlands in freshwater and mildly brackish habitats, most abundantly in the Kearny Marsh and Saw Mill Creek areas. The similar broad-leafed cattail (*T. latifolia*) occurs throughout temperate North and South America. It is also found in freshwater Meadowlands habitats.*

Coneflower (*Echinacea purpurea*), Black-eyed Susan (*Rudbelia hirta*), to name a few. Monarch butterflies were in attendance and a hummingbird moth was identified.

The Eastern Coastal Prairie contained Switch Grass (*Panicum virgatum*), Gay Feather (*Liatris spuata*), Coreopsis (*Corepsis lanceolata*) and Indian Grass (*Sorghastrum nutans*) as well as many of the wildflowers of the Butterfly Meadow.

In the Late Woody Field we found Brilliant Choke-berry (*Aronia arbutifolia*), Glossy Abelia (*Abelia* x *grandiflora*), Gray Dogwood (*Cornus racemosa*), and Smooth Sumac (*Rhus glabra*). Some of the other shrubs present there are considered naturalized rather than native and include the Rugosa Rose (*Rosa rugosa*), Pink Summersweet (*Clethera alniflora*) and Autumn Olive (*Elaegnus unbellata*). St. John's Hidcote (*Hypericum patulum*) was observed in profuse yellow bloom at this time.

The trail moved through the Young Woodland, which contained Summit Green Ash (*Fraxinus pennsylvanica*), Pin Oak (*Quercus palustrus*), Red Maple (*Acer rubrum*) and Cranberry Viburnum (*Viburnum trilobium*).

Lastly, we came upon the Evergreen Forest, which was destined to overshadow all previous natural selection stages. Its botanical residents included White Pine (*Pinus strobus*),

*Duckweed (*Lemna minor*), one of the smallest flowering plants, is found throughout North America on the surface of freshwater ponds, marshes, and other standing or slow-moving waters. Widely introduced outside the natural range, it can be a pest in ornamental ponds, quickly covering the entire water surface. It is a valued food for waterfowl, hence the common name. Duckweed is found in abundance in all freshwater bodies in the Meadowlands; it is especially common in Kearny Marsh, where it forms vast carpets of tiny green leaves on the water in late summer.*

Norway Spruce (*Picea albia*), and I believe, Scrub Pine (*Pinus virginiana*).

There were still two more areas to investigate: the Transco Trail and the Marsh Discovery Trail. The former follows the outer rim of the Kingsland Tidal Impoundment Marsh and is a graveled pipeline right-of-way that originates near the Gulf of Mexico and terminates in New Jersey. Along this trail we encountered milkweed, thistle and hibiscus which were just coming into flower. Walking the pipeline trail we came upon the Marsh Discovery Trail; it is a floating pedestrian trail made of recycled plastic milk cartons! This trail through the freshwater marsh cuts across the Kingsland Tidal impoundment and the principal flora to be found here is the invasive reed known as Phragmites. Atlantic cedar stumps can be seen here, the last botanical remnants of another time and another environment. A groundsel tree was found about halfway across the marsh and salt hay and switch grass grow here in abundance.

Riordan's practiced eye was not trained exclusively on the plants; he took note as well of the park's profusion of wildlife:

> Bird observation stations are situated at strategic points along this trail and we stopped at them to take note of the bird life; moorhens, mallards, snowy egrets and sandpipers were in residence in the marsh as our journey's end approached.
>
> Along with plant communities, wildlife in abundance cohabits the Hackensack meadows. From butterflies to hawks and other birds, mammals and multitudes of aquatic creatures, all are reclaiming their native lands and waters. My mind's eye flashed back to the slide presentation at the Environment Center and the "before" pictures of the landfill garbage mountain. One word: "Transformation!" That which we had destroyed was now on a good start toward restoration. The DeKorte Park is man's attempt to correct the ravages of industrialization and the impact of the modern world. Still in its early stages, the park's many successes far outnumber its setbacks. Time will tell as nature takes its course here.

As an enhancement of its educational offerings, the HMDC in 1989 designed and built a unique "garbage museum" at the park's environmental center. Created by Newark artist Robert Richardson, the exhibit is a walk-though, floor-to-ceiling "jumble of trash" designed so that it appears the rubbish is about to collapse and engulf the visitor. The artist told a reporter that the viewer would "feel that the garbage climbing up the walls is overwhelming and at some point might fall over," adding, "That's good." The exhibit primarily contains packaging materials and lacks organic refuse, soil, demolition debris, or sludge— all major components of a real landfill—for obvious sanitary reasons.

Today, the real dumps are very nearly a thing of the past in the Meadowlands. The seventeen acres of the Bergen County landfill at Lyndurst and the fifteen acres surrounding the county garbage baling facility in North Arlington are the only waste-processing sites still active in the Meadowlands. These dumps are being phased out through a $125 million HMDC landfill closure plan. According to the HMDC, the closure process involves few steps:

> 1) The construction of a cutoff wall or dike, generally made from a clay slurry around the site perimeter to

contain the leachate and prevent it from polluting the surrounding groundwater. The cut-off wall extends down into a layer of clay which is found throughout the meadowlands and which was deposited when the last ice age [glacier] retreated. This clay layer acts as a vertical barrier to the spread of leachate, while the cut-off wall acts to restrict horizontal flow. The construction of the cut-off wall or dike, therefore, creates a giant bathtub-like structure which confines the contaminates.

2) Installation of a leachate collection system/pumping system to collect and transport the leachate to a proper treatment and disposal facility.

3) Installation of an impervious cover material across the top of the site to minimize rainwater infiltration which minimizes the quantity of leachate generated by the landfill.

4) Installation of a methane gas collection system.

Despite the cessation of dumping in the Meadowlands District, the HMDC is nonetheless considering a plan to reopen the old Keegan landfill in Kearny. This one-hundred-acre landfill, closed in 1971, would be opened to receive about 1,500 tons of nonorganic construction debris daily, 300 tons of which would be recycled. If the state request to reopen the Kearny dump is granted by the state Department of Environmental Protection, the landfill will be contained by a fifty-foot-deep clay wall to prevent the leaching of any contaminants into the surrounding terrain. The alternative is to export: most demolition rubble generated in New Jersey is shipped out of state today.

One advantage of reopening the old Keegan landfill would be its eventual, proper closure. Even though the landfill is currently inactive, its compacted refuse still leaches about 65,000 gallons of contaminated liquids a day into the freshwater Kearny Marsh. The US Environmental Protection Agency has documented the presence of mercury, lead, chromium, and polychlorinated biphenyls (PCBs) at the site. Another old landfill a few miles to the south is even more environmentally virulent. The ninety-four-acre 1D Landfill on the Passaic River is reportedly leaching as much as 250,000 gallons of toxic effluent, including motor oil and heavy metals, into the river daily. In total some 375,000 gallons of liquid leachate per acre flow from uncapped Meadowlands dumps per year, all of it ending up in the Hackensack and Passaic Rivers and thence in the ocean. According to *The Record*, a 1991 HMDC study revealed that this "witch's brew" of chemical wastes consists, in part, of "an estimated 4,800 pounds of hydrocarbons, 1,210 pounds of zinc,

743 pounds of nickel, 561 pounds of lead, 572 pounds of arsenic, and 523 pounds of chromium. . . ."

Thus, for both the HMDC and environmental activists, while the goal is within sight (ecological resurrection for the Hackensack estuary), the road there is likely to be a long and rocky one.

TEACH YOUR CHILDREN WELL

Charles Reich, in his then-controversial, now almost quaintly naive *Greening of America*, wrote in 1970 of the widening gulf between modern technological Americans and their natural surroundings. "Economic progress destroys nature, adventure, traditions and the local

Canada geese and winter ice patterns, Kingsland Creek, DeKorte Park.

community," he asserted. As evidence, Reich pointed out, for example, the "Disney-fication" of reality in the growing popularity of theme parks: "As the families flock to the clean, sunny happy enclosure, how many of them realize that something precious has been taken from them, that they are being charged for a substitute that offers only sterile pretense in place of real experience? How many find the chief experience at Disneyland to be a sense of loss of all that they are seeing?" He also lamented the fact that children nowadays are first exposed to the mysteries of their world "earliest and most universally, on television. The television-world is what our society claims itself to be, what it demands that we believe."

Might hands-on education of the young be an antidote to the pervasive "virtual reality," the bogus experience, of modern entertainment and consumerism? Is education in the stuff of nature—including our ancient ties to it and our need for it—the key to preserving the Meadowlands?

Robert Sikora, an environmental education specialist with the HMDC, thinks so. A true educator—the kind of enthusiastic and committed teacher-naturalist that has staffed nature centers and science museums for as long as they have existed—he doggedly refuses to yield to pessimism in the face of today's grim environmental forecasts. He is fond of quoting a Senegalese proverb: "In the end we will conserve only what we love; we will love only what we understand; we will understand only what we are taught." He was delighted to see that the verse was printed above a picture of African wildlife on the T-shirt I wore the day we met.

*The beautiful, racy black skimmer (*Rynchops niger*) is found on beaches and other coastal habitats from Cape Cod to South America. Common in the Meadowlands during the warmer months of the year, it is observed regularly at the Kingsland Impoundment in DeKorte Park and at Saw Mill Creek and the main stem of the Hackensack River. This bird nests in colonies and may breed on spoil banks and isolated landfills in the Meadowlands.*

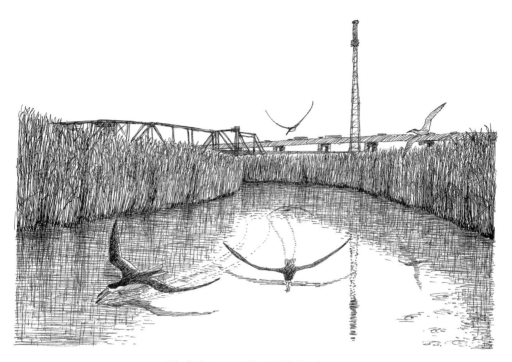

Black skimmers, Saw Mill Creek area.

When I visited him at the HMDC's environment center at De-Korte Park, he gave me a tour of the public exhibits and talked a little about the natural and human history of the Meadowlands. Then, as we stood on the enclosed passageway between the center and its observation rotunda watching the life outside, on the grayish, wind-riffled waters, he ticked off the bird species observed there: "the Canada geese, peregrine falcon, lots of shorebirds, teal, shovelers. . . ." As if on cue, a pair of black skimmers zipped in over the reeds and began coursing over the water, razor-sharp bills scribing the surface. "And skimmers!" he shouted. "Oh, look at that! Isn't that great?" It was indeed; and the sight of those long-winged, exotic inhabitants of our once empty coastlines, right there, right in front of the HMDC's environment center, seemed to lend a wordless confirmation to the ultimate worth of everything the agency is trying to accomplish here.

I asked Sikora how he sees his role as educational point man for the Meadowlands, and how receptive his audience is to his message: "Kids are keenly aware of global environmental issues," he said. "What they are often not aware of is that they have the resource in their own backyard. There is a sense of wonder in kids from more densely populated communities, more appreciation of the remaining open space here. They sense that there is an abundance of life worth being a part of, right in their own backyard—a hidden life in the Meadowlands that most people are just not aware of.

"Kids are open to the ideas of having this intimacy with nature, and that you don't have to go to the rain forests or the Pacific Northwest forests; you can come here and be a part of that web of life. School districts come from all over the state, from as far away as Connecticut and Maryland. There is a sense among children that this place is important, that they want to be a part of it."

We were looking eastward over the meadows at what is arguably the most famous skyline in the world: that of Manhattan Island. On the distant, sun-glinting Hackensack River, at a spot just to the left of the twin towers of the World Trade Center, a small, low-slung boat chugged northward. The craft appeared to have a group of people on its open deck and even at that distance looked much like an eco-tour pontoon boat. This prompted me to solicit Sikora's opinion of the highly vocal grassroots opposition to the SAMP from private groups like the Hackensack Estuary and River Tenders, and his thoughts on their role in the future of the Meadowlands. He responded carefully but without hesitation: "I believe that any organization that brings about a heightened awareness of the river can only be a positive influence. It's important to get all perspectives, all input. Without it you would not have had a SAMP proposal put together." I suspect that the type and volume of development proposed by the SAMP was not a result of input and cooperation from activists like Bill Sheehan, but I can appreciate Sikora's unquestionable sincerity and conviction.

*The glossy ibis (*Plegadis falcinellus*) is an attractive wader widespread in Eurasia, Africa, and Australia; in North America it inhabits the seacoast from Massachusetts south to Florida and the West Indies. The range has gradually expanded northward over the past 25 years. This striking tropical waterbird is now a common summer resident of the Meadowlands region, though it is not yet known to breed here.*

*The marsh fiddler crab (*Uca minax*) occurs from Cape Cod to Florida and Texas, and from the West Indies to Colombia. Fiddlers can be found throughout the Meadowlands in suitable habitats—firm mud banks exposed daily by low tide—and they are most abundant in the Sawmill Creek area. This may be a sign of resurgence. Surveys conducted in the early 1970s revealed that fiddler crabs had become very scare in the Meadowlands, due primarily to oil contamination and past use of the insecticide DDT.*

As a naturalist and educator as well as an employee of the HMDC, Bob Sikora might be expected to effect something of a tightrope act when asked to express his personal perspective on events here. He indeed views the SAMP as "a workable solution" to the alternative prospect of "runaway, unplanned development" in what remains of the meadows. It is, he says, an example of "sustainable growth in an urban ecosystem." Sikora, like many other modern environmental educators, insists that the reality of people must be included in any plans for the resurrection of urban ecosystems; yet he sees a hopeful future for a place that can never again be the untrammeled wilderness it once was. It's too late, he argues, to turn back the clock. The future of these meadows is more a matter of their acceptance as they now exist and, perhaps, a reverence that comes with knowing. "I see a long-term outlook on one's place in nature that's going to be very positive," he says. "There's a much stronger awareness today of the need for open space; the students understand their connection to the natural world. One day, people will say with pride, 'Yes, I grew up on this river. . . . I lived on the Hackensack River in New Jersey.'"

The ultimate fate of the Meadowlands—indeed, the continuing miracle of its existence as a biological community in any state of integrity—can perhaps be better contemplated by placing this landscape within the

Muskrat running an aquatic errand in Saw Mill Creek. These large rodents are by far the most noticeable mammals, other than humans, in the Meadowlands.

context of the state in which it lies. The New Jersey of the 1990s is a very crowded place and destined, like most of the rest of the United States, to become ever more so. Demographers predict that the nation's population, now about 260 million, will increase to 275 million by the turn of the century and then soar to 385 million by 2050–a

50 percent increase over the 1990 level. Perhaps a good deal of that growth will occur farther west and south. Right now, 8.9 percent of the total US population lives within fifty miles of the central Jersey city of New Brunswick. This expanding mass of humanity, if it brings along with it the unchecked spread of random urban growth, will surely render futile most if not all attempts to preserve our remaining natural enclaves in anything even remotely resembling a pristine state. That crucial time, arriving now in other parts of the world, where it still might be possible to keep the original ecosystem intact, has already passed for the Hackensack meadows. Industrial civilization is a fait accompli here, and no force under heaven can alter or reverse this now.

Historian Paul Kennedy, in *Preparing for the Twenty-first Century*, notes that the present, uncertain circumstances in which humankind finds itself today were a long time in the making. They had their genesis in the social and political upheavals that occurred in Europe at the close of the eighteenth century and on the eve of the Industrial Revolution. Concerns for the ominous and growing mismatch between us humans and the finite resources available to us were perhaps best expressed by the English curate Thomas Malthus, who in his 1798 *Essay on Population* warned that the greatest peril facing future humanity was "that the power of population is indefinitely greater than the power of the earth to produce subsistence for man." Kennedy, too, states the case succinctly: "Because of the population explosion and humankind's striving for higher living standards, we may now be subjecting our ecosystem to more pressure than it can take," he wrote. Today, he finds little support for the pie-in-the-sky fantasy of unlimited growth. As the planet reacts to our collective abuse, it "threatens us, rich and poor alike, with the consequences of having tampered too much with the earth's thin film of [life-sustaining] matter."

There is also, of course, the matter of sustaining our souls—of rediscovering our roots in nature.

Voices

JOHN MUIR, 1912

"Everybody needs beauty as well as bread, places to play in and pray in, where Nature may heal and cheer and give strength to body and soul alike. This natural beauty-hunger is made manifest in the little window-sill gardens of the poor, though perhaps only a geranium slip in a broken cup, as well as in the carefully tended rose and lily gardens of the rich, the thousands of spacious city parks and botanical gardens, and in our magnificent National parks—the Yellowstone, Yosemite, Sequoia, etc.—Nature's sublime wonderlands, the admiration and joy of the world. Nevertheless, like anything else worth while, from the very beginning, however well guarded, they have always been subject to attack by despoiling gain-seekers and mischief-makers of every degree from Satan to Senators, eagerly trying to make everything immediately and selfishly commercial, with schemes disguised in smug-smiling philanthropy, industriously, sham-piously crying 'Conservation, conservation, pan[-]utilization,' that man and beast may be fed and the dear Nation made great."

Message on an Observation-Blind Wall

Veteran New Jersey newspaper editor and political observer James Ahearn has carefully analyzed the many environmental, social, and economic factors at work in the Meadowlands today, and he does not see the preservation ambitions of the environmental activists as being in the cards for the Hackensack Meadowlands. "I don't think they will win, once [the SAMP] is adopted, and I think it *will* be adopted," Ahearn wrote in his syndicated column in September 1995, adding that today's political climate is basically hostile toward "the [SAMP] opponents' preferred alternatives, tax-paid land acquisition and restoration." Ultimately, Ahearn is convinced, leaving the remaining marshland acres of this glacial estuary just as they are "just isn't going to happen."

Over the long term, he is probably right. Although Meadowlands issues have garnered much media exposure during the course of the spirited public debate on the SAMP, and major concessions have already been made to reduce the density of the development that will be permitted, too few people yet view this river and estuary as anything other than a degraded environment whose day has passed. And still, the ambitions of the expanding megalopolis press in from every side, and will surely continue to do so.

Andy Willner and the others struggling to gain a stay of execution for the meadows are well aware that poor public image is one of the Meadowlands' liabilities. "We talk a lot about 'sense of place.' You can't get people protective about a place if they don't know it," Willner acknowledges. He knows that the campaign to preserve what remains of

*The double-crested cormorant, or sea crow (*Phalacrocorax auritus*), breeds on the Atlantic Coast from Newfoundland and the Gulf of Saint Lawrence to southern Maine—far from New Jersey. It is, nevertheless, a common and familiar waterbird in the Meadowlands, often seen flying in long, loose formations above the New Jersey Turnpike or the Pulaski Skyway. It is most abundant here in spring and fall, though nonbreeders may remain in the Meadowlands throughout the summer.*

the natural Meadowlands is nothing more than a desperate race between the intangibles of the human spirit, such as that ethereal "sense of place" and the desire to protect it for some distant posterity, and the relentless demand of the very tangible and immediate needs of those same human occupants of the expanding cities (who would, in fact, benefit from the meadows' preservation, if only they knew).

The race is not always to the swift, but time is nonetheless running out for the Hackensack Meadowlands.

In our youth we are bathed in that wonderful perceived light of immortality. We cannot see the end of our time. But as we age we learn the truth that we and our surroundings

Marsh Discovery Trail "boardwalk." This unique, self-guided trail, constructed of recycled waste plastic and floating on the waters of the Kingsland Impoundment, offers today's Meadowlands visitor easy entrance to a once virtually inaccessible habitat.

are finite. We may abrogate our responsibilities at any time, but collectively and individually we are always responsible–always. No excuses will suffice or be accepted by those who will inherit our legacy.

(*Michael Katakis,* Sacred Trusts)

Journal ✌

DeKorte Park, July 1995

I am alone on the Marsh Discovery Trail, an oddly rustic, floating "boardwalk" made of recycled plastic that ushers visitors across the dense reed beds and coffee-colored waters of the Kingsland Impoundment. Standing here, under a blazing sun and freshening breeze, I am struck by the unexpected beauty of this place and somewhat surprised that I am the only traveler—on a delightful summer Saturday.

This little corner of the "new" Meadowlands, rescued just in time from the encroaching twentieth-century glacier of garbage and groomed to perfection by the HMDC, is the park's crowning jewel. It is only in such mitigated, reconstituted habitats that a taste of the ancient meadows can be made available to the hurried people of the surrounding city. Today, interested suburbanites may casually stroll where once muskrat trappers and rail hunters found the going rough.

Tree swallows over Kingsland Impoundment, seen from the Marsh Discovery Trail, DeKorte Park.

Mallards, Kingsland Impoundment, DeKorte Park.

The wind is out of the southwest, muting the roar of the Turnpike's western spur, not a quarter mile to the east. But I am surrounded by nature here: a wall of reeds, ten feet high, green and shining and moving in the wind, creates the illusion of primal solitude. Beyond, an expanse of dun-colored water, corrugated by the breeze and set sparklingly afire by the sun, pushes against rafts of accumulated debris and dense mats of floating vegetation. The silhouettes of waterfowl dance and tremble on the bright water; in the superheated air squadrons of swallows and insects course by in busy, swirling confusion. A pair of egrets, necks folded and startlingly white against the blue, kite against the breeze overhead. A rail, hidden deep within the shadowed green reeds, begins to call—a dry, monotonous ticking sound, like two pebbles tapped together: *tickitickitick tick tick tick.* . . .

As I walk on, the view eastward opens up, and I see the familiar skyline of the city. The art deco spire of the Empire State Building and, to the south, the futuristic monoliths of the World Trade Center rise through the haze. The skyline, wavering, rippling in the burning air, seems an elusive mirage, but it is only too real, and so close to this vest-pocket wilderness that its thundering pulse can almost be felt.

Everything that has been accomplished here, in the Richard W. DeKorte Park, has been part of the concerted effort to turn an environmental sow's ear into an ecological silk purse containing natural treasures to be examined and marveled at—and, above all, appreciated, by a people who have long since ceased to expect them in such an unattractive setting, a place once synonymous with malevolent odors, with acres of soulless factories and warehouses, obscured by the smoke of burning dumps. The optimistic educators of the HMDC's environment center, people like Anne Galli, Don Smith, Ken Scarlatelli, and Bob Sikora, are convinced that the ancient message of the meadows— the positive one—will be duly passed on to the generations that will inherit them. And they believe that DeKorte Park is the best of all possible meadows worlds from which to deliver it. They sense a willing and receptive ear out here, particularly among the young, who have always been open to new ideas and faultless ideals: "Unless you turn and become like children, you cannot enter the kingdom."

Children are among the most enthusiastic participants in the center's environmental programs, Sikora has told me. They have few preconceived notions, or prejudices, on the ultimate worth of the Meadowlands as a place of communion with that part of their world they instinctively sense to be the truly meaningful part, and the part that is vanishing from their own future.

The many people who have had a hand in crafting DeKorte Park's carefully managed landscape look at what they have wrought and

Tree swallows at nest box, Marsh Discovery Trail, DeKorte Park. This species is
one of the commonest and most observable summer birds at DeKorte Park; the
nesting aggregations are always found near water. Tree swallows consume
enormous quantities of insects, including mosquitoes.

are not unhappy with the result, given the alternative. They, like the
activists of the Baykeeper and the River Tenders, have a sense of pro-
prietorship here. There may be deep disagreement among the environmental players in the drama of the Meadowlands, but the overall
unity of purpose is there. All of them love this river.

Other ecosystems in less peopled parts of our country are in danger of being loved to death by humanity, but the Hackensack estuary is

not one of them. It has been named one of the most threatened rivers in the United States; so the Hack's admirers are taking to the trenches, trying to nourish in others the love they have for these meadows. With love comes commitment, hopefully total.

As I stroll this softly bouncing walkway, made of ground-up plastic bottles and floating upon a swamp, I reflect on the novel values that permitted such a place to be opened for the edification of the people. Such a concept, on behalf of what had been universally regarded as forbidding wasteland, would have been inconceivable a generation ago, when I was a kid and prowled the swamps of the Overpeck to the north. For nearly all our history as a nation, in fact, places like wetlands had only few defenders: those who drew on the marshes' resources for their survival, or those rare individuals who were gifted with insight into the critical function of marshes in the cosmic scheme of things. Always a minority, the marsh advocates were usually found in the ranks of the academics, or among the "little people," those vaguely eccentric "nature lovers" with little or no authority to effect changes in public policy.

The impassioned conflict over the future of the Meadowlands has demonstrated that the balance of power has shifted somewhat in our age; the Meadowlands, the real Meadowlands, finally have their spokespeople. Whether their voices will be heard or heeded, and whether their long-term ideals will be incorporated into the biological entity that this ecosystem becomes in the next century, one cannot say right now.

I have arrived now at one of the rustic wooden observation blinds constructed at strategic points along the Marsh Discovery Trail. The little shed, modeled on the utilitarian simplicity of an old meadows gunner's blind, looks weathered and "woodsy" enough, but is only a few years old. It fronts on another wide lagoon and, beyond, the distant nub of Snake Hill with its Turnpike shackle. It is late afternoon, and the sun floods the open back of the hut with bright warmth. The corners of the blind are dusky with cobwebs; spiders lurk everywhere, trembling on their airy snares in predatory intensity. I peer out over the lagoon through the blind's narrow binocular and camera slot. Swallows flit by; a solitary sora rail emerges from the green gloom of the nearby reeds and pads tensely across the exposed mud. It places its long-toed feet very carefully, cocks its head, left and right, and flicks its short stubby tail like a chicken. The bright, shining bodies of insects fill the air in a living blizzard, and a quartet of egrets rises from the reeds across the lagoon and beats away into the wind. They resemble nothing more than dazzlingly white modern-day pterodactyls soaring against the blue.

I am suddenly aware that I have company. A middle-aged woman,

*Common egrets beating into the wind over Kingsland Impoundment,
DeKorte Park.*

lean and suntanned and dressed in hiking garb and sneakers, stands at
the next slot. She peers intently out at the lagoon through her binoculars, then turns to me and asks, "Is that a coot over there, or a gallinule?" She seems completely at ease, unafraid of addressing a male
stranger in a place quite far removed from the safety of crowds. I take
a look at the object of her interest: a darkish waterbird swims along the
flank of reeds at the edge of the lagoon, some ninety or a hundred feet
away. It pumps its head back and forth mechanically as it goes, like a
windup toy duck. Through my glass I note the bird's slate-gray body
and black head, the white shield on its forehead: "It's a coot," I inform
her. Very faintly, we can hear the bird clucking and grating to itself as it
swims.

We exchange pleasantries, and then the woman offers something
that rather surprises me: "You know," she said, "I can't tell you how
much I love this place; I come here all the time, all year." As though
to emphasize her conviction, she lifts her shoulders and inhales deeply
of the pungent marshy air, looking brightly about at the windy reeds,
the blue sky. Sensing the opportunity for an impromptu interview, I
shamefully ask her a leading question: What makes these surroundings

so special—what is there to love about a reconstituted swamp cheek by jowl with the New Jersey Turnpike?

"Are you kidding?" She has to shout, for a jet is passing overhead, on its way to Newark. "Where else could I get a close-up look at the glorious life in a living marsh, so close to New York?" She tells me that she lives in the city, works at "a fairly good job," and loves walking and bird-watching. "But I'm leery of Central Park." She says she cannot afford expensive journeys to the exotic, faraway places visited by "the 700 Club people" of the birding fraternity, so The Gateway's Jamaica Bay Wildlife Refuge and the Hackensack Meadowlands are the next best thing. "I have a thing about birds, and water," she says. "I love the sight and sound of the one and the smell of the other." On cue, we both turn into the wind, testing its offerings of water, and mud, and wet seaweed.

"I think places like this are kind of a confirmation," she says, "that we're not *all* bad, that we can save a place just because it's beautiful and worthwhile. So that everyone, people like me, can come and see it and experience it. Don't you agree?" I do, of course. I smile: "It's certainly much more meaningful than a theme park, right?"

*The common moorhen (*Gallinula chloropus*) (left) occurs from southern Canada to Argentina; in the Old World it is found in marsh habitats in Eurasia and Africa. Formerly called the common gallinule, it is a familiar breeding bird in Kearny Marsh and the Saw Mill Creek area and may be encountered elsewhere in suitable habitats, including the mitigated marshes. The closely related coot (*Fulica americana*) breeds from north-central Canada to northern South America, wintering as far north as ice-free conditions can be found. It is known to breed in Kearny Marsh East and West and the Saw Mill Creek area and is common in the Kingsland Impoundment and elsewhere as a winter resident.*

Female marsh hawk skimming over reeds on a hunt for mice, Lyndhurst Nature Reserve, DeKorte Park. The World Trade Center can be seen in the distance.

I am struck by this woman's almost childlike enthusiasm for this place. I can detect not a hint of the bitter cynicism sometimes evident in "nature types" who often pessimistically regard such small victories as a mere stay of execution for global nature. She did not mournfully recount the lost natural glories here, but rather she saw what had been gained. To her, this part of the world, set aside and then groomed for visitors like her who seek a link with nature, represents a kind of enclosed urban Eden. Nothing at all can be done about the past; it is only what exists here now, in the present moment, that matters. She seems not to question the motives of those who angled and arm-twisted and negotiated to forgo developing this place or filling it completely with garbage, or of those who finally relented and gave up their claim to what is now this park in the interest of posterity; it was, in the long run, simply wonderful that they did so.

As we stand here in the blind, feeling the sun's heat on our necks

and arms and talking about this particular little miracle in the Meadowlands, my eyes wander over the walls and then stop at a spot on the
unpainted boards, near a corner. Someone has scrawled a graffito, left
a message in crude, spiky block letters–a bold pronouncement loaded
with demand, at eye level, impossible to ignore. My companion follows my gaze, and we both step over and read the words. The writer
has asked a rhetorical question:

> *Where is your glorious earth?*
> *Where is your promised land?*
> *It has been beaten into submission,*
> *by the society you so covet.*

He, or she, then warns:

> *WAKE UP!*
> *I say unto you, I am*
> *the Mad Poet & I am God.*

I glance at the woman, waiting for a reaction. She sniffs with dis-
gust. "What crap–*here* is our glorious earth, right here!" she nearly
shouts, pointing down at the wooden planking we stand upon. She an-
grily moves to banish the desecration from the wall with a forefinger,
but the vandal, doubtless with malice aforethought, had used a permanent marker. "God!" she huffs. "Why, God is the very force that made
it possible for goodness to prevail here–for people to do the right thing
and preserve this instead of destroy it!"

But her outrage passes quickly. She realizes, I think, that fruitless
remonstrations are something of a thief here, of time perhaps better
spent in receiving the minute-by-minute gifts of the remaining day and
storing them as living memories for those far ahead. She smiles a bit
sheepishly and shrugs, perhaps embarrassed at having displayed such
deep emotion before a total stranger.

We bid each other a pleasant farewell and she steps off quickly,
before I think to ask her name. I note her progress up the walkway: she
walks briskly but stops frequently, now taking in the long view with her
binoculars, now leaning over the railing and peering intently down into
the mud and reeds at some small object or event of interest. She appears finely attuned to all happenings, like a small bird, determined to
miss nothing of the action and life to be found here. She is, I reflect, the
embodiment of the perennially enthusiastic "curious naturalist" of yore.

✍ ✍

Headquarters and environment center (right) of the Hackensack Meadowlands Development Commission, viewed from the Marsh Discovery Trail, DeKorte Park.

Later, while noting down our conversation for my journal, I found myself remembering another little encounter in the meadows, many years before. I had taken my twelve-year-old brother on a hike through what remained of the Overpeck's marshes one fall afternoon in the early 1960s. As we pushed our way through the tangle of burdocks and ragweed at the edge of the town dump, a cock pheasant blasted from cover right in front of us and rushed off over the reeds, shouting its raucous, rattling crow as it went. It was a heart-stopping event for both of us, but while I laughed it off as old hat, having jumped many pheasants before, my brother clearly regarded the bird's explosive flush as a major milestone in his life. "Wow, oh wow," he repeatedly breathed as we watched the bird race away, its long tail feathers streaming madly behind it like the exhaust flame of a rocket. He recounted that incident often to any family members and friends who would listen in the days and weeks after, and the experience was one of those outdoor encounters that prompted him to take up birding and then to pursue a career in the natural sciences.

I realized that my companion on the DeKorte Park boardwalk had

Service road, DeKorte Park. This view combines contrasting images of the region's vanishing rural past, in the lonely meadows road, and its fast-approaching high-tech future, expressed in the soaring monoliths of the World Trade Center.

somehow retained that coveted sense of wonder that biologist Rachel Carson spoke of as essential to understanding our world and then coming to love it. The woman at the park within the shadow of the city must have clung fiercely through her life to what my young brother had—an innocent, youthful vitality and interest in the world around her uncontaminated by the cumulative abrasion of cynicism. She had proven the Mad Poet wrong, and I envied her for that. For it is she, and all those who share her yearning for that elemental truth in wilderness, for whom the remnant natural Meadowlands are being fought for, preserved from destruction, and made ready for the new century.

POSTSCRIPT

"In the good society," writes economist John Kenneth Galbraith in his recent book of the same title, "voice and influence cannot be confined to one part of the population." To allow otherwise, he warns, is to ensure that money and power are "controlled by the affluent . . . and the business interests, and to them much political talent is inevitably drawn." Money and power are two social factors very close to the heart of the Meadowlands drama. For three hundred years, the acquisition of both has figured prominently in the actions of the many people who have effected great physical change in this estuary. It still does.

But Galbraith also insists that people have "an instinct, immediate or eventual, for what is right." If so, in that inherent sense of rightness lies the natural Meadowlands' only hope for survival. And the need here is immediate, not eventual.

Recently, the US Army Corps of Engineers held a public hearing on a proposal to build a giant shopping mall and office complex on a 206-acre tract in the Meadowlands. The project, called Meadowlands Mills, is the brainchild of the Mills Corporation, a Virginia-based developer. Empire Limited, a major Meadowlands player, has owned the tract since 1952. The Corps is involved because Mills proposes to pump dredge-fill onto the 206 acres, trading off the consequent wetland destruction with the mitigation of an adjacent 320 acres of phragmites. The mall complex will be, the developer says, but one-third the size of the sprawling Meadowlands Towne Center originally proposed for the site under the SAMP. But if it is built, Meadowlands Mills will be the largest mall in New Jersey, which already has plenty of big malls.

More than two hundred persons showed up for the hearing, which was held in East Rutherford's high school auditorium, at the edge of

GREEN HERON

BLACK-CROWNED
NIGHT HERON

GREAT BLUE HERON

HERONS

The great blue heron (Ardea herodius) occurs from southern Canada to Mexico. It is most often observed in freshwater and coastal marshes, on tidal flats, and along lakeshores. This tall, elegant, slate-gray wader is fairly common throughout the Meadowlands; it is most often seen in the Kingsland Impoundment and along the main stem of the Hackensack River. The species apparently does not breed within the district.

The green heron (Butorides striatus) is found in a wide variety of aquatic habitats, from lakeshores and stream sides to freshwater and brackish marshes. Formerly called the green-backed heron, it is common throughout most of the Meadowlands; look for it at the edges of meadows where trees and other upland vegetation provide both cover and nesting sites.

The black-crowned night heron (Nycticorax nycticorax) occurs in Eurasia, Africa, and the Americas, from southern Canada to Argentina; it is found in both fresh and brackish marshes and coastal habitats, usually near forested areas, where it roosts in trees. In the Meadowlands this night heron is fairly common in Kearny Marsh, the Saw Mill Creek area, and in the mitigated marshes.

the meadows. Sentiments seemed to be about equally divided between pro and con. Much of what was said by those testifying has been said dozens, maybe hundreds of times before in the Meadowlands debate, but this fact did not diminish the speakers' conviction or passion. Many of those present had plenty of money, power, or both; others simply wanted to acquire or ensure a little slice of it for themselves. Most of them spoke up for viable jobs and the ultimate welfare of people.

The environmental faction talked of long-term stewardship of the land and of respect for nature and its complex workings, without which neither people or jobs would long survive. Local environmental activists know that the fight to preserve what remains of the real Meadowlands has always been an uphill one. For despite the protestations of the development side, economic expansion, and not environmentalism, has determined the nature of the Meadowlands of today and will likely continue to do so. That's where the odds really are.

At the hearing, everyone who wanted a voice was granted one. Whether the testimony given in opposition to the project will influence its outcome remains to be seen. Probably it will not, for even the mall's most determined foes concede that the project's approval and completion is all but a foregone conclusion, the hearing a mere formality.

The testimony given at the hearing did offer, if nothing else, a clear summation of the conflict that has raged here for a generation. Robert Hillier, the project's architect, called Meadowlands Mills "a tremendous resource for the entire region" and insisted that "our children will be much better served" by its presence in the meadows. Richard Fritzky of the Meadowlands Regional Chamber of Commerce praised the project as "sound regional planning" and "a plan for the bold, not for the timid."

Andrew Willner of the New York–New Jersey Baykeeper voiced the environmental credo that land is not merely a commodity, an anonymous expanse of earth and rock to be bought and sold and put to the economic plow. Labeling the mall proposal "environmentally unjust," Willner said its proponents are blind to an elemental truth of the planet. "This marsh is not real estate; it belongs to the public trust, to all the people of the United States." Environmentalists oppose the project in part because its developers "have not even prepared an environmental impact statement," which, they say, violates the Corps of Engineers' own regulations concerning wetlands protection.

A representative of the state's building trades unions was unswayed by this argument. "I don't have a degree in environmental impact–I got a street degree," he grumbled; adding, "we have to get back to basics, back to worrying about people. We got a multitude of unemployed people out there."

And thus it went. Dozens got their ten minutes at the microphone.

AMERICAN EGRET

CATTLE
EGRET

SNOWY EGRET

EGRETS

The cattle egret (Bubulcus ibis) is native to southern Eurasia and Africa. It migrated to North and South America around the turn of the century and is now found along the Atlantic Coast form Florida to Massachusetts; it has also been introduced in Hawaii. This small, stocky egret is fairly common throughout the district; it usually associates with snowy and American egrets.

The large, all-white American egret (Casmerodius albus) occurs locally as a breeding bird throughout eastern North Amer-ica. It favors larger lakes and rivers, marshes, and coastal habitats. Also called the great egret, this strikingly graceful bird could well be considered the unofficial mascot of the Meadowlands District, as it appears on the HMDC logo. It may be seen almost everywhere in the meadows, especially near water.

The snowy egret (Egretta thula) occurs from the northern United States south to Argentina, usually in swamps and marshes, on tidal flats, or in coastal ponds. A common resident and breeder, this little egret is certainly one of the more familiar waders of the Meadowlands.

Some were dressed in business suits; many wore jeans, T-shirts, and baseball caps. They were shod in wing tips, high heels, Docksiders, and work boots. The diversity of the human fauna engaged in the debate over the Meadowlands is nearly equal to that to be found out there among the reeds and tidal creeks.

After the hearing I drove north through the streets of Carlstadt and, on impulse, turned onto one that offered a wide panorama of the Meadowlands to the east. I stepped from the car and took in the view. Out where the ancient Hackensack River makes an easy curve, near a pair of big white gas tanks and the western spur of the New Jersey Turnpike, lay the tract of land whose fate was being decided. From the street, the area had the look of the meadows of old, the forbidding expanse of reeds and water that the colonial Dutch found here and quickly determined to bring to heel as productive farmland. Surrounded by roads and the city, the Empire tract was somehow isolated from it all—a windy, green field of sun and grass beneath a sky filled with great mountains of cloud and wheeling gulls. It was really quite beautiful, and it seemed to be suspended in time, as though waiting for something.

As I scanned the scene, I noticed that here and there, all about the periphery of the meadows, could be seen heavy machinery—cranes, backhoes, bulldozers—the tools of human progress, the machines that have helped us reshape a continent. Most of them were motionless, silent, poking above the landscape like so many massive sculptures in some sort of industrial Jurassic Park. They, like the rippled sward of reeds at the center of this old glacial valley, seemed for the moment to be suspended in time, poised in watchful waiting.

In and of themselves these machines are powerless, but on command they will work wonders here. So instructed, our machines will move mountains—or marshes—on our behalf. And then, yard by yard, acre by acre, mile by mile, the green vistas of this prehistoric estuary will continue the long journey toward their ultimate destiny.

September 1996

Epilogue

The rock cannot be broken. It is the truth. It rises from land
and sea and covers them.

WALLACE STEVENS, *Credences of Summer*

Snake Hill, one of the better-known geological features on the
East Coast, rises nearly two hundred feet above the town of Secaucus. It is a unique and seemingly out-of-place natural feature on this
flat coastal plain—a small mountain you can climb, in the marshes.
Though assaulted by quarrymen over the decades and today bisected
by the eastern spur of the New Jersey Turnpike, "the rock," as this
rugged outcrop is known to those familiar with it, has persisted against
considerable odds. It is a monument to the long ages required in its
creation, and one of the physical symbols of the modern Meadowlands.

The hill's familiar profile was, in fact, the home-grown inspiration
for the Prudential Insurance Company's famous "Rock of Gibraltar"
logo. Passing by this meadows prominence northbound on the Turnpike's eastern spur that bisects it, a motorist can still readily recognize
the craggy monolith as the model for the Pru's distinctive trademark.
At various times over the past two hundred years, the big hill has supported an almshouse, a state mental institution, and a collection of
squatters' shacks; it also served as the shooting location for an early
twentieth-century war movie.

Today, the rock rises from a fragmented and industrialized landscape, simply existing for what it is—an extruded plug of Triassic diabase. Subterranean magma, as differentiated from surface-flowing lava,
is the the product of volcanic activity deep within the earth, and this
forms the matrix of Snake Hill. Its rock was molten, underground, during an age that witnessed the genesis of the dinosaurs. Geologists know

Snake Hill. The rock's familiar profile looms beside the New Jersey Turnpike's elevated section, eastern spur, in Secaucus.

it as an aberrant extension, or "string," of the nearby Palisades magma as it pushed into the Newark Basin strata about 170 million years ago. As the softer, surrounding rock weathered away, this plug of diabase stood its ground, breaching the surface and then rising above as the surrounding rocks continued to erode. Now an imposing monolith, it seems to be an ancient artifact of magnificent geologic redundancy. Its vast, hazy, and brooding shape standing on the horizon seems that of a reclining giant, at rest for now but marshaling itself to rise up and shrug off the concrete and steel that lash it, Gulliver-like, to an alien ground.

Although I could find no record of Lenape legends concerning Big Snake Hill, it is difficult to believe that it did not have some spiritual significance for the early Lenape peoples. Native Americans have long assigned the more massive and prominent landmarks of their world a special cultural and spiritual standing, if for no other reason than the feeling that such high places brought them closer to the realm of the *manitta*, the beings of the spirit world. At least one Lenape sachem, known by the Dutch only as "Hans," reportedly lived in solitude at the base of the hill in the late seventeenth century.

At that time, three centuries ago, this hill, clothed in lush forest, rose unfettered from a wild and beautiful landscape in every sense worthy of a national park. The early Dutch residents of New Netherland called it *slangenberk*–literally, "snake hill," or "rattlesnake hill," due to the large number of both harmless and venomous snakes they encountered there.

Indeed, the hill's association with snakes is much older, and it survives even now in the name of the borough in which the rock lies. The name Secaucus was derived from two words in the Lenape Munsee dialect: *Sika* ("fright") and *Aki* ("land")–thus, a place to be avoided due to the great number of dangerous snakes found there. The seventeenth-century Dutch knew the current town site as Islandt Sikakes, from the Lenape word meaning "a salt sedge marsh." In any case, the early farmers regarded the firm ground flanking the north side of Snake Hill as highly fertile territory, and many established thriving plantations there.

But the persistent human dread of serpents continued to dominate the historical image of Snake Hill. A seventeenth-century historian reported, doubtless with some exaggeration, that the meadows surrounding the hill were "infested with huge black water snakes, many of them twelve to fifteen feet long." As late as the 1870s the reptilian residents of the place kept human inhabitants at bay. The editor of the *Bayonne Evening News* related a boat trip on the Hackensack River during which he observed that the passing shoreline of Snake Hill "was alive with

*The northern water snake (*Nerodia sipedon*) occurs from Maine and southern Quebec south to northeastern North Carolina, including the Outer Banks. Although not abundant, this harmless though aggressive snake may be found in heavily vegetated freshwater impoundments such as the Kingsland Impoundment in DeKorte Park as well as in mildly brackish habitats like Overpeck and Losen Slote Creeks.*

huge snakes, some of them scintillating with the bronze-like character-
istics of these reptiles when in best condition. For not less than a quarter
mile of shoreline, the steep bank was a mass of hissing, squirming, vil-
lainous water snakes." Big, belligerent water snakes and the common,
entirely beneficial blacksnake are but a memory on Snake Hill today,
though they were apparently still in residence in declining numbers in
the first decade of this century. The only serpents that might be found
among the rocks of the hill now are the city-adapted brown snake (*Sto-
reria dekayi*) and the familiar, mild-mannered garter snake (*Thamnophis
sirtalis*).

As wild creatures retreated from the region under the press of civilization, so too did the vista of unspoiled wilderness. But in 1834 the
view from Snake Hill was apparently still worthy of comment. The
Gazetteer of the State of New Jersey, with descriptions that would seem appropriate even today, noted that the "promontory at the south end of
the 'island called Secaucus' known as Snake Hill has a conical form
that rises into mural precipices," and "from its wood-clad, rocky and
precipitous summit, the spectator may behold the Hackensack and Passaic Rivers almost at his feet, and for several miles dragging their slow
length through a sea of verdure; on the west, populous villages and
ranges of mountains; on the east the great city of New York, and on the
south the wide expanded ocean." In that same year an early climber
to the rock's summit, one Thomas Gordon, referred to Snake Hill as
"a very distinguished elevation."

Perhaps with that noble heritage in mind, Hudson County in 1915
determined that the centuries-old appellation of Snake Hill somehow
denigrated the outcrop; county officials changed the rock's name to
Laurel Hill–"the crowning Laurel of Hudson County." For many years
this sanitized and prettified name fell in and out of common favor; the
prominence has remained, for most residents, the *slangenberk* of the
early Dutch. Today, however, the rock has again been "officially" re-
christened Laurel Hill, and it will be the centerpiece of a planned Meadowlands park.

Preservation may not seem necessary for solid rock, but Snake Hill
was, in fact, a threatened landmark. Such exemplary building material
has many uses, especially when located conveniently close to large
cities. Both Snake Hill and its pint-size neighbor, the densely wooded
Little Snake Hill, are magma eskers, or "pipes," extruded through un-
derlying sandstone; on cooling this magma formed the diabase, or
"traprock," of modern road builders. The term derives from the Swed-
ish word *trapp*, meaning stairs, and was first applied to the towering, colonnaded formations of the three-hundred-foot-high Palisades to
the east.

Before the quarrying started, New Jersey state geologist George

Cook in 1868 described the Meadowlands' traprock hills in all their glorious natural bulk:

> These two trap hills rise out of the salt-meadows, west of Bergen Hill, and on the east side of the Hackensack River. This river washes the western edge of the larger of these hills, for a distance of a quarter of a mile. The hill has its greatest diameter in a northeast and southwest line. This measures half a mile, the circumference of the polygonal outcrop being about one and a half miles. The faces towards the south and southeast are rocky and precipitous. That towards the west is also quite steep. The northeast slope is more gentle, consisting of red shale drift upon red sandstone. . . . otherwise the whole hill is trap, covered in most places by a scanty soil or thin beds of earth and gravel. The maximum height above the surrounding marsh is about two hundred feet. A straggling growth of cedars, with a few oak, hickory and butternut trees crown this rocky mound. Tide-water and salt-marsh surround it except on the north, where a narrow strip of swamp, slightly above high-tide mark, connects it with the low upland of Secaucus, the whole forming a rocky peninsula. . . .
>
> About a quarter of a mile southeast of Big Snake Hill is the small, circular island of rock known as Little Snake Hill. Salt-marsh surrounds it, making it an upland island in the wet meadows. Its form is that of a truncated cone, whose diameters are one hundred and twenty yards long and seventy yards wide. Its extreme elevation above the marsh is seventy-eight feet. The trap of this hill rises abruptly from the marsh on all sides, except the south, where the slope is very steep. No shale or other rock than trap is seen on it, either in situ, or loose, as in drift. A few scattering trees find support in the scanty soil that covers the summit of this rocky knob.
>
> (*The Geology and Geography of New Jersey, 1964*)

The mining of Snake Hill for its traprock commenced in the late 1800s and continued, with interruptions, through the middle years of this century. The American Trap Rock Company set up shop at the south end of the hill, at the point where today the Turnpike overpass casts its shadow on the weathered rock ramparts. Snake Hill is also the stuff of which Manhattan's architectural artifices were made. It had been quarried down as far as it was destined to be by 1982, when excavations ceased.

Nicholas Facciolla, in *Minerals of Laurel Hill*, his delightful 1982

Snake Hill in the early 1870s. From a painting, Snake Hill on the Jersey
Meadows, *by Charles Parsons (1871), courtesy the Hackensack Meadowlands
Development Commission.*

treatise on both outcrops, speaks with some irony of Snake Hill's demolition in spite of its commemorated solidity. Although "Prudential . . .
has strengthened and grown through the years into a gigantic corporation," Facciolla says, "it is sad to report that Snake Hill is being sapped
of all its strength through demolition. In a few more years, it may only
be a memory."

But such was not to be. Snake Hill survived the dynamite of its

would-be destroyers and today rises from an industrial landscape that bears no resemblance to the verdant meadows and lowland forest of yore. Photographs taken in the 1970s, when quarrying was in full swing, show a shattered, hard-edged mound of rubble that has the appearance of a lifeless lunar mountain. Today, a lush crown of vegetation has somewhat softened the outcrop's rugged outline, giving it a far more natural and appealing look. Still, the rock itself is far from pristine.

Snake Hill from the west, showing terraces of quarrying activity. Most of the open area where two figures stand was part of the hill's base; thus some estimate may be gained of the great volume of traprock extracted from Snake Hill.

Facciolla wrote in 1981 of the toll the quarrying had taken on the hill's original mass:

> The major part of the contract to demolish Snake Hill has been completed. The extracted center of the hill is completely leveled off to 3 metres [10 feet] above sea level, with a horseshoe-shaped rim of walls remaining. The west wall which is completely leveled off to the Hackensack River's edge, can be referred to as the open end of a horseshoe. If one were to stand in the open end, facing eastward toward New York City, he would be confronted with exposures of rock and equipment, revealing the past operations and visible geology of Snake Hill as plain as reading a book.

The hollowed-out rock that survives here now remains primeval, still anchored in the earth. It is a monument to the planet itself and a mute reminder, beside the restless Turnpike, that our hurried errands may be stripped of their meaning in the merest blink of time's eye: "Though the generations passeth away, the earth endureth."

Meadowlands naturalist Don Smith, like most of those who appreciate these meadows, has a thing about the rock. He has, on occasion, packed a lunch up to the summit when he felt a need for some solitude. Not long ago I stood with him in the parking lot of the HMDC's environment center, and we looked across the flat, reedy landscape at the hill. There it loomed, as always, half-hidden in a milky scrim of haze, seemingly wired to the earth by the graceful arc of the Turnpike's eastern spur, the city rising in the background.

I asked Smith whether there might be any designs on the remnant, as a consequence of the SAMP. Was the ancient rock destined, as a part of this grand and, hopefully, final plan for the meadows, to be quarried down to the vanishing point, to make way for an office complex? A railyard, perhaps? Another regional shopping mall? Or would it be permitted to stand as a craggy, tree-crowned epitaph to the virgin wilderness this place once was?

"It stays," Smith confirmed, immediately and with emphasis. In fact, he told me, the hill will be incorporated into a new Hudson County riverside park, complete with a boat-launching ramp. He said that while the quarrymen of the past are gone, presumably never to return, modern graffiti artists and off-road-vehicle enthusiasts take a lesser though significant toll on the rocky nub's fragile substrate and vegetation. Dubbed "fraternity rock" by irreverent radio traffic reporters because of the colorful riot of graffiti plastered upon its eastern face, it is still not completely out of danger.

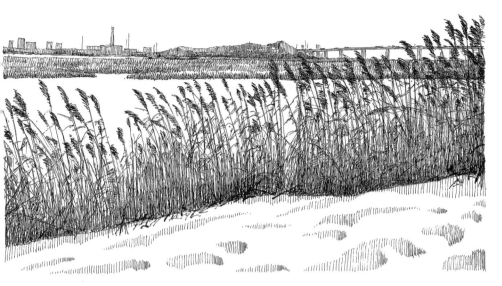

Snake Hill, seen from Kingsland Impoundment, DeKorte Park.

From the edge of the meadows, none of this vulnerability can be seen. Snake Hill has the look of an enormous, exposed vertebra; close up it gives the impression of another, and oddly exotic, world. It has been called an "urban alpine habitat," though such—at a mere two hundred feet elevation—it is not. Nevertheless, it seems a displaced fragment of the primal wilderness, plopped down out of the sky, inviting closer inspection.

Journal ✒

FALL 1995: THE VIEW FROM SNAKE HILL

Although its summit offers spectacular views of the entire New York– New Jersey metropolitan area, from the foothills of the Catskills and the Watchungs to Sandy Hook and the sea beyond, few people are inclined to visit Snake Hill today. In one of the most transportation-intensive regions on Earth, it stands alone in magnificent isolation.

I went there on a bright late-November morning to take what would be my first real look at the place. I had never visited the hill, though it lay a mere seven miles and twenty minutes from my home. I planned to climb to the summit, a rather sharply angled cairn at the south end of the outcrop, topped by a few windblown trees and hardy grasses. I had often glanced up at the modest peak as I passed it quickly among the rushing throng on the Turnpike below. Now I would take a

seat on one of its weathered boulders and try to absorb the view it offers—the long-term, geologic-scale view—of the modern Meadowlands.

The route to Snake Hill passes through surroundings that are de-
pressingly typical of urban America. Secaucus is a meadows town—perhaps *the* archetypal one, for it was at one time completely surrounded
by marshland. The borough has long struggled to live down the stigma
of the infamous pig farms of its past and maintain its sense of community, while simultaneously being swallowed by the industrial and transportation hub that has engulfed the region at large. The pigs were long
ago banished, but today the borough treads water against a rising tide
of upscale retail outlets that have become its modern symbol.

As though in response to this relentless urbanization, the town has
had more than its share of local environmentalists and political gadflies.
Bill Sheehan of the River Tenders is one. Anthony Just, the borough's
current mayor, is both a local historian and an ardent conservationist;
he is a vocal critic of unplanned development in his borough's wetlands and implacably opposed to the huge Allied Junction railroad terminus slated for the town by the SAMP.

Secaucus is also a town dominated by trucks; they transport every
conceivable product, locally and long distance, from perishable goods
to garbage, over the malevolent Route 3 and all the major trunk roads
that section the borough. One of these is County Avenue. For most of
its length, County Avenue is an industrial and commercial roadway, a
place of nondescript buildings, constant noise, and exhaust fumes. I
drove its length, crossing two sets of railroad tracks to the gateway to
the old quarry. Flanked by a county "pre-release" jail complex, it appears in undistinguished, chain-linked splendor.

The environs of the hill have undergone considerable change.
Once an empty, windswept quarry by the river, an isolated and potentially dangerous place, the area today is being groomed for the anticipated arrival of a recreational public. This is a positive prospect, but
somehow, through accessibility and then familiarity, much of Snake
Hill's mystique and symbolism will be taken from it. In the past, when
the rock was called Long Neck or Mount Pinhorne, it was the talked-
about site of prisons, the state "lunatic asylum" and "almshouse," and
other vague "public institutions," not to mention being the haunt of il-
licit midnight dumpers, vagrants, and the ghosts of long-dead Hessians.
In the early years of this century a colony of squatters assembled a tiny
settlement of shacks atop the hill; they were finally evicted and their
Meadowlands Hooverville dismantled when large-scale quarrying began in the 1960s. After the quarrymen packed up and abandoned the
place, few rational people ventured there, especially at night. Snake
Hill stood alone once more, like a forgotten, weed-choked graveyard,

its machine-carved canyons and escarpments echoing with the whispers of the past and the sea wind off the meadows.

As I stood at the base of the hill, on the flat and gravelly plain liberally sown with broken glass, shards of pulverized traprock, and sun-dried grasses, I contemplated the soaring rock flank before me and my ultimate objective, its rubbly, tree-lined summit. The rock waited there, an enormous, shadowy silhouette in the cold morning sunlight, the slanting terraces of the quarrymen cut into its western side. But Snake Hill is not large. It covers a mere twelve acres—in its reduced size, hardly a Mount Washington—though it was larger in the past, before the road builders got to it. Yet the outcrop stands tall, somehow, in the imagination. Maybe it's because it seems so completely out of place here.

On Don Smith's suggestion, I chose the north end of the rock to start my ascent. Here, at the base of a huge, graffiti-scrawled, yellow-brick chimney rising from a crumbling foundation, a rusted chain-link fence proceeds up a steep slope densely clothed in gnarled though sturdy oaks. "You'll have to use the fence as a handrail going up," Smith had cautioned me, warning that last year's oak leaves underfoot would make the going slippery. They indeed did, but as I toiled upward along the fence, almost literally hand over hand, I felt a growing sense of excitement as I watched the brow of the hill, and the bright blue sky, draw ever closer. What would I find just over the first rise?

For much of its length Snake Hill's upland terrain undulates and appears graded, doubtless due to the activities of the excavators and their heavy equipment. Much of it is clothed in a modest "forest" of chestnut oak, red oak, hackberry, black cherry, and other hardy tree species. The rest, particularly along the ridge, or spine, of the outcrop, is a grassy heath of goldenrod, panic grass, mullein, Queen Anne's lace, and a host of other adaptable, survivor-type vegetation. A 1991 survey of the hill's vegetation conducted by the Torrey Botanical Club came up with 115 species of trees, shrubs, and herbaceous plants resident there; the HMDC's own botanical inventory lists 145 species, one of them—the wafer ash (*Ptelea trifoliata*)—ranked as an endangered species in New Jersey.

By and large, the ridgetop environment seems one of untrammeled nature, for little of the trash and litter one might expect in such a place is to be seen among the trees and the scree. Two plastic five-gallon pails and a battered folding chair nestled among a tangle of briars; they appeared weathered, and I wondered how in the world they came to be discarded here. As I walked on through this odd little urban woodland in the bright November sun the roar of the nearby Turnpike was muted by the trees, and I heard the familiar call of a cardinal; the

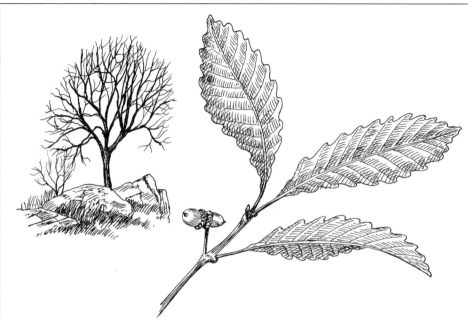

*The chestnut oak (*Quercus prinus*) occurs in eastern North America from New England south to Georgia, mostly at higher elevations. Also known as the rock oak, this tree is partial to dry, rocky soils of the type found on the ridge and summit of Snake Hill. The chestnut oak occupies a narrow outcrop habitat there, which it shares with red and black oaks, hackberry, and staghorn sumac.*

bird streaked away through the trees, a wonderfully bright flash of red among the grays and browns of November. A few feet away a late-season gray-cheeked thrush scratched industriously in the leaf litter, and a blue jay screamed a little higher up; I was both surprised and pleased that not a street pigeon, starling, or house sparrow was within sight or sound.

As I walked on, I soon found myself confronted by a narrowing of travel options. Ahead and to the left, the wooded slope became steeper and the challenge of the climb much greater. To the right, the narrow spine of the hill gradually rose toward, I hoped, the still-invisible summit, and although a tangle of undergrowth and a cairn of large angular boulders barred the way, I decided that this was the route to take.

Along the irregular spine of the ridge the trail meandered but was fairly well defined, apparently having been kept open by the occasional youthful climber armed with a spray can and an artistic flair. As I neared the summit, the ridge narrowed so that I felt as though I were treading gingerly upon the keel of an overturned ship; on one side the woods sloped away toward the Turnpike, on the other, the abyss. Then the path dipped into a steep gully—a crevasse of sorts—and just ahead lay the final obstacle to the peak itself. It was a series of "steps" in the jumbled cascade of traprock rubble that led roughly ten feet up to a large rounded rock face. Looking at this craggy Everest-in-miniature before me, I saw here, in miniature, a confirmation of a nineteenth-century climber's awe at "the savage grandeur of riven rock and contorted glacier" of the Alps. Here, ages ago, the ice had done its work on Snake Hill as well.

This modest, seamed rock face was all that now stood in my way; it would have to be scaled, and the rest of the way to the top would be, presumably, the figurative piece of cake. But here, right at the brink of success, I had a completely unexpected recurrence of my old, though usually dormant, fear of heights. As I hauled myself to the very lip of the shelf, huffing with the effort, I squatted on the last rocky step and glanced down. A brisk wind poured up the eastern flank of the ridge, bringing with it the roar of the Turnpike traffic; on the other side, the rocks shelved off for about ten feet and then dropped straight to the ground below. I glanced up; five or six feet higher, over the rim of the breastwork, lay the path to the peak. As I realized that I would have to come to a standing position on the narrow step and pull myself over the edge, I felt my heart rate pick up speed. The sun was burning the back of my neck, the traffic din rising unabated from below; I felt a strange and disturbing panic rising within me. Could I accomplish so simple an effort as turning around, standing up, and climbing six more feet of rock—two hundred feet above the Meadowlands below? At that moment, as I computed the height and my heart pounded and my breathing accelerated, I had my doubts.

Why, I asked myself, on the very cusp of success, am I going to be denied it? I mean, for God's sake, this isn't a big mountain; it's not even a mountain at all! Think of all the people who have been here before—kids with spray cans. Teenage girls probably, for crying out loud! Chicken, coward. . . .

But it was no good; the fear whispered in my ear, snuggled close, wrapped its cloak around me. I considered going back, photographing the summit from the first, and safer, ridge. But it wouldn't be the same, not at all; and as I fought to control my strange, debilitating panic, a memory crept into my mind. Twenty years before, I, as a neophyte mountaineer, had climbed the nine-hundred-foot-high White Horse Ledge in northern New Hampshire in the company of experienced climbers. I had brashly (having had more than a few drinks) accepted a cocktail party challenge issued by a rock-climbing friend. I would soon live to regret it.

Equipped with helmets, ropes capable of bearing the weight of a

Volkswagen, and all manner of foolproof climbing gear with odd names like piton and carabiner, it took the four of us more than half a day to reach the forested top of the ledge. Part of the climb—the final third—was made over faces of near-vertical rock with handholds about as wide as a fingernail. In our preclimb briefing, I and the other newcomer to the sport were assured that there was no danger if we followed instructions and that we would at all times be secured by ropes to those who knew what they were doing up there.

Halfway up the cliff, after a relatively easy ascent up a forty-five- to fifty-degree slope, we arrived at a narrow shelf known to local climbers as "the lunch ledge." Here, devouring our spartan trail mix of peanuts, granola, and raisins and downing volumes of water, our legs dangling over the abyss, we reviewed the strategies ahead; I tried to envision what this lonely place might be like in the middle of winter, the winds howling out of the valley below, the cliff sheathed in iron-hard ice. At the same time I privately pondered the social repercussions of turning back. Although the climb had not been overly taxing so far, the reality of my situation was hammered home as I watched a small plane fly by about two hundred feet below us. The lunch ledge was at least seven hundred feet above terra firma, and as I leaned out and gazed upward, what I saw terrified me.

I began to doubt that I had the courage to crawl over a sheer rock wall like the human spider I most assuredly was not, ropes or no ropes. But we were all trapped by our own machismo. I knew that I could not back down; it would be an admission of cowardice. There was also the fact that I could not, in any case, make it back down the ledge unaided. And the certainty of this, that there was no turning back, brought with it the realization that I was engaged in what now seemed a pointless and foolish exercise.

Somehow, without betraying my fear to the others, I managed to talk myself back to a level of control that enabled me to go on. Although my memory of the remainder of the climb is perhaps mercifully obscured by the passage of time, I do remember tension-filled belays across great curved breastworks of rock during which we could not see one another. Our leader drove fresh pitons into cracks when he did not trust those left by previous climbers, and we clipped and unclipped our carabiners to these reluctantly abandoned safe-stations as we slowly made our way skyward. We managed, nearly two hours later, to attain the blessed safety of the woods nearly a thousand feet above the cliff's base. I suppressed an impulse to kiss the damp, leafy litter of the forest floor. We hooted in triumph, punched each other, threw food around, and generally acted like "real guys." But it took a long time for the terror to subside within me.

Back on the Snake Hill ledge, I felt my breathing rate slow as I relived the memory of that past climb, not only the terror but also the immense satisfaction we had all felt at its completion. Although I knew that a slip and fall from a two-hundred-foot height could kill you just as dead as one from seven hundred feet, I knew that here, a mere thirty paces from my objective, I would not allow that old, crippling fear to carry the day.

I briskly surmounted the last obstacle of humped rock, crawling over its smooth lip, and stood up; about sixty feet of rocky incline lay between me and the summit. Above was the rich blue vault of the sky. To my left the sunlit, mixed red and black oak forest fell steeply away to the Turnpike; to the immediate right, a mere two or three paces distant, the spine of the hill ended abruptly and then fell away in a sheer drop to the gritty, shadowed plain far below. I felt the morning sun on my face and impulsively looked down and waved my arm overhead; a tiny shadow-figure on the ground far below responded in kind. I felt like Sir Edmund Hillary, the pinnacle of my own private Everest an easy walk away.

The very top of the Snake Hill outcrop is an interesting little piece of the planet. The spectacular view aside, there can be few other microhabitats like it in the Northeast. The summit is a gently sloping plateau of exposed and weathered rock interspersed with a substrate of soft and surprisingly rich humus. I saw that there had apparently been a recent fire, as much of the naked and sere earth was littered with burned and blackened plant detritus. Among the rocks, flattened mats of tiny, bright green, round-leafed plants hunkered out of the reach of the winds. Although the peak was rumored to be an alpine habitat magically transplanted into the middle of the megalopolis, the vegetation in fact is that characteristic of the higher rocky elevations found in Sussex County or the Ramapo Mountains. Alpine is defined as "being between four thousand and six thousand feet altitude, not two hundred feet," a member of the New Jersey Native Plant Society had reminded me.

A small vanguard of the knob's unique chestnut oaks, looking surprisingly robust and healthy, graced the path to the top. Sparse and hardy black cherry, hackberry, staghorn sumac, and ailanthus trees, seemingly few of branch and contorted of form, as though in anguished recoil from an unforgiving environment, stood at the highest point itself and comprised the "alpine forest" at this heady altitude.

As I walked up to the peak, following the angle of a rusting pipe set upon stanchions and running right up to the top, I marveled at the variegated tapestry of the omnipresent graffiti; some of it was old, very faded, but much of it was obviously fresh and quite colorful. "Gino" and "Patty Spatz" had been here sometime in 1993; the "Beaste Boys"

Summit of Snake Hill. Most of the available rock surfaces are scrawled with graffiti. The actual peak is something of a geological cliché: the sharply pointed rock just right of center in the drawing.

White rock, Snake Hill summit. Graffiti artists covered this entire boulder with a coat of dazzling "appliance white" paint before inscribing it with multicolored designs. This rock is starkly visible, even at night, from the Turnpike below. The raptor is a red-tailed hawk, a species often observed riding thermals up the flank of this urban minimountain.

left their calling card on "8/8/94." "Ryan Caldwell" had paid a visit to the peak in 1980. The nearly perfectly triangular boulder that is the actual peak of Snake Hill had been claimed as a canvas by a kid named "Jay Luty." Maybe he was a thirtysomething fellow raising a family by now, for the faded whitewashed script had doubtless been there for years. On a south-facing flank of rock, it was announced to Turnpike riders that "WE" had looked down on them, the word accompanied by a huge, freestyle caricature of a human face.

I marveled at the ancient desire of humankind to leave a record of its passing, a desire that surely persists into the Age of Technology. Do these graffiti belong to the prehistoric tradition of rock art, or are they merely desecration, a form of expression no longer appropriate? Flowering upon the rocks in intricate, bright configurations in a rainbow of turquoise, white, red, orange, and green hues, the Snake Hill graffiti has an odd beauty that might, if one is enough of an anthropologist, be viewed as a valid artifact expressing the enduring creativity of the human spirit.

I found very little trash at the peak: three beer cans (one of them stuck on the end of a tree branch), a rusted and crumbling aerosol can, a couple of lengths of telephone cable, and what appeared to be the valve spring of an auto engine. I had once read that a Sierra Club crew had hauled a half-ton of trash off the "pristine" summit of Alaska's Mount McKinley. All things considered, Snake Hill had gotten off lucky.

Standing on the brow of the eastern escarpment, overlooking the Turnpike, I spotted a familiar object: a rusted climber's piton, sprouting from a seam in the living rock. As observed from the highway below, it is evident that some of Snake Hill's "paintings" are situated on vertical rock faces accessible only by rappelling down a rope; one had to admire the determination and bravado required to reach these lofty galleries!

Studying the lay of the land at the summit, I had no idea whether these very same square yards of rock and muddy soil once hosted a Lenape warrior, or perhaps offered a seat to climber Gordon in 1834. Given the relentless will of weather and gravity over the centuries and the work of quarrymen over the decades, I had my doubts. The jumbled mass of boulders making up the south flank of the mountain looked hard-edged and fresh, in disarray, as though quarrying had indeed ceased there only recently. Was the present summit, in fact, all that remained of an even higher prominence? Although the old accounts gave the outcrop's original elevation as 202 feet, I had read somewhere that the systematic extraction of its traprock over the years had resulted in a revised height of 160 feet. From my vantage point, the ground below seemed awfully far away—surely farther than 160 feet; the loaded dump trucks lumbering dustily over the service road to the Amtrak construction project under the Turnpike span looked no bigger than Matchbox toys. I looked to the west, toward the broad Saw Mill marsh. I noted the deep, semicircular amphitheaters and the angled terraces that had been gouged into the western side of the hill and lent the place the look of a Western "big sky" canyon; their sheer size clearly represented a huge volume of extracted rock. They gave the scene a stark, angular kind of beauty, like that of a manufactured Bryce Canyon. The sunlit traprock, a striated and brilliant reddish and tan, stained with what was surely the collective rainstorms of centuries, lay shadowed in delicate reds, blues, and purples wherever fissures and carved caverns broke the regularity of the walls.

It was altogether a wildly beautiful and almost spiritual place, a cathedral whose blasted and shaved arches and machined galleries seemed meant to resound with song. The acoustics of this artificial canyon were such that the rich warbling tunes of a mockingbird concealed

Rock climber's piton near the summit of Snake Hill. This climbing aid, more often used in the Alps or the Rockies, was probably hammered in by a graffiti artist determined to reach a particular overhang visible from the Turnpike.

Western view from the ridge of Snake Hill, 1970s. This scene takes in the extensive Saw Mill Creek area, the western spur of the New Jersey Turnpike, and the low ridges of the Watchung Mountains in the far distance. From a photo courtesy the Hackensack Meadowlands Development Commission.

far below on the rutted flatland at the hill's base were carried up to my ear on the southeast wind off the meadows. It was a moment made for contemplation; so I walked to the south face of the peak, found a convenient rock warmed by the sun, and sat in quiet reflection of the amazing scene that unfolded before me.

Looking south over the Meadowlands from Snake Hill, toward the gray ramparts of Jersey City, the grimy industrial tangles of Bayonne and Kearny, and the forest of chimneys and standpipes busily pumping the "smell of money" into the patient atmosphere, one might be forgiven the impulse to tap one's forehead rhythmically against the graffitied wailing wall of Snake Hill in atonement for our many sins against this lovely little planet. Surely, this New World glacial estuary now harbors but a transplanted Old World Glasgow or Ruhr valley in all its profligate and toxic ugliness. But standing there, atop my isolated little mountaintop, I found myself overcome by emotion as the sheer power and humanity of the place washed over me from below. The solid mass of the hill beneath me rose like the prow of a ship, and against it broke a continuous wave of sound. The roar, which seemed to come from the Turnpike below, nonetheless seemed to have a pulse, like that of a gargantuan heartbeat. As its waves struck and swept up the rock and flooded past my ears, I realized that its true source was the entire valley itself. Contained here, between the sea and the low hills to the west, were a multitude of living things so beyond counting that the scene's dimensions could not be fully grasped by a mere human. Everywhere I turned, in every quarter where the landscape shelved away in receding horizons of hazy buildings, convoluted roadways, and marshy flatlands, the ceaseless motion of machinery and living things was evident. The sun winked from the windshields and chrome of a hundred thousand moving cars and trucks; they plied the roads and bridges, coming and going, from all points of the compass.

Aircraft rose, glinting in the sun, from Newark Airport far to the south. Clearly here was a ponderous and directionless migration in progress; valleys have always been convenient and logical settings for the movement of life. And there was something timeless, in the flight of "all these, all the *generations* of these enormous and microscopic beings, harvested through a time beside which Earth time itself is a watch-tick . . . in layers unnumbered light-years deep."

The sun warm on my face, I closed my eyes and tried to imagine this valley, the scene from this rock, twelve thousand years ago, when the retreating glacier lay on the northern horizon of today's Rockland

Looking east from the summit of Snake Hill. Immediately to the right of the figure, the low hump of Little Snake Hill rises from surrounding marsh and landfill.

County. What manner of human or beast had traveled here then? I heard the rush and clatter of half a million caribou, moving up the valley from the sea, following the receding glacier and the barren tundra at its base; then, the distant voices of men in aboriginal hunting parties following the beasts as they fled the valley. Did they, perhaps, gaze up at these very rocks from the primeval cedar forests below and speculate on the advantage of the view from here? I thought I heard the mournful call of a loon, far below, on the river, as it may have flowed here through a Pleistocene landscape of boreal loneliness and splendor. Then I asked myself: what was this place like before there were human beings?

What I had been hearing and feeling was not just noise; it was the collected energy, the vital force, if you will, of all this life—eons of it—that had been picked up by the wind and delivered to the wall of the mountain, from there to be swept heavenward. Sitting there in the November sun, assailed by the noise of a hundred thousand machines, the collective voices of perhaps a million people and half a billion birds, I found my convictions as a naturalist challenged by the overpowering visual and auditory assault. I saw and heard this exultation not as a craven offense against nature but rather as a spectacular confirmation of it. We speak of "change" so often today that it has become a meaningless, politicized buzzword. But change—constant, subtle, and eternal—is indeed an incontestable rule of nature.

The contradictions are at once evident from this lofty perspective, for blinking in the sun and enduring the sting of engine exhaust and power plant emissions here on the hill, I am convinced that this is a toxic place. I know that such an environment surely cannot be an improvement over the "pristine" river valley that lay under a November sun of two thousand, or ten thousand, years past. But for better or ill it is a world of our own making, and we have, to the best of our short-term-gain abilities, adapted to it. It is still a livable place, in all its fierce vitality and tensions.

Look at the roadway roaring out of the south and past the hill.

On impulse, I waved both arms overhead, signaling my fellows zipping impersonally by, two hundred feet below. I had always glanced up at the tip of the outcrop whenever I passed by on the Turnpike, but would others take notice of a lonely figure flagging them down from that defaced heap of rocks? Did others ever ponder the presence of this weathered rampart, what it was and how it got there? Did they realize how old it was, what it had witnessed, standing here long before there were people on Earth capable of even conceptualizing a superhighway, much less building it and the conveyances that would use it? Somewhat to my surprise I was greeted by a small chorus of beeps and air

Snake (or Laurel) Hill, peregrine falcon, and New Jersey Turnpike, Secaucus. The endangered peregrine falcon is often seen near this outcrop, feeding on the numerous rock doves that frequent the Turnpike bridge superstructure.

horns. Not many, given the hundreds of vehicles streaking by at that moment, but enough to tell me that Snake Hill was not, for at least a few of the travelers on the New Jersey Turnpike, an invisible feature of their environment, like a decrepit billboard or an abandoned warehouse or, perhaps, the Meadowlands themselves.

I found a curious sense of fulfillment and community in that fleeting contact with fellow voyagers who would forever remain anonymous to one another. It seemed that we were all, in the end, card-carrying members of that diverse and often fractious entity known as the "human family."

With the sun at noon I left the peak and, lowering myself over the warm rocks and sliding down the north slope through the now-helpful windrows of oak leaves, reached the ground in less than an hour.

I walked away from the hill, across the wide gritty flats, and through the groves of sparse weedy poplars that would, one day soon, become transformed into the green and inviting parkland of a lovely retreat by the side of a once lovely river. The Snake Hill of old, the

Juvenile black-crowned night heron (Snake Hill in background), Saw Mill Creek Wildlife Management Area. Pencil drawing.

despised "place of snakes" and haunt of squatters, reprobates, and eccentrics, would soon be but a memory. It would be set aside, carefully protected from further indignity, and perhaps even venerated, at last, as the unique geologic symbol of the new Meadowlands: that place of marvelous contrasts—those of utility and beauty—a place that we humans are now in the process of shaping around our own perceptions of what a Cenozoic estuary should look like in the twenty-first century.

I turned and gazed up at the familiar craggy silhouette, looming high above the Turnpike and the river of many bends. Somehow, I knew this rock would always stand here, its time of trial now passed, a silent reminder that, in the end, the planet itself is far more patient and enduring than we are. There were the ageless rocks, delicate blue and lavender in their shadowed recesses, rich and tawny under the sun; there was the endless motion of the roadway, there the fierce glint of the November sun on the river. The scene, in spite of its contradictions, was one of considerable beauty.

In writing of my journey to Snake Hill and of the visual and spiritual impressions gained from its summit, I find that a scrap of three-hundred-year-old verse, passed on to me by a helpful friend years ago, seems oddly appropriate to the experience. The four lines are those concluding an inspirational poem, dated 1692, found on the wall of a Baltimore church. Their sentiments were intended to comfort and reassure the residents of an age far less complex than ours, but to me, they express perfectly the essence of the triumph and the tragedy contained in the continuing story of the Hackensack Meadowlands:

> *Whatever your labors and aspirations,*
> *in all the noisy confusion of life keep peace with your soul.*
> *With all its sham and drudgery and broken dreams*
> *it is still a beautiful world.*

Exploring the Meadowlands

Swamps have traditionally not lent themselves to casual exploration, especially on foot. This, for the most part, has been the case in the Meadowlands throughout their long association with humankind. Over the past twenty-five years, however, the opportunities for recreation have improved.

Although the Meadowlands are not yet akin to a national park, the advent of planning by the Hackensack Meadowlands Development Commission and the publicity afforded the activities of environmental groups have made the Hackensack River and its marshes much more accessible to the public. The river itself has long been a popular route of travel for recreational powerboaters and canoeists, but few people other than dedicated birders, naturalists, muskrat trappers, or scrap collectors braved the reedy expanses inland on foot or wandered the network of unpaved service roads (often the racetracks of dirt bikers). In the not-so-distant past, the Meadowlands were also regarded as a place of potential criminal assault, and female birdwatchers were routinely advised to avoid solitary excursions there.

Today, while still rather limited due to lack of ready access to many areas, active participation in Meadowlands nature study and observation is available. Nature programs and river cruises offered by both

Skein of Canada geese passing high above a rank of phragmites.
Both of these adaptable and often problematic species are biological symbols of
a degraded but recovering environment.

the HMDC and private environmental groups, for example, have increased in recent years. In addition, private canoe clubs offering Hackensack River cruises are enjoying a resurgence. A number of municipal parks abut the Meadowlands, and they, too, offer at least limited access to the interested hiker and explorer, without the threat of becoming lost among the towering reeds.

Here I list some of the Meadowlands parks, trails, and points of accessibility that will allow you to become familiar with this unique environment. The information has been assembled with the aid of several individuals and organizations: I am especially grateful to Captain Bill Sheehan of the Hackensack Estuary and River Tenders; Steve Barnes of the New York–New Jersey Baykeeper, Greg Renaud, John Pontodicorno, and Martin Wellhoffer; and Don Smith and Bob Sikora of the HMDC.

BY BOAT

Powerboats, sailing craft, and canoes are probably the most enjoyable way to view the Hackensack River and explore its tributaries and mitigated marshes. In recent years personal watercraft, commonly called Jet Skis, have appeared in some numbers on the river; these vessels are generally too noisy and fast-moving to serve as nature-observation vehicles.

Winds and tides may limit the mobility of boaters on the Hackensack River. Most winds present no problem for powerboaters, but the strong prevailing winds encountered on the wider portions of the lower river, usually out of the southwest or northwest, may prove daunting to inexperienced canoeists attempting to paddle against them. The Hackensack River is subject to tidal influence all the way to the Oradell Dam, and all boaters should be aware that groundings or collisions with submerged objects are possible at lower tide levels. The extreme turbidity of the water does not permit visual sighting of the bottom anywhere on the river. Canoeists who make landfall to camp or explore should do this on a rising tide, so as not to become stranded by an expanse of soft mud that may emerge between solid ground and the water as the tide goes out. A current tide table, normally available at all marinas and sporting goods stores, should *always* be consulted before planning a canoe cruise or onshore camping.

In my experience, the outgoing tide in the Hackensack River is usually stronger than the incoming, and canoeists of moderate arm strength and endurance should consider planning a cruise that runs with the tide rather than against it. Bucking a strong tidal flow in combination with a brisk headwind will make for an exhausting rather than

Least bittern on nest, Kearny Marsh. These tiny, shy bitterns spend most of their time creeping furtively through dense reed beds and are seldom seen by the casual observer.

Least bittern nestlings, Kearny Marsh. When disturbed, young bitterns instinctively assume the motionless, heads-up pose of their elders in order to escape detection.

an enjoyable river paddle. In most cases it is much wiser to arrange for a drop-off and paddle one-way—with the tide—to a vehicle waiting at the destination. Trust me on this one!

Powerboating

Several private marinas on the lower Hackensack offer refreshments, ample parking, restrooms, and launch ramps. These are listed below in the section on canoe launch sites. Daily launch fees at the private marinas on the Hackensack River are typically seven to ten dollars.

Powerboating on the Hackensack involves few risks if the operator sticks to the main channels. Closer to shore or in the river's many tributaries, submerged objects and mudflats may present a threat of collision or stranding at lower tide levels. Throughout the estuary the water is not clear enough to allow you to see submerged pilings, boat wrecks, and old docks or bulkheads. Speeds at or below the no-wake speed of five knots are strongly recommended whenever the powerboater strays from the main stem of the river!

While passage beneath the New Jersey Turnpike's eastern spur overpasses at high-tide levels is not a problem for canoes and smaller motorized craft, a larger powerboat may become stranded on the eastern side of the 'pike until the tide falls. Always check current tide tables before planning a cruise involving areas that may become isolated from the river due to high or low tide levels.

Canoeing

The canoe and kayak are without a doubt the most effective craft for wildlife watching, and meadows waterfowlers and rail hunters have used them for generations, often poling them through the reedy channels. Silent in operation and of shallow draft, a canoe can penetrate areas of the Meadowlands very much off-limits to larger boats. In a canoe, it is difficult to run hard aground in the meadows!

The lower Hackensack River is canoeable for its entire thirty-five-mile length, from Newark Bay to the dam at Oradell. Many sections, including those in the northern Meadowlands and through parts of Teaneck, Bogota, and River Edge, are still quite attractive and lend an aura of rural yesteryear to a day cruise; just don't contemplate drinking the water! It is possible to put ashore at many places along the river, even those of an unattractive, industrial nature, though again, careful attention must always be paid to the tide schedule to avoid an onshore stranding. It is also wise to explore tributaries and creeks on a rising tide, as these meandering waterways can empty with surprising speed on a falling tide, often leaving barriers of exposed mud banks or formerly submerged debris to block escape.

Saw Mill Creek canoeists.

At this writing there are no "official" Meadowlands campgrounds along the river, although the adventurous may pitch a tent anywhere dry and firm ground can be found above the high-tide mark. My wife and I have canoed and camped the river on several occasions. We were neither challenged nor hassled by anyone and found the experience of drifting off to sleep in our pup tent pitched among the reeds, bathed in the soft nocturnal glow of Giants Stadium, to be a unique one!

Commercial boat traffic on the Meadowlands portion of the Hackensack is rather light these days, being limited to the occasional oil and cement barge and to tugs hauling barges loaded with sludge from the Bergen County Utilities sewerage plant in Little Ferry. The lower river is wide enough so that the canoeist or small-boater may easily avoid the wake of the occasional tug or barge that does pass by.

Canoe Launch Sites

Officially sanctioned, or "legal," canoe launch sites are rather scarce on the Hackensack River, a sign of its regrettable status as a waterway still regarded as industrial. Although much of the shoreline acreage is in private hands, Steve Barnes of the Baykeeper stresses that private citizens are assured access to riparian lands through the Public Trust Doctrine. Access to the river should be more or less guaranteed the canoeist via municipal and county parks and other such publicly owned lands. If you are denied access and feel the action is unwarranted, contact the Baykeeper for possible action on the matter.

Access to some launch sites, such as the municipal bird sanctuary behind the Riverside Square Mall off Route 4 in Hackensack and the gravel river beach at the city's Foschini Park, is generally reliable, but it is always wise to check before arriving with boats in tow. Below, in north-to-south progression, are listed some of the better-known launch sites that have been used by veteran Hackensack River canoeists.

Ridgefield Park: TLI Heliport. The heliport, formerly the site of the Waterfront Airways seaplane base, is located at the dead end of Bergen Turnpike at the south end of the village. The proprietors have allowed canoeists to use their seaplane ramp as a launching site. For advance permission call (201) 440-5050.

Nearby, just beyond the dead-end barrier of Bergen Turnpike, a small gravel and rubble beach affords good access to the river at higher tide levels. I have used this access point many times and have never had a problem with leaving my van (legally) parked on the street. I would recommend, however, that canoeists leaving their vehicles anywhere on public streets or private riverside property either get prior permission from the police or owner to do so or leave an explanatory note on the dashboard.

Overpeck Creek. Access to the impounded Overpeck Creek above the tide control gates at the New Jersey Turnpike is extremely limited. The west bank of the creek is rendered virtually inaccessible due to the impassable barrier of Interstate 95 and the presence of the Overpeck Corporate Centre at the southern end. The east bank can be reached by parking in the turnaround at Overpeck County Park just south of Fort Lee Road in Leonia. You will have to carry your canoe across the park lawn and through the reeds to the creek bank. The impounded part of the creek is not tidal, so access is unlimited regardless of the time of day.

Access to the tidal portion of the Overpeck—west of the Turnpike—near its juncture with the Hackensack River may be had off Bergen Turnpike in Ridgefield Park, immediately west of the village's creekside McGowan Park. A small section of the shoreline is within a few feet of the road, though the water is reachable only at high tide; the village is considering developing this spot as a small park. Check daily parking regulations before leaving a vehicle on the street there.

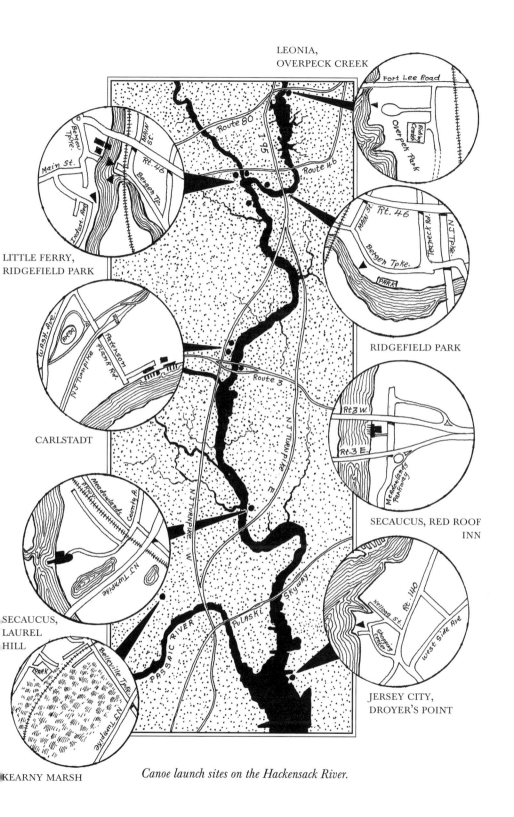

LEONIA,
OVERPECK CREEK

LITTLE FERRY,
RIDGEFIELD PARK

RIDGEFIELD PARK

CARLSTADT

SECAUCUS, RED ROOF
INN

SECAUCUS,
LAUREL
HILL

JERSEY CITY,
DROYER'S POINT

KEARNY MARSH

Canoe launch sites on the Hackensack River.

Little Ferry: Pirate's Cove Marina (formerly Meadowlands Boat Yard–Yacht Club). Located at 120 Industrial Avenue, this marina has a boat ramp that may be used by canoeists. For information on launch fees and parking: (201) 440-4554.

Little Ferry: Tracey's Nine Mile House. The current owners of this venerable and highly popular meadows restaurant, located on the river at 4 Bergen Turnpike in Little Ferry, do not object to canoeists' putting in there if their presence does not interfere with the business's operation. It is best to call first and seek permission to launch and leave a car in their lot: (201) 440-1100.

Secaucus: Laurel Hill. Canoes may be launched at the new HMDC launch ramp at Laurel Hill Park, located at the foot of the famous Meadowlands rock outcrop formerly (and alternatively) known as Snake Hill. There are no launch fees, and parking is free. Directions to this excellent, centrally located launch site are detailed below in the section on foot exploration. For information call the HMDC: (201) 436-8300.

Secaucus: Snipes Park. Access is good at this small municipal park; canoeists are advised to park their cars in the adjacent Channel 9 lot off Meadowlands Parkway and carry canoes the short distance to the river. As there are beds of new *Spartina* emerging on the banks of the river at this site, canoeists are urged to exercise care in walking through the vegetation and sliding canoes into the river.

Secaucus: Red Roof Inn. Located at 15 Meadowlands Parkway, between the east and west overpasses of Route 3, this hotel has adequate parking and a large marina that offers fine access to the river; it is the home port of the HMDC's river cruise pontoon boat. Launch fees are payable at the inn's registration desk. For information: (201) 319-1000.

Secaucus: The Old Mill, Mill Creek. Captain Bill Sheehan says this restaurant, located at the mouth of Mill Creek near the Mill Creek Mall in Secaucus, has "a ramp suitable for launching canoes and small power boats." Ramp fees are charged.

Carlstadt: The Meadowlands Golf Center and Marina. The home port of the Hackensack Estuary and River Tenders group, this popular facility is located off Washington Avenue at the end of (56) Paterson Plank Road on the river. The Golf Center and Marina offers refreshments, a golf driving range, ample parking, and a large marina with a good

*The pied-billed grebe (*Podilymbus podiceps*) is a shy, unobtrusive little waterbird whose presence often goes unnoticed. It occurs from southern Canada to Argentina, breeding in freshwater marshes, ponds, and lakes; it winters in coastal bays and brackish marshes, where it builds bulky floating nests of vegetation. The pied-bill, or water witch, is a regular summer resident and nester in freshwater impoundments in the Meadowlands and may remain in the area during mild, ice-free winters.*

launching ramp for both canoes and powerboats. For directions and information on launch fees: (201) 507-5656.

Carlstadt: The River Barge Cafe. Located on Outwater Lane adjacent to the Meadowlands Golf Center and Marina, the River Barge Cafe offers excellent food and atmosphere and a fine launch ramp. For information on launch fees and parking: (201) 531-0700.

Kearny Marsh. A three-hundred-acre freshwater wetland habitat filled with life, Kearny Marsh has long been a favorite of waterfowl hunters, birders, and ecologists. It is divided into two sections: Kearny Marsh East and West. Isolated from the tidal influence of the Hackensack River by old dikes, tide gates, and roadways, the marsh is alive with nesting waterfowl, rails, grebes, bitterns, coots, and gallinules during the warmer months and has a large muskrat population. Kearny Marsh West is the site of a black-crowned night heron rookery and has a large population of American bitterns.

Kearny Marsh West is accessible to canoeists by way of the Gunnell Oval, a public park off Schuyler Avenue in the township of Kearny.

The HMDC offers warm-weather canoe cruises in Kearny Marsh West, guided by staff naturalists who explain the ecology of the marsh and its history. Call the HMDC Environment Center for details: (201) 436-8300.

Canoe Clubs

In the early decades of this century there were perhaps twenty active canoe and kayak clubs located along the Hackensack River, most of them focusing on the upper river from Hackensack to the New York State line. Today there are perhaps four active groups, one of the oldest

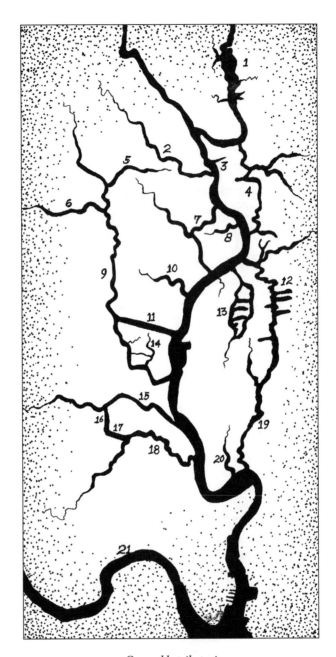

Canoeable tributaries

1. Overpeck Creek	8. Doctor Creek	15. Kingsland Creek
2. Losen Slote Creek	9. Berrys Creek	16. Williams Creek
3. Public Service Plant Outflow	10. Bashes Creek	17. Vreeland Ditch
4. Bellmans Creek	11. Berrys Creek Canal	18. Saw Mill Creek
5. Peach Island Creek	12. Cromakill Creek	19. Penhorn Creek
6. Ackermans Creek	13. Mill Creek	20. Fish Creek
7. Moonachie Creek	14. Fish Creek	21. Passaic River

being the seventy-year-old Wanda Canoe Club. This club, affiliated with the American Canoeing Association, has about forty-five active members and sponsors numerous cruises and endurance races on the Hackensack River. Fleet Captain John Ponticorvo says the club conducts regular thirteen-mile races on the lower Hackensack River, and members train on the river in preparation for national and Olympic competition. The club sponsors an annual thirty-five-mile race in September in conjunction with the Hackensack River Festival held on the river in Carlstadt. For information on membership, contact Ponticorvo at (201) 868-5241 or Karen Siletti at (201) 525-1594.

The Hackensack River Canoe Club is another active group that regularly holds river regattas and informal cruises throughout the Meadowlands. For information on membership contact Eric Nelsen at (201) 866-2788.

River Cruises

Guided river cruises are offered on a regular basis by both the HMDC Environment Center and private operators. These half-day trips usually involve the use of twelve-passenger pontoon boats departing the dock at 8:00 A.M. or 12:00 noon. Canoe excursions to Kearny Marsh are also offered by the HMDC.

Hackensack Estuary and River Tenders Eco-Cruises. The HEART eco-cruises, conducted by Captain Bill Sheehan of Secaucus, have been growing in popularity over the past three years. Offered during the warmer months, the cruises utilize a motorized pontoon boat of shallow draft able to penetrate most of the major tributaries of the river and surrounding marshlands. The HEART cruises are usually half-day events that originate at the Meadowlands Golf Center and Marina in Carlstadt, at roughly the halfway point of the lower river. A cruise may travel north from the marina to the Route 46 bridge at Little Ferry–Ridgefield Park or south from the marina to the Jersey City–Newark Bay area, depending on demand. All-day cruises or special itineraries are available on request. Sheehan offers a running commentary on the history of the river and its ecology and protection.

For information on the eco-cruises, write HEART at P.O. Box 1397, Secaucus, NJ 07096 or call (201) 866-8996.

HMDC River Cruises. The HMDC Environment Center offers regularly scheduled motorized river cruises and canoe trips for a modest registration fee at most times of the year, weather permitting. The pontoon boat cruises may depart in the early morning, early afternoon, or evening depending on the trip objective and time of year; staff

*The least bittern (*Ixobrychus exilis*) occurs from southeastern Canada to South America; it is a secretive inhabitant of freshwater marshes and bogs, and occasionally brackish and salt marshes. This reclusive little bittern is fairly common throughout the Meadowlands, breeding mostly in Kearny Marsh East and West and the Saw Mill Creek area, though probably elsewhere in suitable cattail and sedge habitats. The larger American bittern (*Botaurus lenti-* ginosus*) occurs from central Canada to the Gulf of Mexico, wintering south to Panama. Found in freshwater and brackish marshes and heavily vegetated pond and lake margins, this species is common throughout the marsh areas of the district, especially in Kearny Marsh. It is more often heard than seen. Its call, a throbbing* unk-a-lunk unk-a-lunk, *repeated over and over like an old-time pump, explains its old "thunder pumper" nickname.*

naturalists provide commentary on Meadowlands wildlife, ecology, and human history. The Kearny Marsh canoe trips are scheduled for the warmer months and feature a guided tour of this unique ecosystem emphasizing its breeding bird populations and the environmental changes that have occurred over the years. You may use your own canoe or arrange to use one of the Environment Center's fleet.

The river and canoe cruise schedule is listed in the HMDC Environment Center's periodically issued *Schedule of Events*. To receive the events schedule or for information on specific cruises, call the center: (201) 460-8300. Preregistration is generally required.

The Baykeeper Boat Auxiliary Program

The New York–New Jersey Harbor Baykeeper of the American Littoral Society offers a program in which volunteers use their own boats to patrol the Hudson River harbor and estuary waters, including the Hackensack River. Owners of private pleasure boats or commercial fishing and charter craft are invited to participate in the patrolling of regional waters in search of pollution, polluters, stream encroachments, illegal dredging, and unusual natural developments within the harbor and estuary. Program participants are instructed to act as observers only and not to interact or directly interfere with people engaged in suspected illegal activities; reports must be filed with the Baykeeper office (1-800-8BAYKPR) for further action.

Participants receive hats, shirts, and boat banners that identify them as auxiliary members and are periodically asked to attend informational meetings and take part in special surveys and wildlife inventories.

For information on the auxiliary program contact the Baykeeper: (800) 822-9577.

FISHING

Until the latter decades of the nineteenth century the Hackensack River and its tributaries were a veritable cornucopia of aquatic life, and fishes and crustaceans formed a major item in the diet of residents. Marine, brackish, and freshwater fishes abounded, and the Hackensack was famous for the abundance and quality of its blue crab population. As the twentieth century progressed and pollution began to overwhelm the river's ability to purge itself of toxins, the situation changed. Today, although many fish populations are recovering and the blue crab is still abundant in the tidal reaches of the river, the Hackensack is for the most part a "catch and release" sportfishing waterway: PCB and heavy metals persist on the bottom sediments, and toxins continue to leach from closed landfills.

Both the Bergen County Department of Health Services and the state Department of Environmental Protection have issued advisories against eating striped bass, bluefish, eels, and blue crabs caught in the Hackensack River below the Oradell Dam. According to health officials, pregnant women, nursing mothers, and children under the age of fifteen should not eat striped bass, American eel, bluefish over six pounds, white perch, or white catfish caught anywhere in the Hudson River–Newark Bay drainage more than once a week.

Since it is obvious that many subsistence anglers on the Passaic, Hackensack, and Hudson Rivers regularly disregard these health warnings, officials have noted that most of the contaminants in larger food and game fishes accumulate in the fat, dark meat, and entrails. They note that the health risk can at least be reduced by removing these before preparation for the table. The green gland of collected blue crabs should always be removed before eating.

ON FOOT

Foot travel in the Meadowlands has historically been described as being fraught with peril. Many older residents of nearly every town surrounding the district will say they have either known or heard of someone who "went into the swamps and never came out," and breathless tales of bottomless quicksands, of isolated, mysterious clearings among the reeds "where all the air had been sucked out of the place," and of hordes of bloodthirsty "Jersey mosquitoes" draining the meadows traveler dry have frequently appeared in print over the years, usually in context with earnest justifications to drain and reclaim these wetlands.

While the meadows were and are far from the "green hell" their detractors accused them of being over the years, there is no doubt that foot travel through the reeds and along the meandering creek banks has never been akin to a stroll in a municipal park. There is no true quicksand in the Meadowlands (that natural phenomenon is a product of the shifting, semiliquid sands of river deltas), but you do risk becoming bogged down like a mastodon in the deep and clinging mud of a low-tide river flat. And attempting to blaze a trail through dense stands of twelve-foot-high reeds can be an arduous procedure; you may even

*The striped skunk (*Mephitis mephitis*) has a very extensive range, occurring from north-central Canada and southern Labrador to Florida, Texas, and Baja California. It has been reported in a wide range of Meadowlands habitats, being most abundant in the surrounding suburbs. Its presence, like the racoon's, is often unsuspected due to its nocturnal habits. The skunk is both scavenger and hunter, eating everything from birds' eggs and fledglings to insects, carrion, vegetables, and garbage.*

lose your sense of direction, since a horizon cannot be seen in the depths of a phragmites thicket.

Nowadays most Meadowlands adventurers avoid the large expanses of trackless reeds. There are countless obscure but well-defined foot trails that enter the meadows where they abut corporate parks and suburban dead-end streets, most of them kept open by successive generations of adventurous kids. In addition, miles of unpaved pipeline and landfill service roads lace the district, and many of these are used regularly—both legally and illicitly—by birders, hikers, utility crews, and off-road vehicle enthusiasts.

Those seeking the meadows hiking experience without the risk of being interrogated by a Public Service foreman or run down by a speeding dirt biker will find ample and interesting trail mileage in the Richard W. DeKorte and Losen Slote Creek Parks described in the next section. Other trail networks either already in existence or in the planning stage include several described in the following paragraphs.

Laurel Hill Park

The 104-acre Laurel Hill Park, incorporating the famous outcrop of Laurel (or Snake) Hill in the borough of Secaucus, was formally dedicated in October 1995 with the opening of a public boat launch ramp. When completed, the park will include a ball field, a river walkway, a nature trail, and a restored wetlands habitat on the riverfront. Use of the public boat launch, constructed by the HMDC with matching Green Acres funding, is free.

Laurel Hill Park is the first new park built in Hudson County in seventy-five years. It is reached by following County Avenue south from Secaucus, bearing right on New County Road just before the New Jersey Turnpike overpass. Follow this road for about one mile, over two sets of railroad tracks and past the county jail prerelease complex (on the left) into Laurel Hill Park. To date, the boat launch area is the only part of this park that has been fully developed; turn right at the park entrance and follow signs to the public parking area at the boat launch.

The Meadows Path

Conceived in 1983 as "a coastal urban trail system" in the Meadowlands, the Meadows Path, when completed, will comprise a twenty-two-mile trail following the western bank of the Hackensack River from Losen Slote Creek Park in Little Ferry to Kearny Marsh and then east to the 720-acre Saw Mill Creek Wildlife Management Area on the Hackensack River. It is being planned as a pedestrian and bicycling artery that will connect two regional parks and the wildlife area of Kearny Marsh. The HMDC says the completed Meadows Path will

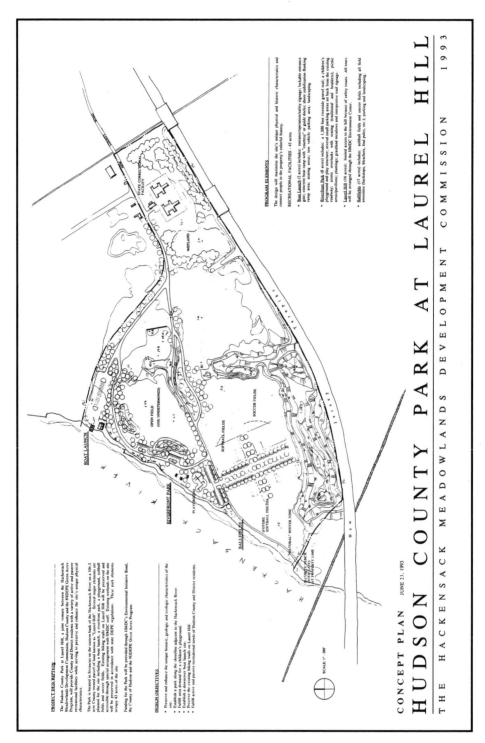

Plan for Laurel Hill Park and boat launching ramp.

"serve both public and private interests by creating continuous access to thousands of acres of parks and wetlands in the Hackensack Meadowlands." Much of the wetland area is currently accessible primarily to boaters.

The Meadows Path exists today in several sections in DeKorte Park and the borough of Lyndhurst. Begun in 1993 with a $50,000 state design grant, to complete it will cost $600,000, and will rely on cooperation between private and public interests and agreements between the HMDC and public utilities involving rights-of-way. About five miles have been built.

Where it passes through the meadows, the trail follows existing dikes and service roads, which will limit the impact on wetlands. At its northern terminus in Little Ferry, the Meadows Path will connect with the Sierra Club's projected Hackensack River Pathway, which would parallel the west bank of the river north to Oradell. The path is slated for completion in 1998.

Secaucus Linear Park

A self-guided trail system, Secaucus Linear Park is the result of collaboration between private property owners and the HMDC. It seeks to "provide passive recreational opportunities for . . . both resident and office populations" in a highly office-commercial section on the west bank of the Hackensack River. The park offers wildlife observation as well as "the opportunity to celebrate the river, a unique resource of the Meadowlands," according to the HMDC.

The North Bergen Urban Trail

According to the HMDC, the North Bergen Urban Trail was proposed to "create a two-mile pedestrian corridor in the northeastern quadrant of the Hackensack Meadowlands District on West Side Avenue in North Bergen." Citing a dearth of open space and walkways in this area of warehouse and distribution centers, planners of the Urban Trail noted that it would offer residents and workers a place for "strolling, picnicking and kickball" as well as for "spontaneous lunchtime ball games." The trail also features a nature observation tower, decorative plantings, a lawn area, and descriptive signage. The 15-acre park overlooks an adjacent 160-acre mitigated wetland.

PARKS AND OTHER FACILITIES

The Richard W. DeKorte Park

The 2,000-acre Richard W. DeKorte Park is the crown jewel of the HMDC's recreational planning for the Meadowlands District. Carved

RICHARD W. DEKORTE PARK • LYNDHURST, NEW JERSEY

Richard W. DeKorte Park

out of abandoned landfills and utilizing pipeline rights-of-way and access roads, the park serves as the site of the HMDC's headquarters and its popular Environment Center. At the center of the park is the 80-acre Kingsland Impoundment, a managed freshwater and brackish marsh that has become a birding hot spot in recent years. Among rare or unusual species sighted here are the bald eagle, purple martin, black tern, peregrine falcon, white pelican, and whimbrel. The impoundment area has a large summer population of tree swallows and waterfowl, including the threatened ruddy duck, and is heavily utilized by shorebirds in late summer and early fall.

The impoundment is accessible via the twenty-three-hundred-foot floating Marsh Discovery Trail, which features strategically located "hunter-style" wooden blinds for observation and photography. This trail was constructed from recycled polyethylene and is supported by foam-filled floats, eliminating the need for pile driving and heavy machinery.

Also included within DeKorte Park are the Transco Trail, a formerly private utility dike and service road that forms the southern and eastern boundaries of the impoundment, and the Environment Center, described below under "Education." The 3.5-acre Lyndhurst Nature Reserve is an adjunct of the Kingsland Impoundment.

All trails in DeKorte Park are barrier-free. Outdoor trails are open daily from 8:00 A.M. until dusk, weather permitting. For information: (201) 460-8300.

The Lyndhurst Nature Reserve

A minipark built on a former "garbage island," the 3.5-acre Lyndhurst Nature Reserve has both wetland and upland habitats, and is geared toward environmental education. Brackish wetlands, sand beaches, a small freshwater pond, and a "northeast inland woody plant community" were carefully re-created on the old dump site, and a network of trails, bird blinds, and a stone seating amphitheater enhance the reserve's function as an outdoor classroom.

Among the reserve's more interesting features are "sighting tubes" made of PVC pipe situated along the reserve's trails. These fixed viewing "scopes" focus the visitor's attention on prominent area landmarks including Snake Hill, the New Jersey Turnpike, the World Trade Center, and the Empire State Building.

Bird species that are known to have nested in the reserve's environs include the tree swallow, American kestrel, barn owl, and osprey.

Access to the reserve is partially restricted during the nesting season in order to protect sensitive species and habitats; during spring and

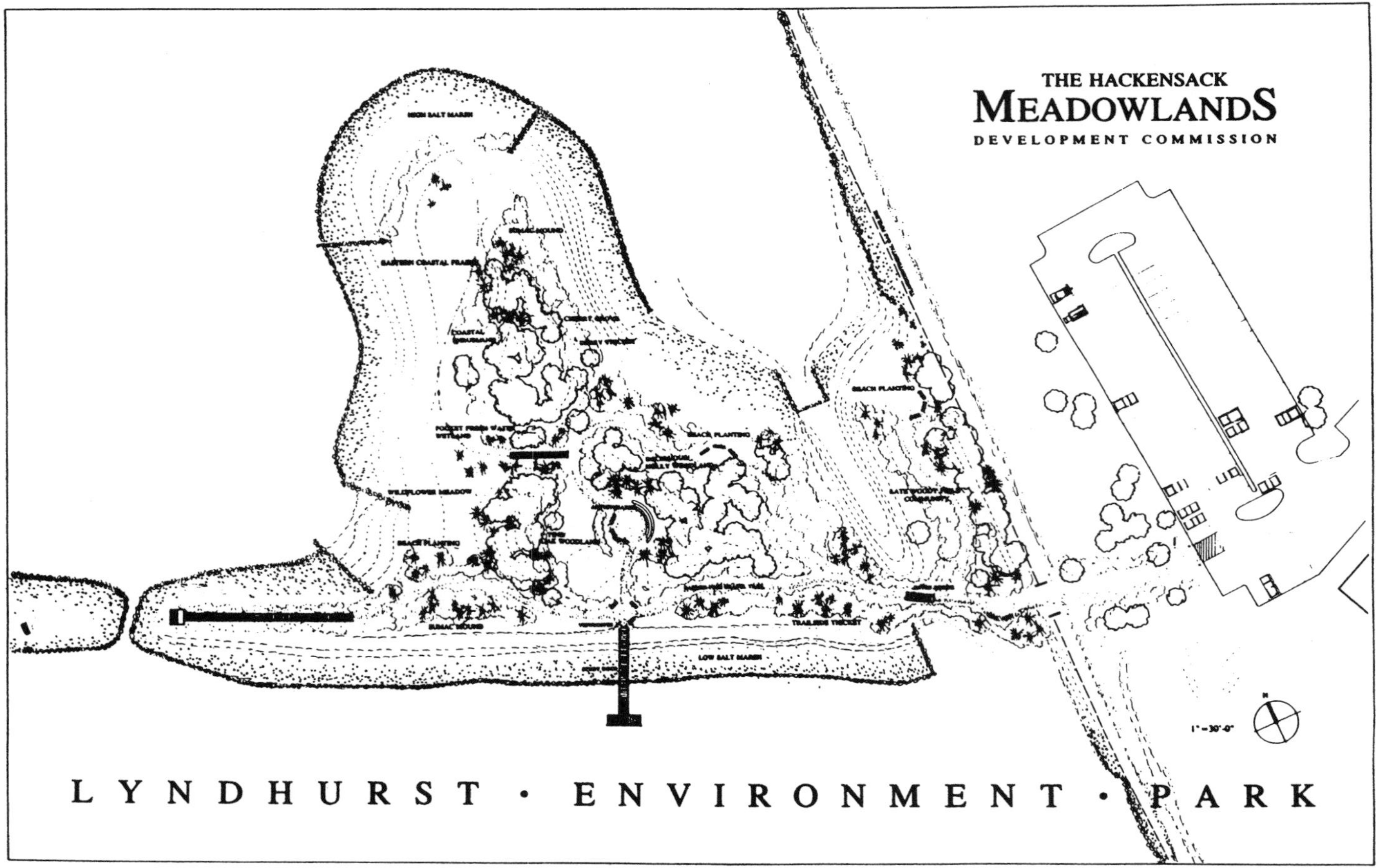

THE HACKENSACK
MEADOWLANDS
DEVELOPMENT COMMISSION

LYNDHURST · ENVIRONMENT · PARK

Lyndhurst Nature Reserve.

Jersey City and the Manhattan skyline from Lyndhurst Nature Reserve, DeKorte Park.

summer months, visitors should inquire at the Environment Center in adjacent DeKorte Park before entering the reserve.

Losen Slote Creek Park

Located in the borough of Little Ferry, this 28-acre lowland forest and meadow habitat was protected in 1990 by agreement between the town and the HMDC. The park consists of a 2-acre active recreation unit, which includes a children's playground and regulation-size roller hockey rink, and a 22-acre passive (or preservation) section, which seeks to protect the sole remaining remnant of lowland forest in southern Bergen County. The HMDC notes that "botanically, this woodland is a treasure."

Losen Slote Park centers around Mehrhof Lake and the impounded Losen Slote Creek, a former tidal tributary of the Hackensack River; it features nature trails and discreet clearings suitable for use as outdoor classrooms. The area is used by both the HMDC and private groups as a field trip destination and science lecture site.

Bergen County Utilities Authority Nature Preserve

One of the newest additions to the Meadowlands park system, the 60-acre Bergen County Utilities Authority Nature Preserve and trail system was dedicated in June 1996. It is located on BCUA property at the end of Mehrhof Road in Little Ferry. The facility, adjacent to Losen

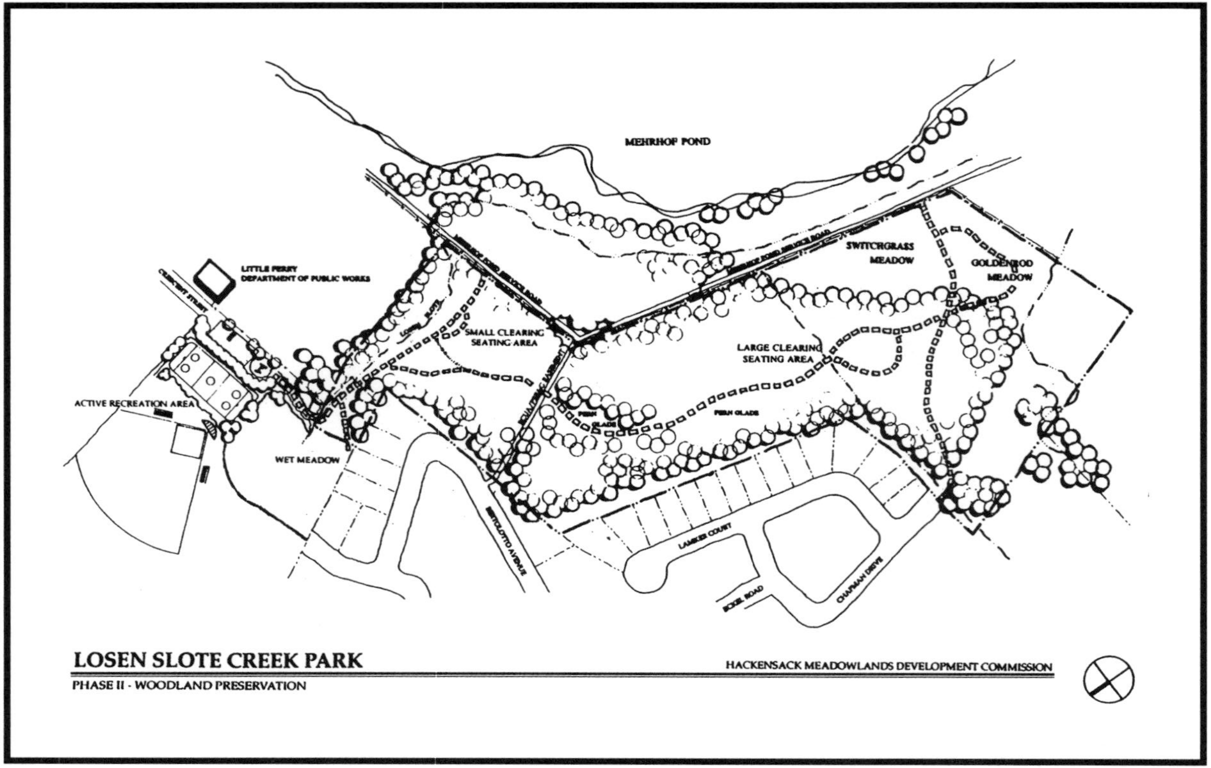

LOSEN SLOTE CREEK PARK

PHASE II - WOODLAND PRESERVATION

HACKENSACK MEADOWLANDS DEVELOPMENT COMMISSION

MEHRHOF POND

COTTONWOOD MEADOW

SWITCHGRASS MEADOW

LARGE CLEARING SEATING AREA

FERN GLADE

CHANNEL DRIVE

LARCH COURT

BOX ELDER ROAD

SMALL CLEARING SEATING AREA

BERTOLOTTO AVENUE

LITTLE FERRY DEPARTMENT OF PUBLIC WORKS

WET MEADOW

ACTIVE RECREATION AREA

Losen Slote Creek Park.

Slote Creek Park, includes a one-and-one-half mile trail that circles Merhrhof Pond and offers visitors a look at one of the last tracts of lowland forest in Bergen County. A section of the HMDC's Meadows Path will transect the preserve.

Over time the preserve will be fully developed as an environmental education facility featuring informational literature, interpretive trailside signs, and "outdoor classrooms." Plans include a more formalized educational format geared toward enhancing grade-appropriate environmental curricula. Lori Tarzia, the BCUA's education coordinator, says plants attractive to butterflies will be reintroduced to the preserve, making the park "a butterfly-watchers' hot spot."

For information on hours and registration for tours and classes, contact the BCUA: (201) 807-8692.

Schmidt's Woods, Secaucus

Located on Mill Ridge Road near the sewage disposal facility at Mill Creek, this park encompasses a remnant lowland forest of pin oak, sweet gum, and maple and is an important oasis for migrating songbirds. This woodland and the small forest at Losen Slote Creek Park in Little Ferry are the only public lowland forest preserves in the Meadowlands. Part of Schmidt's Woods Park is geared toward active recreation, though most of the area is natural woodland with a varied shrub layer very attractive to resident and migrant wildlife.

Overpeck County Park (Bergen County Park Commission)

First proposed in 1954 as a sprawling 1,100-acre active-recreation area that would rival New York City's Central Park, the Overpeck Marine Park of the mid-1950s today presents a somewhat less grandiose appearance. The brainchild of A. Thornton Bishop, then-president of the Bergen County Park Commission, the design for the original Overpeck Park incorporated miles of roadways and pedestrian hiking trails with an eighteen-hole golf course, several boat basins, picnic areas, acres of tennis courts, and a soaring bell tower and carillon donated by the government of the Netherlands. A reclaimed and purified Overpeck Creek would also be stocked with bass and pickerel for anglers. A newspaper report of the period summed up the universal optimism : "Three miles long and about a half-mile wide, the Overpeck County Marine Park will make these marshes just a memory."

Today, the Overpeck meadows are indeed a memory. But the fifteen-acre golf course in the Teaneck segment, a small area in Palisades Park, and the larger Leonia sections of the present park (Leonia North and South), on the east bank of Overpeck Creek, are the only

The short-eared owl (Asio otus) is often seen crossing above the Meadowlands during daylight hours, in contrast to the nocturnal habits of most owls. The species is of circumpolar distribution and breeds very locally throughout much of the northern United States, and in Canada to the Arctic. It is reported as declining throughout much of the range, including the Meadowlands, and can be considered uncommon in the district; a few pairs are known to breed in isolated areas of abandoned landfills.

sections of "one of the biggest park projects ever undertaken by a County government in the United States," as *The Record* called it, that are fully developed and geared toward active recreation. The 100-acre Leonia North and South sections, which straddle Fort Lee Road, features such active recreation facilities as a fitness trail, tennis courts, the Overpeck Riding Center (a horse riding and boarding unit), and extensive ball fields and picnic areas. This area is heavily utilized during the warmer months. Other, smaller sections of county parkland exist in the towns of Palisades Park and Ridgefield Park.

Administered by the Bergen County Park Commission and unconnected to the Meadowlands District, Overpeck Park, though it has fallen short of expectations, nonetheless preserves open space where it is sorely needed in overdeveloped Bergen County. The undeveloped portions of the park, mostly fallow, weed-covered landfill in Overpeck West, attract a wide variety of birdlife at all times of the year, and many rare and uncommon species have been reported there. Among the more unusual bird species observed at Overpeck Park West are the LeConte's, clay-colored, and Henslow's sparrows, the European kestrel (sparrow hawk), the dickcissel, and the yellow rail.

The open, undeveloped areas of Overpeck Park are accessible via unpaved roads that lead from the public parks in Leonia on the east bank and from Ridgefield Park's public recreation area on the west side of the creek. As these former landfill access roads are gated to bar unauthorized vehicles, they must be traveled on foot.

For information on the park's Leonia and Palisades Park sections, call (201) 944-7474. For the Ridgefield Park section, located at the end of Challenger Road, call (201) 807-0201.

EDUCATION

The HMDC Environment Center Museum

The Environment Center is the keystone facility of the Richard W. DeKorte Park. Operated by the HMDC and funded by the New Jersey Sports and Exposition Authority, the center's education programs have hosted more than ten thousand students annually. The unit, which is adjacent to HMDC headquarters and overlooks the Kingsland Impoundment, boasts a 288-seat auditorium, a certified research laboratory, lecture and conference rooms, and a glass-enclosed visitor center.

Canada geese waiting out a February blizzard at DeKorte Park. Snake Hill and the Manhattan skyline are dimly visible through the curtain of snow.

Kingsland overlook.

The center's lobby area contains a striking three-dimensional Meadowlands diorama, a bookstore, and the unique "trash museum," which opened in 1985.

Most of the Environment Center's programs target the ecology and recovery of this urban ecosystem, as well as the dimensions of the "garbage crisis" and other environmental threats that challenge us today. Presentations on acid rain, groundwater contamination, and wetlands protection are also offered.

The center's laboratory functions as an educational, research, and monitoring agency, analyzing and monitoring air and water quality throughout the district. The work done here has been crucial to the HMDC's program of closing landfills and establishing public parks and wildlife areas on these reclaimed tracts. The lab also provides opportunities for student internship and graduate research.

Most Environment Center education programs and events have a preregistry requirement. To receive the current "Schedule of Events" flyer listing programs, workshops, and special events, contact the center at 2 DeKorte Park Plaza, Lyndhurst, NJ 07071, or call (201) 460-8300.

The Environment Center is open Monday to Friday, 9:00 A.M. to 5:00 P.M., and Saturday from 10:00 A.M. to 3:00 P.M. Adult admission is two dollars; children under twelve are admitted free.

The Hackensack Estuary and River Tenders (HEART)

In addition to its popular eco-cruises, HEART works with local conservation and school groups in the development of science-oriented programs stressing the understanding of wetlands ecology and the preservation of intact habitats in the Meadowlands. Captain Bill Sheehan and other members of HEART are available to speak to interested groups on the importance of wetlands and clean water to a healthy biosphere and the history and future of the Hackensack River estuary. For information: (201) 866-8996.

The Hackensack River Coalition

Founded in 1986, the Hackensack River Coalition has as its central philosophy "the commitment to preserve open space along the river, to work to improve water quality and to increase the recreational potential of the Hackensack estuary." Director Margaret Utzinger says the HRC was founded in direct response to increasing development pressures in the Meadowlands, and the group seeks to educate both its membership and the general public about the irreplaceable natural resources that will be lost should the remaining wetlands be destroyed.

The HRC encourages its membership to become politically involved in matters concerning the Meadowlands and seeks to increase

Low-tide mud, DeKorte Park. This mud quickly dried and broke up into geometric patterns in the intense heat of a late summer sun.

grassroots involvement in decisions affecting the ecosystem. Current membership is between 350 and 400.

For information, write to the HRC at P.O. Box 4233, River Edge, NJ 07661, or call (201) 652-9239.

Association of New Jersey Environmental Commissions (ANJEC)

ANJEC offers many opportunities for political involvement and a variety of educational programs on the state's natural areas, including the Hackensack Meadowlands. The group is currently undertaking a freshwater wetlands campaign that seeks to ensure protection of the state's remaining wetlands under the terms of the Clean Water Act.

For information on ANJEC programs and membership, write to the group at 300 Mendham Road, Box 157, Mendham, NJ, or call (201) 539-7547.

The American Littoral Society

This venerable and active conservation organization, founded in 1962, has a large membership and branches in many states. Based at Sandy

Muskrat venturing out on a snowbank, Transco Trail dike, DeKorte Park.

Hook in the Gateway National Recreation Area, the ALS has long maintained a high profile in efforts to protect the wetlands of the Hudson River estuary and the New York Bight, including the Hackensack Meadowlands. The group conducts a wide variety of seminars, lectures, and field trips that focus on aquatic ecology and conservation. The ALS is strongly opposed to further development in the Meadowlands and other fragile coastal habitats.

For information on programs, field trips, and membership write to the ALS at Sandy Hook, Highlands, NJ 07732, or call (201) 291-0055.

American Rivers

A Washington, D.C.–based not-for-profit conservation group, American Rivers works to protect the nation's waterways and estuaries and stresses education in its public presentations. The group annually compiles a list of the ten "most endangered" rivers and twenty other "highly threatened" rivers in the United States. In 1996 the Hackensack River won the dubious honor of placement on the group's "threatened" list. The listing was due both to the Hackensack River's standing as a long-polluted, industrialized waterway and to the perceived impact the HMDC's proposed preservation-with-development plan (SAMP) would have on the river and its dwindling wetlands.

For information, write to American Rivers at 1025 Vermont Ave. N.W., Suite 720, Washington, DC 20005, or call (202) 547-6900.

Hackensack River Festival

This popular annual event, designed to foster awareness of the Hackensack River and the Meadowlands and held in either June or September, features canoe and kayak races, arts and crafts displays, and games and events, including miniature golf, pony and helicopter rides, and pontoon boat eco-cruises on the river. The festival's key racing events are the twenty-two-kilometer Hackensack River Marathon and the Meadowlands Cup races. The event is held at the Meadowlands Golf Center and Marina in Carlstadt and is sponsored by the Hackensack River Canoe Club and the Wanda Canoe Club. For information on time and date and entering races or exhibiting at the festival, contact Karen Siletti at (201) 525-1594 or John Ponticorvo at (201) 868-5241.

Bibliography

ATKINSON, BROOKS. *This Bright Land*. Garden City, N.Y.: Doubleday, 1972.

AUGROS, ROBERT, and GEORGE STANCIU. *The New Biology*. Boston: New Science Library, 1987.

BARLOW, ELIZABETH. *The Forests and Wetlands of New York City*. Boston: Little, Brown, 1969.

BATES, MARSTON. *The Forest and the Sea*. Chicago: Time-Life Books, 1960.

BEBOUT, JOHN E., and RONALD J. GRELE. *Where Cities Meet: The Urbanization of New Jersey*. Princeton, N.J.: Van Nostrand, 1964.

BECK, HENRY CHARLTON. *A New Jersey Reader*. New Brunswick, N.J.: Rutgers University Press, 1961.

BERRY, THOMAS. *The Dream of the Earth*. San Francisco: Sierra Club Books, 1988.

BISHOP, GORDON. *Gems of New Jersey*. Englewood Cliffs, N.J.: Prentice-Hall, 1985.

BORCHERT, JOHN R. *Megalopolis: Washington to Boston*. New Brunswick, N.J.: Rutgers University Press, 1992.

BORDEWICH, FERGUS M. *Killing the White Man's Indian: Reinventing Native Americans at the End of the Twentieth Century*. New York: Doubleday, 1996.

BRIDENBAUGH, CARL. "The Foundations of American Urban Society." In *The Urbanization of America: An Historical Anthology*, edited by Allen M. Wakstein. Boston: Houghton Mifflin, 1970.

BURCHELL, ROBERT W., and DAVID LISTOKIN, eds. *Future Land Use*. New Brunswick, N.J.: Center for Urban Policy Research, Rutgers University, 1975.

CALDWELL, LYNTON KEITH. *Environment: A Challenge for Modern Society*. Garden City, N.Y.: Natural History Press, 1970.

CAWLEY, JAMES, and MARGARET CAWLEY. *Exploring the Little Rivers of New Jersey*. 1942. 2d, 3d, 4th eds. New Brunswick, N.J.: Rutgers University Press, 1961, 1971, 1993.

CHAPMAN, FRANK M. *Autobiography of a Bird-Lover*. New York: D. Appleton-Century Co., 1933.

COLLINS, BERYL ROBICHAUD, and KARL H. ANDERSON. *Plant Com-*

munities of New Jersey. New Brunswick, N.J.: Rutgers University Press, 1994.

COMMONER, BARRY. *The Closing Circle.* New York: Bantam Books, 1972.

COX, JAMES. *My Native Land; The United States: Its Wonders, Its Beauties, and Its People.* Philadelphia: Blair Publishing Co., 1903.

CRUMP, J. IRVING, ed. *Biography of a Borough: Oradell.* Borough of Oradell, N.J., 1969.

CUNNINGHAM, JOHN T. *New Jersey: America's Main Road.* Garden City, N.Y.: Doubleday, 1976.

——. *This Is New Jersey.* 1953. 2d, 3d, 4th eds. New Brunswick, N.J.: Rutgers University Press, 1968, 1978, 1994.

DEAN, BRADLEY P., ed. *Faith in a Seed: Henry David Thoreau.* Washington, D.C.: Island Press, 1993.

DIAMOND, SIGMUND, ed. *The Nation Transformed—the Creation of an Industrial Society.* New York: Brazillier, 1963.

DOLAN, EDWARD F. *The American Wilderness and Its Future.* New York: Franklin Watts, 1992.

DUBOS, RENÉ. *Man Adapting.* New Haven: Yale University Press, 1965.

EHRLICH, PAUL R. *The Machinery of Nature.* New York: Simon & Schuster, 1986.

——, and Anne H. Ehrlich. *Healing the Planet: Strategies for Solving the Environmental Crisis.* Reading, Mass.: Addison-Wesley, 1992.

EISELEY, LOREN. *The Immense Journey.* New York: Random House, 1957.

——. *The Invisible Pyramid.* New York: Charles Scribner's Sons, 1970.

ELDREDGE, NILES. *The Miner's Canary: Unraveling the Mysteries of Extinction.* Englewood Cliffs, N.J.: Prentice-Hall, 1991.

ERRINGTON, PAUL L. *Of Men and Marshes.* New York: Macmillan, 1957.

FACCIOLLA, NICHOLAS W. *Minerals of Laurel Hill.* Teaneck, N.J., 1981.

FELL, BARRY. *America B.C.* New York: Quadrangle Books, 1976.

FOGARTY, CATHERINE M., et al. *Bergen County: A Pictorial History.* Norfolk, Va.: The Donning Co., 1985.

FREEDGOOD, SEYMOUR. *The Gateway States.* New York: Time Inc., 1967.

GABOR, DENNIS. *The Mature Society.* New York: Praeger, 1972.

GALBRAITH, JOHN KENNETH. *The Affluent Society.* Boston: Houghton Mifflin, 1958.

——. *The New Industrial State.* Boston: Houghton Mifflin, 1971.

GILL, DON, and PENELOPE BONNETT. *Nature in the Urban Landscape: A Study of City Ecosystems.* Baltimore: York Press, 1973.

GILLESPIE, ANGUS KRESS, and MICHAEL AARON ROCKLAND. *Looking for America on the New Jersey Turnpike.* New Brunswick, N.J.: Rutgers University Press, 1989.

GOLDSTON, ROBERT. *Suburbia: Civic Denial.* New York: Macmillan, 1970.

GORE, AL. *Earth in the Balance.* New York: Houghton Mifflin, 1992.

GRAHAM, FRANK. *Since Silent Spring.* Boston: Houghton Mifflin, 1970.

GRUEN, VICTOR. *The Heart of Our Cities.* New York: Simon & Schuster, 1964.

HEADLEE, THOMAS J. *The Mosquitoes of New Jersey and Their Control.* New Brunswick, N.J.: Rutgers University Press, 1945.

HILLARY, SIR EDMUND, ed. *Ecology 2000.* New York: Beaufort Books, 1984.

HUXLEY, JULIAN, ed. *Man, Nature, and Ecology.* Garden City, N.Y.: Doubleday, 1974.

HUXTABLE, ADA LOUISE. *Will They Ever Finish Bruckner Boulevard?* London: Macmillan, 1970.

HYER, RICHARD, and JOHN ZEC. *Railroads of New Jersey.* Self-published, 1973.

KANE, RICHARD, and DAVID GITHENS. *Hackensack River Migratory Bird Habitats; with Recommendations for Conservation.* Franklin Lakes, N.J.: New Jersey Audubon Society, 1996.

KELLY, KATIE. *Garbage: The History and Future of Garbage in America.* New York: Saturday Review Press, 1973.

KENNEDY, PAUL. *Preparing for the Twenty-First Century.* New York: Random House, 1993.

KIERAN, JOHN. *A Natural History of New York City.* Boston: Houghton Mifflin, 1959.

KOEHLER, FRANCIS C. *Three Hundred Years: The Story of the Hackensack Valley, Its Settlement and Growth.* Chester, N.J.: Lew Biebigheiser, 1940.

KOELSCH, WILLIAM A., and BARBARA G. ROSENKRANZ, eds. *American Habitat.* New York: Free Press, 1973.

KRAFT, HERBERT C. *The Lenape: Archaeology, History, and Ethnography.* Newark: New Jersey Historical Society, 1986.

LAUNER, DONALD. *A Cruising Guide to New Jersey Waters.* New Brunswick, N.J.: Rutgers University Press, 1995.

LEIBY, ADRIAN C. *The Revolutionary War in the Hackensack Valley.* New Brunswick, N.J.: Rutgers University Press, 1980.

LEVENSON, DAVID. *A Sense of the Earth.* Garden City, N.Y.: Natural History Press, 1971.

LINTON, RON M. *Terracide.* Boston: Little, Brown, 1970.

LONG, ROBERT EMMET, ed. *The Problem of Waste Disposal.* New York: H. W. Wilson, 1989.

MABEY, RICHARD, ed. *Second Nature.* London: Jonathan Cape, 1984.

MATTSON, CHESTER A. "The Hackensack Meadowlands: An Ecological Perspective." Thesis, Temple University, 1970.

MCHARG, IAN L. *Design with Nature.* Garden City, N.Y.: Natural History Press, 1969.

MCKIBBEN, BILL. *The End of Nature.* Garden City, N.Y.: Doubleday, 1989.

MCMICHAEL, A. J. *Planetary Overload.* New York: Cambridge Univerity Press, 1993.

MEADOWS, DONELLA H., et al. *The Limits to Growth.* New York: Universe Books, 1972.

MEEK, RAY L., and JOHN A. STRAAYER, eds. *The Politics of Neglect: The Environmental Crisis.* Boston: Houghton Mifflin, 1971.

MELZER, ARTHUR M. *The Natural Goodness of Man: On the System of Rousseau's Thought.* Chicago: University of Chicago Press, 1990.

MORRIS, RICHARD. *The End of the World.* Garden City, N.Y.: Doubleday, 1980.

NEW JERSEY AGRICULTURAL SOCIETY. *Some Early Industries of New Jersey.* (Salt hay.) Trenton: Harry B. Weiss, 1965.

NEW JERSEY BELL. *Journal: Managing New Jersey's Growth.* Vol. 10, no. 3, 1987.

NEW JERSEY STATE CHAMBER OF COMMERCE. *New Jersey: The Year 2000.* Morganville, N.J.: Business Journal of New Jersey, Feb. 1989.

NEW JERSEY TURNPIKE AUTHORITY. *1985–90 Widening: Technological Study.* Vol. 4, *Cultural Resources.* Feb. 1986.

OCEANUS, WILLIAM H. MACLEISH, ed. *Estuaries.* Vol. 19, no. 5, 1976.

PACKARD, VANCE. *The Waste Makers.* New York: David McKay, 1960.

POMFRET, JOHN E. *The Province of East New Jersey 1609–1702.* Princeton, N.J.: Princeton University Press, 1962.

PONTING, CLIVE. *A Green History of the World: The Environment and the Collapse of Great Civilizations.* New York: St. Martin's Press, 1991.

PORTNEY, PAUL R., ed. *Public Policies for Environmental Protection.* Washington, D.C.: Resources for the Future, 1990.

PRINGLE, LAURENCE. *City and Suburb.* New York: Macmillan, 1975.

——. *Restoring Our Earth.* Hillside, N.J.: Enslow Publishers, 1985.

QUINN, JOHN R. *Our Native Fishes.* Woodstock, Vt.: Countryman Press, 1991.

——. *Wildlife Survivors: The Flora and Fauna of Tomorrow.* Blue Ridge Summit, Pa.: TAB McGraw-Hill, 1994.

RATHJE, WILLIAM, and CULLEN MURPHY. *Rubbish! The Archaeology of Garbage.* New York: HarperCollins, 1992.

REIGER, GEORGE. *Wanderer on My Native Shore.* New York: Simon & Schuster, 1983.

REILLY, H. V. PAT. *From the Balloon to the Moon: New Jersey's Amazing Aviation History.* Oradell, N.J.: HV Publishers, 1992.

ROBICHAUD, BERYL, and MURRAY F. BUELL. *Vegetation of New Jersey.* New Brunswick, N.J.: Rutgers University Press, 1973.

ROCKEFELLER BROTHERS FUND. *The Use of Land: A Citizen's Policy Guide to Urban Growth.* A Task Force Report of the Citizen's Advisory Commission to the Council of Environmental Quality. New York: Thomas Y. Crowell, 1973.

ROTHSCHILD, EMMA. *Paradise Lost: The Decline of the Auto-Industrial Age.* New York: Random House, 1973.

RUBLOWSKY, JOHN. *Nature in the City.* New York: Basic Books, 1967.

SCHUBERTH, CHRISTOFER J. *The Geology of New York City and Environs.* Princeton, N.J.: Princeton University Press, 1968.

SERRAO, JOHN. *The Wild Palisades of the Hudson.* Westwood, N.J.: Lind Publications, 1986.

SHABECOFF, PHILIP. *A Fierce Green Fire: The American Environmental Movement.* New York: Hill and Wang, 1993.

SNYDER, JOHN P. *The Mapping of New Jersey.* New Brunswick, N.J.: Rutgers University Press, 1973.

STILL, HENRY. *The Dirty Animal.* New York: Hawthorn Books, 1967.

——. *In Quest of Quiet: Meeting the Menace of Noise Pollution.* Harrisburg, Pa.: Stackpole, 1970.

STOCKTON, FRANK R. *Stories of New Jersey.* New Brunswick, N.J.: Rutgers University Press, 1961.

TANNER, OGDEN. *Urban Wilds.* New York: Time-Life Books, 1975.

TERRELL, JOHN UPTON. *American Indian Almanac.* New York: World Publishing, 1971.

THAYER, THEODORE. *As We Were: The Story of Old Elizabethtown.* Elizabeth, N.J.: Grassmann Publishing, 1964.

TRUST COMPANY OF NEW JERSEY. *History of Hudson County & of the Old Village of Bergen.* New York: Bartlett Orr Press, 1921.

WACHTEL, PAUL L. *The Poverty of Affluence.* New York: Macmillan, 1983.

WARNER, MATT. *Your World, Your Survival.* New York: Abelard-Schuman, 1970.

WEINER, JONATHAN. *The Next One Hundred Years.* New York: Bantam Books, 1990.

WESTERVELT, FRANCES A., ed. *History of Bergen County, New Jersey.* New York: Lewis Historical Publishing Co., 1923.

WHISENHUNT, DONALD W. *The Environment and the American Experience.* Port Washington, N.Y.: Kennikat Press, 1974.

WIDMER, KEMBLE. *The Geology and Geography of New Jersey.* Princeton, N.J.: Van Nostrand, 1964.

WILLIAMS, MICHAEL, ed. *Wetlands: A Threatened Landscape.* Cambridge, Mass.: Basil Blackwell, 1991.

WILSON, BILLY RAY. *Environmental Problems.* Philadelphia: J. B. Lippincott, 1968.

WILSON, HAROLD F., ed. *Outline History of New Jersey.* The New Jersey History Commission. New Brunswick, N.J.: Rutgers University Press, 1950.

WILSON, KENNETH D. *Prospects for Growth.* New York: Praeger, 1977.

WRIGHT, KEVIN W. *The Hackensack Meadowlands: Prehistory and History.* Hackensack Meadowlands Development Commission, 1988.

Index

(Page numbers in italics indicate illustrations.)

About the Author

John R. Quinn is an artist-naturalist of more than forty years' experience. A native of the Village of Ridgefield Park, at the northern boundary of the Meadowlands, he has explored, fished, and canoed the Hackensack River and its marshes since childhood. Quinn is the author of ten books on nature and science subjects, including *One Square Mile on the Atlantic Coast*, *Wildlife Survivors*, and *The Winter Woods*, a Book-Of-The-Month Club selection. He is a former editor of *Tropical Fish Hobbyist* magazine and has served on the exhibit design staffs of the Academy of Natural Sciences of Philadelphia, the Science Center of New Hampshire, and the Bergen Museum of Art and Science.